# The Northern Ireland Peace Process 1993-1996

## A Chronology

Paul Bew and Gordon Gillespie

Serif
London

First published 1996 by
Serif
47 Strahan Road
London E3 5DA

Copyright © Paul Bew and Gordon Gillespie 1996

**British Library Cataloguing-in-Publication Data.**
A catalogue record for this book is available from the British Library.
**Library of Congress Cataloging in Publication Data.**
A catalog record for this book is available from the Library of Congress.

ISBN 1 897959 28 1

Designed by Ralph Barnby
Photoset in North Wales by
Derek Doyle and Associates, Mold, Flintshire
Printed and bound in Great Britain by
Biddles of Guildford and King's Lynn

# Contents

To the memory of
Barry Phillips

# Introduction

This volume, a sequel to *Northern Ireland: A Chronology of the Troubles 1968-1993*, is the public record of the 'Irish peace process' (or, as some preferred, the Northern Ireland peace process) which began to gather momentum in 1993 and came to an end with the Canary Wharf bomb in February 1996. We do not suggest that it is impossible to re-establish another peace process – indeed, we sincerely hope that it is – but this particular process was a self-contained one with a beginning, a middle and, sadly, an end, which had a certain ambiguous internal logic. This peace process depended on the belief that a working assumption could be made, despite the IRA's refusal to use the word, that the IRA's 'complete' cessation of military operations was a permanent one. A new process may well duplicate such a difficulty, but this time with many more cynics and with fewer people willing to put the most optimistic interpretation on events.

The confrontation between Orange marchers and the police at Drumcree in July 1996 made the likelihood of a renewed peace process even more remote. After Drumcree and the Orange parade through Belfast's lower Ormeau Road, mainstream, moderate nationalist opinion was alienated as never before, and many nationalists blamed Unionist leader David Trimble personally for the disorder: a UUP-SDLP accommodation, once apparently possible, became much less likely. The SDLP moved much closer to Sinn Fein, although some SDLP moderates could be expected to draw back should IRA violence increase. Neither the SDLP or Sinn Fein believe that a British withdrawal from Ireland is feasible, principally for economic reasons: withdrawal would leave Northern Ireland a wasteland with the Republic unable to pick up the bill. Both parties do, however, seem to want the British government to impose something unpleasant on the unionists, such as giving some executive power in the province to Dublin, rather than seeking the agreement of local parties The confrontation at Drumcree raises a very significant question in relation to this political desire: if Ulster's unionist community will sustain such massive and violent disruption to prevent the re-routing of a fifteen-minute parade, what will it not do in the event of a more serious challenge?

This is a public record: it is explicitly not the 'secret story' behind the Irish peace process. Yet in a situation in which the aspirations, interests and even self-deceptions of the main protagonists are easy enough to ascertain, the public record has a certain value. We have tried to ensure that the items selected for inclusion in this chronology were chosen on an objective basis. We would like this book to be a useful source of reference for all readers, regardless of their views on the contemporary Irish question. We also hope that the short interpretative essays which accompany the chronology at key moments during the period are also objective but here, it must be admitted, it will be harder to please everyone.

The public record does permit a relatively simple and unproblematical resolution of some of the key controversies of the peace process – for example, who said what, and when, about the arms issue? Was Gerry Adams really unaware of the British government's viewpoint before the ceasefire? What did the Irish government say?

The role of the Frameworks Documents is also highlighted. What part did they play in securing the ceasefire? What is the difference between the Frameworks Documents as they finally appeared and the Irish Department of Foreign Affairs documents leaked to journalist Emily O'Reilly in November 1993?

Readers will note how frequently Northern Ireland Secretary of State Sir Patrick Mayhew insists that the British government will not act as a persuader for Irish unity; is this perhaps also an important part of its reaction to the Hume-Adams proposals? How much does this tell us about the British approach to the Downing Street Declaration and the Frameworks Documents? As for the Reynolds government, was it committed to support for joint authority over Northern Ireland, a notion which Gerry Adams had hinted might be a way forward? Was the Irish government committed to the 'triple lock', as formulated by John Major, that any agreement would have to have the support of the Northern Irish parties, the Northern Irish people and the parliament of the United Kingdom?

Did the Ulster unionists continue to dream of a military victory over republicans or was their involvement in the peace process more complex? What did James Molyneaux actually say about the Spring principles or the Downing Street Declaration and how did his views differ from Ian Paisley's? Did all unionists view the IRA ceasefire as a ruse or did any unionist hold out the hand of reconciliation to the republicans?

A number of myths may already be developing around the peace process, in part because Irish sources, including prime ministerial and official sources, have been much keener to give their side of events than the British. Despite the fascination of some of the Irish accounts, these have tended to be, as is the nature of such things, one-sided. It is all the more important, therefore, to take note of the public press accounts of, say, the June 1994 Corfu meeting between the two premiers.

Some of the 'secrets' of the Irish peace process are still shrouded in mystery. Some of the key questions – for example, why did the British government make so little effort to sell the Frameworks Documents to the Ulster Unionist leadership? But outlining the public record allows readers, whatever their final view, the opportunity of reaching a well grounded conclusion.

# 1993

**8 June** The IRA detonates a bomb at a gas-holder at Gateshead in Tyneside. The following day another bomb explodes at a disused petrol depot in North Shields.

**9 June** The independent Opsahl Commission, which received 550 submissions from 3,000 individuals, publishes a report based on a wide range of submissions from groups within Northern Ireland. The report makes 25 recommendations including the creation of a power-sharing administration for NI and an equal say for each community in the area of law-making. The report also recommends that the government open informal channels of communication with Sinn Fein and that the party be admitted to talks if it rejects violence.
In West Belfast the UFF launches a grenade attack on the home of Sinn Fein leader Gerry Adams.

**11 June** Gerry Adams and SDLP leader John Hume hold a meeting and say that their talks will continue.
The Queen pays a one-day visit to NI.

**16 June** In London the British and Irish prime ministers, John Major and Albert Reynolds, call for the resumption of political talks on NI.

**18 June** Irish President Mary Robinson faces a storm of protest from unionists after she shakes hands with Gerry Adams during a private reception for community leaders in West Belfast. It later emerges that the British government had advised against the visit going ahead.

**21 June** In a speech in Belfast, Fine Gael leader John Bruton supports Mary Robinson's decision to visit West Belfast but claims she should not have met Gerry Adams.

**23 June** The body of a Belfast man, murdered by the IRA because it claims he was an informer, is found on the border.

**25 June** Sir John Wheeler is appointed to the NIO in succession to Michael Mates. Mates resigned the previous day following the controversy surrounding his defence of fugitive businessman Asil Nadir.

**26 June** On a two-day visit to NI John Major calls for the resumption of talks between constitutional parties.
In Belfast UVF member Brian McCallum is fatally wounded and eighteen others are injured when a grenade explodes during an Orange march which was being held back from the peace line on the Springfield Road.

**28 June** It emerges that a 1992 Labour Party discussion document, which had been supported by Labour's NI spokesman Kevin McNamara, suggested that local parties be given six months to agree a form of devolved administration. Had the parties failed to reach agreement within this period, the British and Irish governments would then begin talks aimed at bringing about joint British-Irish authority over the North. 'Options for a Labour Government' proposed that joint sovereignty should last for a period of twenty years and would be supported by a three-person panel elected from within Northern Ireland. The proposals are generally welcomed by nationalists but totally rejected by unionists.
A grenade attack on an Orange parade on the Shankill Road leaves 30 people injured. Sir Patrick Mayhew causes fury among unionists by commenting, after leaving an opera at Castleward, Co. Down, 'Well, nobody died. At the end of this opera everybody's dead.'

**2 July** The funeral of UVF member Brian McCallum is followed by serious rioting in Protestant areas of North and West Belfast. Rioting and loyalist attacks on the RUC occur in Belfast, Bangor and Lurgan over the following days.
A Sinn Fein election worker is injured in a UVF gun attack in Antrim.

**3 July** Eight entrances to the City of London's financial area are sealed by permanent roadblocks in an attempt to prevent further IRA bomb attacks.

**4 July** In a *Sunday Tribune* interview Gerry Adams says republicans might be prepared to accept joint authority as 'part of the process towards the end of partition'.

**5 July** A 1,500 lb IRA bomb explodes in Newtownards, Co. Down.

**8 July** In an interview with the *Guardian* Irish Deputy Prime Minister and Foreign Minister Dick Spring says that if there is not clear evidence that NI inter-party talks will restart in the late summer, the British and Irish governments should negotiate a framework agreement for NI without any input from local parties. The resulting agreement would be put to a referendum in both the North and the Republic. Spring says that there can be no real objection to Sinn Fein participating in the political process once it abandoned violence, adding, however, 'You cannot expect to sit down at the negotiating table while keeping a 1,000 lb bomb in a van outside.' Sir Patrick Mayhew criticises the proposals for breaking the 'cardinal principle' that constitutional change would require cross-community support. UUP leader James Molyneaux accuses Spring of inciting support for the paramilitaries.

**10 July** In a radio interview John Hume says he believes that the IRA wants to end its campaign, although this will require enormous moral courage. A 300 lb bomb is defused in Belfast city centre.

**11 July** UUP leader James Molyneaux claims that British government representatives held secret negotiations with the IRA in 1992. The *Sunday Life* report claims that the British government had proposed a ceasefire plan which the IRA had rejected. The NIO says the report is untrue.

**12 July** The *Irish Times* reports that senior unionist politicians are alleging that British officials have held secret negotiations with the IRA. Despite a UDA statement that there will be no further rioting in Protestant areas, there are attacks on the RUC in Belfast, Derry, Newtownards and Ballycastle, Co. Antrim.

**15 July** A UVF statement admits that the organisation carried out the May 1974 bombings of Dublin and Monaghan.

**17 July** An IRA sniper shoots dead a soldier in Crossmaglen, Co. Armagh.

**19 July** Former Conservative minister Lord Tebbit says that Articles 2 and 3 of the Irish constitution will only be removed when Dublin has suffered bomb attacks on the same scale as Belfast or London. Bombs are found planted under the cars of SDLP members Joe Hendron and Brian Feeney.

**22 July** Ulster Unionists support the Conservative government in a vote of confidence over the Social Chapter of the Maastricht Treaty; an Opposition amendment is defeated on the casting vote of the Speaker. In the Commons John Major says that no deal has been done with the

Unionists in return for their support. UUP MP Revd Martin Smyth says, however, that he expects a Commons Select Committee on Northern Ireland to be established soon.

**26 July** The UFF claims that it has the expertise necessary to make fertiliser-based bombs similar to those used by the IRA.
In the Republic there is unease over the possibility of an agreement between the British government and the UUP. Albert Reynolds states, however, that his government will accept that no deal has been done 'until the facts establish the contrary'. The following day Reynolds says that the establishment of a Northern Ireland Select Committee could undermine the Anglo-Irish Agreement.

**27 July** The UFF carries out gun and bomb attacks on the homes of a Sinn Fein councillor in Belfast and an SDLP councillor in Glengormley, Co. Antrim.
Laurence Kennedy, leader of Northern Ireland's Conservatives, resigns his seat on North Down Council in protest at the apparent Conservative-UUP agreement.
It is announced that NI is to receive £1,040 million from European Community structural funds in the period 1994-99.

**2 August** The government approves the opening of three new integrated schools, bringing the total in NI to 21.

**4 August** A 1,000 lb bomb attached to a tractor crashes into a field at Belleeks, Co. Armagh.

**5 August** An arson attack by the Red Hand Commando destroys a Gaelic Athletic Association clubhouse at Glengormley, Co. Antrim. On 9 August the same group damages another GAA clubhouse in Portaferry, Co. Down.

**6 August** Belfast High Court rejects the plea of Joseph Doherty that he have the nine years' imprisonment he spent fighting extradition from the US deducted from his sentence for the murder of an SAS captain in 1980. Michael McKee, who had been convicted in connection with the same case, was initially permitted to take into consideration time served in the Republic while facing extradition, but this ruling was subsequently overturned following an appeal by the NIO.

**8 August** An internment anniversary rally supported by Sinn Fein is attended by several thousand people, the first time a republican rally is permitted to take place at Belfast City Hall.

The UFF murders the son of Sinn Fein councillor Bobby Lavery at his home on Belfast's Antrim Road.

**11 August** In a *Belfast Telegraph* interview former NIO Minister Michael Mates suggests that NI public expenditure be cut so that 'people would be pressing for a settlement'.
Following earlier suggestions that representatives from the Catholic Church might act as intermediaries with paramilitary groups, Cardinal Cahal Daly says they 'would not be willing to meet with representatives of any organisation engaged in a campaign of violence'.

**12 August** Three men are arrested after the RUC forces the IRA to abandon a 3,000 lb van bomb in Portadown.
In Dublin Gerry Adams calls on the Irish government to seek a new agreement with the British based upon the right of the Irish people to self-determination.

**13 August** Six IRA incendiary devices explode in Bournemouth. The English seaside town's pier is also damaged by an IRA bomb.

**18 August** An IRA car bomb explodes in Belfast city centre causing £750,000 worth of damage.

**19 August** The American ambassador to Dublin, Jean Kennedy-Smith, makes her first visit to Northern Ireland and says that a US 'peace envoy' is an 'option for the future'.

**22 August** A *Sunday Times* report suggests that a 60-point peace plan had been drawn up by the British army late in 1992 but no action had been taken because the IRA had rejected pressure from SF leaders for an extended Christmas ceasefire.

**24 August** Following criticism from within nationalist circles of the continuing Hume-Adams talks, the *Irish News* defends the talks and says that they offer 'the best prospect for peace'.
On ITV The Cook Report alleges that leading Sinn Fein member Martin McGuinness was the 'man in charge' of the IRA. The following day McGuinness denies he is 'an IRA activist or strategist'.
Incendiaries planted by the UVF are defused at bus stations in Dublin and Dundalk.

**25 August** NIO Minister of State Sir John Wheeler claims that the IRA is 'already defeated'. The following day the IRA states that it is ready for 'a meaningful peace process' but 'utterly determined' to resist failed

British policies.

The Red Hand Commando states that it will attack bars or hotels holding Irish folk nights, saying that the music is part of the 'pan-nationalist front'. The organisation withdraws the threat the following day.

**26 August** Ten prison officers are injured during clashes with UVF inmates at the Maze prison.

The UFF threatens to attack civil servants involved in North-South co-operation.

**28 August** A small IRA bomb is detonated by police inside the City of London control zone.

**29 August** A *Sunday Tribune* story discloses that former Irish diplomat Michael Lillis has held two private meetings with Gerry Adams at the latter's request.

**30 August** The UFF shoots dead a Catholic woman at her home in North Belfast. The loyalist group later expresses 'regret' for the murder and says its target had been her husband.

**31 August** An IRA bomb explodes at a supermarket in South Belfast causing nearly £1 million damage.

**1 September** The UVF murders a Catholic van driver in East Belfast and a prison officer at his home in the North of the city. The following day the UVF threatens to kill more prison officers unless there are reforms in prison conditions; the threat is withdrawn on 10 September.

**3 September** The centre of the town of Armagh is severely damaged by a 1,000 lb IRA bomb.

**6 September** The European Commission on Human Rights rules that the claim by relatives of the IRA members shot by the SAS in Gibraltar that the killings had breached Article 2 of the European Convention is admissible.

**7 September** An independent American delegation led by former US Congressman Bruce Morrison arrives in Ireland for a fact-finding visit. The group meets Mary Robinson and Albert Reynolds, Sir Patrick Mayhew and the UUP the following day and Alliance, SDLP and Sinn Fein representatives on 9 September. The visit coincides with a week-long lull in IRA activity.

**8 September** Ulster Unionist MP John Taylor says that 'in a perverse way' the increasing fear among Catholics might prove useful in helping them to 'appreciate' Protestant fears.

**11 September** In a speech to the British Irish Association in Cambridge, Sir Patrick Mayhew attempts to re-launch inter-party talks stating, 'I can report to you not only my belief that the objectives of the talks process remain valid, and that their achievement remains a possibility; I can report in addition that there is rational, and not self-deluding, ground for hope that that possibility will be fulfilled in an agreed settlement.'

**12 September** Gerry Adams says that republicans are more willing than ever to explore new avenues towards a settlement, but calls talk of a ceasefire 'an unhelpful distraction'.

**13 September** A Protestant man is shot dead by the Red Hand Commando at his home in Newtownards, Co. Down.

**14 September** During a visit to the US, Albert Reynolds says that any package for a political settlement would involve changes in Articles 2 and 3 of the Irish constitution.

**15 September** A Catholic haulier is shot dead at his home near Lisburn, Co. Antrim. The IRA claims that he had carried out work for the security forces.

**16 September** After a meeting with John Major in London, John Hume says that he does not 'give two balls of roasted snow' for critics of his continuing talks with Gerry Adams. The following day SDLP deputy leader Seamus Mallon says that his party's patience with regard to IRA violence is 'finite'.

**17 September** After presenting his party's policy document 'Breaking the Logjam' to the Prime Minister in London, DUP leader Ian Paisley describes the Hume-Adams talks as 'pan-nationalism'.
SDLP MP Joe Hendron says that although his position in West Belfast had been undermined by the Hume-Adams talks he still supports John Hume. On 19 September the West Belfast MP also questions the value of the talks continuing indefinitely if IRA violence continues. On 20 September the SDLP MPs give their full support to the Hume-Adams talks.

**18 September** DUP spokesman Sammy Wilson says the GAA is

perceived by loyalists as 'the IRA at play'. Earlier in the week the UFF had attacked a GAA hall in West Belfast and another near Banbridge, Co. Down.

**20 September** In Dundalk Albert Reynolds says that if inter-party talks in the North need to proceed without the DUP, 'So be it.'

**21 September** The UFF launches bomb attacks on the homes of Dr Joe Hendron MP and four SDLP councillors. The UFF says the attacks are a consequence of the Hume-Adams talks.

**22 September** NIO Minister Michael Ancram meets SDLP MPs at the start of a fresh round of political talks with NI parties.

**23 September** In South Armagh a heavy machine-gun and rifles are recovered following an exchange of gunfire between the IRA and an army helicopter.

**25 September** John Hume and Gerry Adams issue a statement saying, 'Our discussions, aimed at the creation of a peace process which would involve all parties, have made considerable progress. We agreed to forward a report on the position reached to date to Dublin for consideration. We recognise that the broad principles involved will be for wider consideration between the two governments. Accordingly, we have suspended detailed discussions for the time being in order to facilitate this.

'We are convinced from our discussions that a process can be designed to lead to agreement among the divided people of this island, which will provide a solid basis for peace. Such a process would obviously also be designed to ensure that any new agreement that might emerge respects the diversity of our different traditions and earns their allegiance and agreement.'
In response to the joint statement Sir Patrick Mayhew says, 'We have made it clear that we do not negotiate with people who support the use of violence for political ends.'

**26 September** As John Hume flies to Boston as part of a business delegation, the Hume-Adams statement released the previous day is greeted with a range of reaction from British and Irish government scepticism to unionist hostility. Hume urges critics to suspend immediate judgement and, in Boston, creates some confusion by saying that no report has yet been sent to the Irish government.

**27 September** An *Irish Times* report claims that the Hume-Adams agreement calls on the British government to declare it has no long-term interest in Ireland and that it will actively pursue unionist consent for a united Ireland. IRA violence would be ended if the government made a formal declaration that the Irish people as a whole had a right to national self-determination.

A 300 lb IRA car bomb explodes in Belfast city centre causing widespread damage. Later in the day a 500 lb bomb causes extensive damage in South Belfast.

The UDA calls on unionist politicians to withdraw from all institutions of government.

**29 September** Sir Patrick Mayhew rejects the idea of self-determination 'by the Irish people as a whole'. He also rules out the idea of joint authority.

**30 September** At the Labour Party conference in Brighton the party's spokesman on NI, Kevin McNamara, suggests that the British and Irish governments establish new arrangements in the North should local parties fail to reach agreement.

**1 October** The DUP says that it will not become involved in political talks unless the Prime Minister rejects the Hume-Adams proposals.

**2 October** Three IRA bombs explode in Hampstead, North London, damaging a number of shops and flats. On 4 October another five devices explode in North London, injuring four people.

**3 October** A statement from the IRA welcomes the Hume-Adams initiative and says that, 'If the political will exists or can be created, it could provide the basis for peace. We, our volunteers and our supporters, have a vested interest in seeking a just and lasting peace in Ireland. Our objectives which include the right of the Irish people to national self-determination are well known. Our commitment remains steadfast.'

**4 October** Police in the Republic find half a tonne of explosives and three heavy mortars in Co. Louth; another mortar is found the following day.

**5 October** A UVF letter bomb addressed to Dick Spring is discovered at Belfast sorting office.

Albert Reynolds says that there will have to be a cessation of violence by the IRA before Sinn Fein can become involved in political talks on Northern Ireland. The following day Reynolds says that a referendum to amend Articles 2 and 3 of the Irish constitution would be held in the context of an overall settlement.

**6 October** The UFF murders a Catholic man and wounds two others in a bar in West Belfast. The UFF claims the attack is in response to the Hume-Adams talks and the 'pan-nationalist' front. A bomb, planted by the UVF, explodes outside a Sinn Fein office on Belfast's Falls Road.

**7 October** After a meeting involving John Hume, Dick Spring and himself, Albert Reynolds says that the SDLP leader has provided them with a document setting out broad principles upon which a peace process might be established.
In London the trial of three former police officers accused of perjury and conspiracy to pervert the course of justice in the case of the Birmingham Six is terminated because of what the judge describes as the 'saturation' publicity surrounding the trial.

**9 October** Speaking on Radio Ulster, Sir Patrick Mayhew says that the people of Northern Ireland alone have a right to self-determination. Sinn Fein could only become involved in talks when 'a sufficient period' had elapsed after IRA violence ended. During an RTE radio interview the following day Mayhew says that the IRA will have to make its guns and explosives available in order to show that its violence was over.

**10 October** A statement by UUP MP Martin Smyth that Sinn Fein could join political talks if it openly rejected violence leads to a dispute within the Unionist Party.

**12 October** A UVF gun attack on a workers' van near Shorts aircraft factory in East Belfast leads to Joseph Reynolds being killed and five others being wounded. Another Catholic man is wounded in a separate UVF attack in North Belfast. On 15 October 1,000 people, including workers from Shorts, take part in an East Belfast protest rally against Mr Reynolds's murder.
Police find sufficient semtex at a house in North London to make twenty explosive devices. Four days earlier two IRA bombs had exploded in the area.

**13 October** Gerry Adams says that peace will be the result of 'total demilitarisation' and not a prerequisite. Sinn Fein chairman Tom Hartley announces the party's plans to open a European office.

**15 October** A Catholic man is murdered by the UFF in the New Lodge area of Belfast.

**16 October** At the UUP conference in Craigavon James Molyneaux says that the Hume-Adams proposals seek 'to determine Ulster's future outside the United Kingdom' and adds, 'When fellow-travellers end their exploitation, intimidation and racketeering and all arms and explosives are surrendered then there will be a lengthy period of quarantine before access to the democratic processes can be even considered.'

**17 October** At the annual Wolfe Tone commemoration at Bodenstown, Co. Kildare, Albert Reynolds says there can be 'no secret agreements or understandings between governments and organisations supporting violence as a price for its cessation'.

**21 October** A Protestant man is shot dead by the IRA at his home in Glengormley, Co. Antrim. Staff of the company he worked for had been repeatedly attacked by the IRA because it undertook work for the security forces. The following day the IRA issues threats to five firms believed to be carrying out work for the security forces.
The Alliance Party wins a North Down council by-election brought about by the resignation of leading NI Conservative Laurence Kennedy.

**22 October** In the House of Commons Sir Patrick Mayhew, commenting on the Opsahl Commission's report, remarks, 'Alas, the commission also suggested that the government should open informal channels of communication with Sinn Fein to test its commitment to the constitutional process without resort to the justification of violence, and that they should persuade the IRA to move towards the de-escalation of violence and, eventually, a ceasefire. We want an end to violence as much as anyone does, and perhaps more than some do. The government's position on the matter is quite clear, Sinn Fein must end the violence and demonstrate its commitment to democratic constitutional politics ... Until then, there should be no doubt that the government will not conduct talks or negotiations with anyone who perpetrates, threatens or supports the use of violence for political ends.'
Also in the Commons John Hume says of his talks with Gerry Adams, 'I have said that this is the most hopeful dialogue and the most hopeful chance of lasting peace that I have seen in twenty years. At the end of the day, as our statement made clear, this process must involve both governments, and all parties. Its objective is an agreement that has the allegiance and agreement of all traditions ... I believe that we have a real process of lasting peace and a total cessation of violence on the basis that I have just stated. I am saying to them, "Hurry up and deal with it".'
In an interview with the *Belfast Telegraph* Gerry Adams says that Sinn Fein 'has never been merely a Brits out party. Brits out is presented quite cynically as meaning get rid of the Protestants – that is not the case. We may have to change – and you may argue that we already have changed in

discussions with John Hume – but we want to see an Irish national democracy. We don't want Northern Protestants to be outside of that.' On the right of unionists to maintain the Union, Adams says, 'They don't have that right anyway. Are you telling me that if the British government and all the people of the UK decided to end the connection they would let this tiny percentage here stop them?' He also adds that, 'Unionism is the antithesis of democracy.'

On the question of the IRA ending its campaign, Adams says, 'We know that isn't going to happen. None of the elements who are involved in armed campaigns are of their own volition going to give them up. Of course it would be better if everyone stopped and there were no prisons but the reality is that all these are part of the problem. They are symptoms ... It is quite valid to say the IRA should stop. My response is to say I am prepared to go to the IRA when I think I have something to govern the future conduct of their campaign. I would like to be able to make definitive proposals. For four or five years Sinn Fein's policy has been total demilitarisation. We want to see all the forces in the conflict setting aside their weapons – right now, today.'

**23 October** An IRA bomb explodes in a fish shop on the Shankill Road, Belfast, killing ten people and injuring 57. Those killed include the shopkeeper and his daughter and one of the bombers, Thomas Begley. The Provisionals say that the bomb was intended to kill members of the UFF who they claimed were meeting in a room in the former UDA office above the shop.

John Major describes the incident as 'sheer bloody-minded evil' while NIO Minister Michael Ancram says the bombing makes 'a total mockery of any talk of peace on the part of the Provisional IRA'.

John Hume describes the bombing as an 'appalling act of mass slaughter' and Gerry Adams expresses 'deep concern' at the event.

In the wake of the Shankill bombing the UFF says its members will be 'fully mobilised'. Later in the day a Catholic man is critically wounded in the Donegall Pass area and another man is wounded in the Bawnmore area of Belfast. Over the course of the following days there are petrol bomb attacks on a number of Catholic homes in Lisburn.

**24 October** The Anglo-Irish Intergovernmental Conference meeting due to take place on 27 October is postponed as a mark of respect for those killed in the Shankill Road bombing.

Belfast City Council Ulster Unionists say they will break off relations with the SDLP until the Hume-Adams initiative has ended.

In England an IRA bomb explodes on a railway line near Reading and other devices are found at two railway stations. The following day another IRA bomb explodes on a bridge over a railway line in

Buckinghamshire.

**25 October** Sean Fox, a 72-year-old Catholic man, is shot dead by the UVF at his home in Glengormley, Co. Antrim.
Thousands of workers from Shorts and Harland and Wolff in East Belfast march to the scene of the Shankill Road bombing.
At Westminster Sir Patrick Mayhew says that while he recognises John Hume's courage in attempting to achieve a breakthrough, 'It must be understood that there will never be any bargaining with those who in this democracy reinforce their arguments with bombs and bullets or the threat of violence.'

**26 October** Two Catholic workmen are shot dead and five others wounded in a UFF gun attack in West Belfast.
Leading republican Eddie Copeland is wounded when a soldier opens fire on mourners at the home of Shankill bomber Thomas Begley.

**27 October** In the Dail Dick Spring proposes a list of six 'democratic principles' which he believes will produce a sustainable peace: the NI situation should not be changed by the use or threat of violence; any political settlement must depend on freely given consent; there can be no talks between the governments and those who use, threaten or support violence; there can be no secret agreements with organisations supporting violence as a price for its cessation; those claiming to advance peace should permanently renounce the use or support of violence; if violence were to be renounced and this to be sufficiently demonstrated, 'new doors could open' and the governments would wish to respond 'imaginatively'. On 29 October Sir Patrick Mayhew describes the Spring principles as 'very reassuring'.
Gerry Adams is widely condemned after he helps carry the coffin of Shankill bomber Thomas Begley.
Rallies for peace are held in many parts of the Republic, including Dublin, Galway and Limerick.

**28 October** Brothers Gerard and Rory Cairns are murdered by the UVF at their home near Lurgan, Co. Armagh.

**29 October** After a meeting in Brussels, John Major and Albert Reynolds present a six-point statement detailing what they see as the prerequisites for peace: the situation in NI should not be changed by violence or the threat of violence; a political settlement must depend on consent freely given and in the absence of force or intimidation; there can be no talks between the governments and those who use, threaten or support political violence; there can be no secret agreements or understandings between governments and organisations supporting violence as the price for its cessation; those claiming to advance peace in Ireland should renounce violence, or support for the use of violence, for good; if a renunciation of violence was made and demonstrated sufficiently 'new doors could open' and both governments would wish to respond 'imaginatively' to the new situation.

The two leaders describe John Hume's efforts as 'courageous and imaginative', but say they will not adopt or endorse the Hume-Adams proposals. John Major says, 'We want to hear from the Provisional IRA that they are going to repudiate violence. By that I don't mean a short-term ceasefire to be casually tossed away at the first opportunity. I mean the clearest possible indication that they have decided ... to give up violence for good.' Asked about the Hume-Adams proposals, Major says, 'I don't think they are going to run.'

Albert Reynolds comments, 'There is a clear message from both governments that when they cease violence there will be provisions for them. If people want to come in from the cold, we are providing them with the opportunity to do so.' Reynolds' advisor Martin Mansergh later says, 'The Taoiseach agreed to create some public distance from Hume-Adams by agreeing that both he and the Prime Minister had a broader canvas to take into account.'

**30 October** Two UFF gunmen enter the Rising Sun Bar in Greysteel, Co. Londonderry, and fire at random at customers celebrating Halloween. One of the gunmen shouts 'Trick or treat' before opening fire. Seven people, including 81-year-old James Moore, are killed and thirteen wounded. John Burns, the only Protestant killed in the massacre, was an ex-UDR man. The UFF claimed it had attacked the 'nationalist electorate' in revenge for the Shankill bombing. The local MP, William Ross, describes the attack as 'an appalling act of murdering violence'. On 7 November over 3,000 people take part in a peace rally in the village. 27 people die as a result of the Troubles in October alone, the greatest number in any month since October 1976, when 28 people were killed.

In Dublin Sinn Fein chairman Tom Hartley says that 'consent' is a euphemism for a unionist 'veto'. Hartley also says he will be 'disappointed if the British rejected the Irish peace initiative and the Dublin government acquiesced'.

**1 November** At Westminster John Hume asks John Major why he had rejected the Hume-Adams proposals without talking to him about them first. Major replies, 'I reached the conclusion – after having been informed of them by the Taoiseach, as we said in our statement over the weekend – that that was not the right way to proceed.' Speaking about loyalist and republican paramilitaries, Major comments: 'We are dealing with people who are beyond the pale of civilised behaviour, and it does not lie within the remit of any hon. Member to be able to talk them out of their behaviour.' When Labour MP Dennis Skinner says that, 'People outside Parliament understand only too well that the government have dealt with terrorists over the decades,' Major replies, 'As ever, the honourable gentleman is very lucid, and as almost ever, he is entirely wrong. If the implication of his remarks is that we should sit down and talk with Mr Adams and the Provisional IRA, I can only say that that would turn my stomach and those of most honourable members; we will not do it. If and when there is a total ending of violence, and if and when that ending of violence is established for a significant time, we shall talk to all the constitutional parties that have people elected in their names. I will not talk to people who murder indiscriminately.'

**2 November** John Major says he will meet the leaders of the four 'constitutional' parties in preparation for new inter-party talks. He also orders a review of broadcasting restrictions, saying that recent interviews 'stretched the present guidelines to the limit and perhaps beyond'.
The UUP and DUP restate their view that they will not negotiate with the SDLP until discussions with Sinn Fein end.
Reserve Constable Brian Woods dies two days after being shot by an IRA sniper in Newry.

**3 November** After an Anglo-Irish Intergovernmental Conference meeting the British and Irish governments issue a statement saying that they will work together 'in their own terms on a framework for peace stability and reconciliation'. Sir Patrick Mayhew says the Spring principles will be central to this. UUP leader James Molyneaux describes the Hume-Adams proposals as 'a recipe for bloodshed' and says the Spring principles are 'a great improvement'.

**4 November** After a meeting with the Prime Minister at Downing Street, John Hume says that there could be peace within a week if his proposals were accepted.

**5 November** The IRA offers to stop targeting loyalist paramilitary figures if loyalists end their attacks on individuals in the nationalist community. Rejecting the offer, a UDA spokesman says: 'They need to announce a total cessation of violence before the UFF and the UDA will be disbanded.'

**6 November** In Dublin Gerry Adams says the Spring principles are 'not the basis for a peace process'.

**8 November** Writing in the *House Magazine*, Sir Patrick Mayhew states:

'The government will never negotiate with those who support, threaten or perpetrate violence or fail to show their disavowal of such evil is for real.'

**10 November** Replying to a letter from the outgoing Mayor of New York, President Clinton repeats his opinion that Gerry Adams should not be given a US visa 'because of his involvement in terrorist activity'.

**12 November** Rumours that government officials and SF leaders had held secret meetings earlier in the year are described as 'unsubstantiated gossip' by the NIO.
Albert Reynolds says that he is prepared to pursue his own proposals with regard to NI and to 'walk away' from John Major. The following day John Bruton accuses Reynolds of moving away from the Spring principles.

**15 November** At the Guildhall in London John Major says, 'There may now be a better opportunity for peace in Northern Ireland than for many years.' He says that terrorists have to be persuaded to end violence unconditionally and choose the path of democratic political activity. 'Some would deny them that path on account of their past and present misdeeds. I understand that feeling, but I do not share it … But if the IRA end violence for good, then – after a sufficient interval to ensure the permanence of their intent – Sinn Fein can enter the political arena as a democratic party and join the dialogue on the way ahead … There can be no secret deals, no rewards for terrorism, no abandonment of the vital principle of majority consent.'
Reacting to the speech, Gerry Adams says that members of his party have been in 'protracted dialogue' with the British government but that negotiations had been broken off 'at the behest of his [Major's] Unionist allies'.
The *Belfast Telegraph* claims that face-to-face meetings have taken place between Sinn Fein and senior British government officials and that an exchange of documents had been authorised by Downing Street.

**16 November** Sir Patrick Mayhew says, 'There has been no negotiating with Sinn Fein … no one has been authorised to talk or negotiate on behalf of the British government with Sinn Fein.' Republicans claim that a SF delegation, led by Martin McGuinness, has had talks with government representatives and that there is documentary evidence to prove this. On 18 November McGuinness repeats the claim that members of his party have had 'protracted contact and dialogue' with the British government.

**18 November** In the House of Commons John Major says of NI's constitutional position that, 'It is a cast-iron guarantee. The future constitutional position of the people of Northern Ireland is a matter for the people of Northern Ireland to determine and for no one else to determine.' He also states that no party can veto progress.

In Dublin the Special Criminal Court sentences Brixton jail escapee Pearse McAuley to seven years' imprisonment for possession of a loaded weapon.

**19 November** The *Irish Press* leaks a secret plan for the future of Northern Ireland which has been drawn up by Irish Department of Foreign Affairs officials. The plan calls on the British 'to acknowledge the full legitimacy and value of the goal of Irish unity by agreement'. In return the Dublin government would be prepared to include a commitment that constitutional change in the North could only come about with the agreement of a majority within NI. There should be joint North-South administrative bodies with executive powers. New executive and legislative structures should include measures to promote consensual approaches and the mutual acceptance by representatives of both communities of each other's rights. The Anglo-Irish Agreement would be expanded by having representatives of agreed political institutions in the province formally associated with the Anglo-Irish Intergovernmental Conference. The conference 'will be the forum for both governments to jointly guarantee and monitor the commitment ... that such institutions will provide for the equitable and effective participation in power of representatives of both communities'. If the devolved institution were to fail the conference would have powers to intervene.

Reacting to the leaked draft Irish proposals, UUP MP David Trimble says Ulster Unionists 'will not be party to the marginalisation of the unionist community'. Albert Reynolds meanwhile states that, 'No such document has been presented to the Irish government. The Irish government has not authorised such a document.'

**20 November** John Hume and Gerry Adams issue a further joint statement saying that they are assessing the position of their initiative in the wake of Hume's meeting with John Major: 'We naturally hope that the British government will respond positively and quickly to the clear opportunity for peace which this initiative provides ... We remain committed to this peace initiative and to the creation of a peace process which would involve both governments and all parties. We also remain convinced, despite all the difficulties, that a process can be designed to lead to agreement among the divided people of this island which will provide a solid basis for peace.'

**21 November** A *Sunday Life* report says there have been 'authoritative claims' that Martin McGuinness has been involved in talks with a British government representative.

**22 November** A press release from the loyalist paramilitaries' co-ordinating body, the Combined Loyalist Military Command (CLMC), says that they are earnestly seeking peace 'in accordance with the overwhelming desire of the population'. However they also warn that they are preparing for war if peace is 'bought at any price'. The statement also says that their representatives have met government officials twice since the summer. Sir Patrick Mayhew says that, 'Nobody has been authorised to talk or to negotiate on behalf of the British government with Sinn Fein or any other terrorist organisation.'

**23 November** At Westminster James Molyneaux warns, 'There has been a progressive hardening of attitudes in the professional and middle classes, and that is always a bad sign in Northern Ireland. Many of those groups have in the past taken no part whatever in politics, but they are now in such a state of anxiety that they disbelieve any assurance, and suspect betrayal in every sentence they hear or read.' In response an Irish government source says it will not react to 'the rhetoric of a backwoodsman'.

**24 November** Customs officials at Teesport in England discover arms including 300 AKM assault rifles, two tonnes of explosives with detonators and thousands of bullets aboard a Polish container ship. The armaments, valued at £250,000, were believed to be destined for the UVF. NIO Minister Michael Ancram says the leaked Irish government proposals for NI have 'no status whatsoever'.
After a meeting with John Major at Downing Street, Ian Paisley says that the Prime Minister had told him that if he had received the Irish Department of Foreign Affairs document he would have 'kicked it over the house tops'. DUP MP Revd William McCrea, who attended the meeting, is believed already to have received documentary evidence of contacts between government officials and Sinn Fein.
It is disclosed that a special Cabinet group has been set up by John Major to oversee the peace initiative. The key members of the group are Douglas Hurd (Foreign Secretary), Sir Patrick Mayhew (Secretary of State for NI), Malcolm Rifkind (Defence Secretary) and Michael Howard (Home Secretary).

**26 November** James Molyneaux says that there will be 'significant developments' in the next few days with regard to the terrorist campaign.

**27 November** At the SDLP conference in Cookstown, Co. Tyrone,

John Hume says that John Major holds 'the key to peace'. On the same day Ian Paisley tells the DUP conference in Belfast that Ulster faces the greatest threat to the union since the Home Rule crisis.

**28 November** The *Observer* reveals that the British government has had a secret channel of communication with Sinn Fein and the IRA for three years and has been in regular contact since the end of February. Sir Patrick Mayhew later claims that contacts had developed as a result of an oral message from the IRA leadership received on 22 February which stated: 'The conflict is over but we need your advice on how to bring it to a close. We wish to have an unannounced ceasefire in order to hold dialogue leading to peace. We cannot announce such a move as it will lead to confusion for the volunteers, because the press will misinterpret it as a surrender. We cannot meet the Secretary of State's public renunciation of violence, but it would be given privately as long as we were sure we were not being tricked.' Mayhew claims that the government made a substantive response on 19 March stating that, 'Any dialogue would follow an unannounced halt to violent activity. We confirm that if violence had genuinely been brought to an end, whether or not that fact had been announced, then dialogue could take place.' An IRA reply on 10 May did not provide the unequivocal assurance the British sought. Mayhew claims that an IRA message of 2 November stated: 'In plain language please tell us through the link as a matter of urgency when you will open dialogue in the event of a total end to hostilities. We believe that if all the documents involved are put on the table ... that we have the basis of an understanding.' A British response on 5 November stated: 'If, as you have offered, you were to give us an unequivocal assurance that violence has indeed been brought to a permanent end, and that accordingly Sinn Fein is now committed to political progress by peaceful and democratic means alone, we will make clear publicly our commitment to enter exploratory dialogue with you. Our public statement will make clear that, provided your private assurance is promptly confirmed publicly after our public statement and that events on the ground are fully consistent with this, a first meeting for exploratory dialogue will take place within a week of Parliament's return in January.' Gerry Adams denies that republicans initiated contacts with the British government. Loyalists claim that there have been contacts between Protestant paramilitaries and the Dublin government since the spring.

**29 November** Sir Patrick Mayhew faces only limited criticism of his policy of maintaining secret contacts with Sinn Fein when he defends his position in the House of Commons. Ian Paisley notes, however, that, 'These talks were going on, but we had Warrington ... Even when the bombing took place in the Shankill Road, the lines were still open. Surely the Secretary of State cannot think that, after his behaviour, he can have any trust with the Northern Ireland people.' Paisley is asked to withdraw the accusation that Mayhew had issued 'falsehoods'. The DUP leader refuses to withdraw the remark and is ordered to leave the chamber after saying, 'It was a falsehood: it was worse, it was a lie.'

Sinn Fein publishes a set of documents which it says have been exchanged with the British government over the previous months. Martin McGuinness says, 'Patrick Mayhew today read a text which he claims to be a communication sent by me to the British government in late February. I totally refute his claim. The text he read is counterfeit. No such communication was ever sent. It is a lie ... My initial comparison of the version of the 19 March document read out by Patrick Mayhew today indicates that they are now counterfeiting their own documents to meet their current needs.'

## The Contacts Between the British Government and Sinn Fein

After Sir Patrick Mayhew's unambiguous rejection in the House of Commons on 22 October of the Opsahl Commission's advice on precisely the subject of opening channels of communication with Sinn Fein, there was little doubt that the revelation of contacts between the British government and Sinn Fein came as a severe shock to the body politic. On 30 November *Times* correspondent Matthew Parris noted of Sir Patrick's speech at Westminster that, 'No Tory dared ask *the* question – the one on all our minds: why had he said there was no talking? What is the difference between the exchange of messages and a conversation? We were made to feel it was somehow rude to mention it. Like your uncle's toupee, the evidence was plain, but decency forbade discussing the matter. Besides, the politically correct word on the Tory benches is not "talks", let alone "negotiations". It is "contacts".'

It may well be that the government's 'contacts' with Sinn Fein damaged Sir Patrick Mayhew's credibility with unionists to the extent that he was never again able to win their trust – this despite his appointment having been considerably more popular in unionist than in nationalist circles. In particular, Sir Patrick was known to have reservations about the Anglo-Irish Agreement, yet he was never able to cash this in with unionists following the revelation of his contacts with republicans.

The sense of anger, shock and confusion on all sides led many people to miss the force of Sir Patrick's most important defence of his actions – that the government's core position was the same in private as it had stated in public. On 19 March 1993 the British government message ran: 'The British government does not have, and will not adopt, any prior objective of "ending partition" ... unless the people of Northern Ireland come to express such a view, the British government will continue to uphold the union, seeking to ensure the good governance of Northern Ireland, in the interests of all its people, within the totality of relationships in these islands.' Four days later a British government representative told Sinn Fein, 'A North-South settlement that won't frighten unionists. The final solution is union. It is going to happen anyway. The historical train – Europe – determines that. We are committed to Europe. Unionists will have to change. The island will be as one.' Even allowing for the ambiguity of phrasing here, 'The island will be as one,' sounds suspiciously like an 'agreed Ireland' – this is considerably less enticing to republicans than the language used in similar contacts in the mid-1970s, a point surprisingly overlooked in many discussions of the 1993 revelations.

**30 November** A Catholic man is shot dead by the UFF in East Belfast. A 2,000 lb IRA bomb is defused outside Armagh.

**1 December** Sir Patrick Mayhew admits that there are 22 inaccuracies in the British version of the documents covering contacts with republicans.

**2 December** Replying to Labour's NI spokesman, Kevin McNamara, on the question of the government acknowledging the value of the goal of a united Ireland, Sir Patrick Mayhew says, 'The British government cannot join the ranks of the persuaders. Here we differ from the Opposition who wish to persuade the people of Northern Ireland to leave the United Kingdom and join a united Ireland. We believe that it should be for the people of Northern Ireland to determine for themselves, without persuasion from us, whether they wish to remain in the United Kingdom.'
Sinn Fein releases *Setting the Record Straight*, a further set of documents concerning contacts with the government. Martin McGuinness says that the British government had initiated contact with SF in 1990. In 1992 his party had been briefed on the state of inter-party talks by the British and in 1993 the British had sought fuller discussions with SF representatives. On 19 March 1993 SF received a nine-paragraph positional paper from the British. On 10 May the British government was informed that the IRA would call a fourteen-day suspension of operations to enable talks to take place. According to SF the British government was hesitant about deeper involvement because the government was 'under siege'. Subsequent leaks also led the government to give a limited briefing on the talks to the UUP. In July SF passed its eleven-paragraph response (drawn up in April) to the British

communication of 19 March in which SF outlined the conditions under which it would enter negotiations. After this SF said exchanges became less common. On 5 November SF received a document from the British government which purported to be a response to a message from SF three days earlier. SF immediately repudiated the authenticity of the 2 November communication.

A soldier is shot dead by an IRA sniper in Keady, Co. Armagh.

**3 December** John Major and Albert Reynolds meet in Dublin and, after seven hours of talks, agree to negotiate a joint declaration on NI on the basis of an Irish draft.

An IRA bomb with more than 1,000 lb of explosives is defused in West Belfast.

**5 December** Two Catholic men are shot dead by the UFF outside a taxi depot in North Belfast. On 7 December the UFF murders another Catholic man at his home in East Belfast.

**10 December** Prime ministers Major and Reynolds meet during the European Council summit in Brussels. Albert Reynolds later says, 'There are some very difficult issues to be put to bed.'

**11 December** A survey conducted for the *Irish Times* finds that there is 59% support in NI for the continuing talks between prime ministers Major and Reynolds; while 88% of Catholics are in favour of the talks, only 37% of Protestants support them.

**12 December** Two RUC officers are shot dead by the IRA in Fivemiletown, Co. Tyrone.

A report in the *Sunday Press* says that Albert Reynolds plans to call an all-Ireland convention, which will include SF representatives, as soon as IRA violence ends.

In the *Sunday Tribune* Gerry Adams says that NI cannot have a right to self-determination.

The *Sunday Telegraph* claims that former British official Michael Oatley was the intermediary who met Martin McGuinness during the secret contacts between the government and Sinn Fein.

**13 December** A report in the *Financial Times* claims that Sir Patrick Mayhew offered to resign because of the 'transcription and typographical errors' in the documents presented to parliament. The following day Sir Patrick storms out of a Stormont press conference after admitting that he offered to resign over the mistakes in the documents.

In Belfast the UFF shoots dead a man it claims was an informer. The accusation is denied by the dead man's family.

**14 December** A 1,500 lb IRA van bomb is defused in the Markets area of Belfast. A 78-year-old woman dies of a heart attack while the area is being evacuated.

**15 December** In London John Major and Albert Reynolds issue a Joint Declaration on Northern Ireland. The Downing Street Declaration states that, 'The ending of divisions can come about only through the agreement and co-operation of the people, North and South, representing both traditions in Ireland.' The governments commit themselves to 'promote co-operation on all levels' and to recognising international agreements including NI's statutory constitutional guarantee. The governments aim 'to foster agreement and reconciliation, leading to a new political framework founded on consent and encompassing arrangements within Northern Ireland, for the whole island, and between these islands'. (para. 2)
The British government states that it has 'no selfish strategic or economic interest in Northern Ireland. Their primary interest is to see peace, stability and reconciliation established by agreement among all the people who inhabit the island, and they will work together with the Irish government to achieve such an agreement, which will embrace the totality of relationships.

'The role of the British government will be to encourage, facilitate and enable the achievement of such agreement over a period through a process of dialogue and co-operation based on full respect for the rights and identities of both traditions in Ireland.

'They accept that such agreement may, as of right, take the form of agreed structures for the island as a whole, including a united Ireland achieved by peaceful means on the following basis.

'The British government agree that it is for the people of the island of Ireland alone, by agreement between the two parts respectively, to exercise their right of self-determination on the basis of consent, freely and concurrently given, North and South, to bring about a united Ireland, if that is their wish.

'They reaffirm as a binding obligation that they will, for their part, introduce the necessary legislation to give effect to this, or equally to any measure of agreement on future relationships in Ireland which the people living in Ireland may themselves freely so determine without external impediment.' (para. 4)
For the Irish government the Taoiseach states, 'It would be wrong to attempt to impose a united Ireland in the absence of the freely given consent of a majority of the people of Northern Ireland.

'He accepts, on behalf of the Irish government, that the democratic right of self-determination by the people of Ireland as a whole must be achieved and exercised with and subject to the agreement and consent of a majority of the people of Northern Ireland and must, consistent with justice and equity, respect the democratic dignity and the civil rights and religious liberties of both communities.' (para. 5)

Recognising unionist fears, the Taoiseach 'will examine with his colleagues any elements in the democratic life and organisation of the Irish state that can be represented to the Irish government in the course of political dialogue as a real and substantial threat to their way of life and ethos, or that can be represented as not being fully consistent with a modern democratic and pluralist society, and undertakes to examine any possible ways of removing such obstacles.' (para. 6)

He also confirms that, 'In the event of an overall settlement, the Irish government will, as part of a balanced constitutional accommodation, put forward and support proposals for change in the Irish constitution which would fully reflect the principle of consent in Northern Ireland.' (para. 7)

There will be 'institutional recognition' of the links between the people of Britain and Ireland as part of the 'totality of relationships'. (para. 9)

Both governments confirm that, 'Democratically mandated parties which establish a commitment to exclusively peaceful methods and which have shown that they abide by the democratic process, are free to participate fully in democratic politics and to join in dialogue in due course between the governments and the political parties on the way ahead.' (para. 10)

The Taoiseach also suggests that democratic parties consult together about the political future in a Forum for Peace and Reconciliation to be held in the Republic. (para. 11)

The Declaration concludes with the two prime ministers stating their belief 'that these arrangements offer an opportunity to lay the foundations for a more peaceful and harmonious future devoid of the violence and bitter divisions which have scarred the past generation'. (para. 12)

Commenting on the statement John Major says, 'It is a declaration for democracy and dialogue and it is based on consent. It makes no compromise on strongly held principles but it does embody a common view that there is an opportunity to end violence for good in Northern Ireland.' Albert Reynolds states, 'This is a historic opportunity for peace. We hope that everybody will grasp it. There is now a clear political path which is meaningful for all. What we are offering is a framework for peace that prejudices nobody's position or predetermines nobody's future.'

In the House of Commons John Major attempts to reassure unionists by stating: 'I understand the fears and concerns of unionists about the prospects of the British government's entering into talks with Sinn Fein. This period has been a worrying and uncertain time for them. Although they have the primary interest in seeing an end to violence, they are rightly concerned lest this be achieved by selling out the fundamental constitutional principles which the government have always upheld. If they fear that, then they should be reassured by this declaration. It reaffirms the constitutional guarantee in the clearest possible terms. The Taoiseach fully accepts the principle that any constitutional change could come about only with the consent of a majority in Northern Ireland.' He also notes that, 'What is not in the declaration is any suggestion that the British Government should join the ranks of persuaders of the "value" or "legitimacy" of a united Ireland; that is not there. Nor is there any suggestion that the future status of Northern Ireland should be decided by a single act of self-determination by the people of Ireland as a whole; that is not there either. Nor is there any timetable for constitutional change, or any arrangement for joint authority over Northern Ireland. In sum, the declaration provides that it is, as it must be, for the people of Northern Ireland to determine their own future.'

The *Belfast Telegraph* notes that the Declaration 'achieves a balance between the two traditions, a blurring of the edges, but whether it is to satisfy the extremists and lead to a permanent cessation of violence remains to be seen'.

In the Dail Dick Spring says that an end to violence would involve paramilitaries handing over their arms: 'Questions were raised on how to determine a permanent cessation of violence. We are talking about the handing up of arms and are insisting that it would not be simply a temporary cessation of violence to see what the political process offers. There can be no equivocation in relation to the determination of both governments in that regard.' This point is later reiterated by Sir Patrick Mayhew when he says, 'If they hold on to arms, if you know they have got them, then quite patently they are not giving them up for good.'

In an open letter to John Major, Ian Paisley writes, 'Before the latest victim of the IRA murder campaign has been buried, you have been making a deal to get them to the conference table ... It is a tripartite agreement between Reynolds, the IRA and you. You have sold Ulster to buy off the fiendish republican scum and you are prepared to do this notorious deed with such speed that time is not even given for the Christian burial of their latest victim.'

Paisley makes it clear that he feels that republicans are being offered access to all-party talks without the need to give up arms.

**16 December** The *Times* comments, 'Yesterday's declaration was the pinnacle of a close diplomatic relationship which has developed between Dublin and London in the past ten years. Peace broke out between the British and Irish governments long ago: this latest result of that peace is not in itself a guarantee that amity will break out between the other warring parties.'

The Belfast *News Letter* remarks, 'Northern Ireland's majority community may not have been sold out by yesterday's London-Dublin declaration but the Province's position as an integral part of the United Kingdom seems less secure than it was before John Major and Albert Reynolds shook hands on the deal. If the unionist people of the Province still believe they are as British as those in Finchley, they are kidding themselves. For proof they should closely study the statement signed by the two premiers yesterday.'

The *Irish News*, however, says that while much of the document is aimed at calming the nerves of unionists the substance of the document is directed at the republican movement: 'The declaration is a clear and unambiguous attempt to create the conditions for republicans to reject violence and to enter the political process. The document represents a courageous leap of faith and imagination by both governments.'

Asked in a radio interview about the need for the IRA to give up arms before it can become involved in talks, Sir Patrick Mayhew replies, 'What we are saying is that within three months you will be invited to exploratory talks to examine the mechanics, the ways, the means in which you can demonstrate that you have brought violence to an end. At some later stage, and it will be for all the participants in the talks to agree, you can enter the main political talks.' Gerry Adams calls for 'clarification' from the Irish government on parts of the document.

**17 December** In the Dail Albert Reynolds gives his view of how the Downing Street Declaration emerged. He notes that, besides consulting nationalist opinion, he took steps to ascertain what could reassure moderate unionist opinion. He concludes by stating, 'In the final analysis this Joint Declaration is particularly addressed to the people and organisations on both sides who can most directly deliver peace. While none of us can ever condone the deeds committed over the past 25 years, I believe it is right to acknowledge what I believe are serious and courageous efforts that have been made for some time by some in the republican leadership to find a path out of the impasse. I believe when they examine the Joint Declaration closely, together with the proposal for a peace forum ... they should find that they provide the necessary elements for a peace process that will create its own dynamic.'

## The Downing Street Declaration

It has to be conceded that there was no hint of the Downing Street Declaration in Sir Patrick Mayhew's key strategy speech to the British Irish Association in Cambridge on 11 September. In Cambridge Sir Patrick's emphasis was on the renewal of the talks process involving the mainstream constitutional parties, not on the need to draw the 'men of violence' into the political process. Yet by December the Downing Street Declaration appeared with precisely this objective in mind. To explain this shift of emphasis it is helpful to turn to the words of Martin Mansergh, then Albert Reynolds's principal adviser: 'In June 1993, not without much soul-searching on the republican side, the draft [of 'a formula for peace'] was handed over to the British government by the Taoiseach. To say they handled it with kid-gloves would be something of an under-statement. They were prepared to discuss, but not negotiate it, and on several occasions in the autumn of 1993 many of them would have preferred to sideline it. But an initiative that might bring peace was always going to be more important than attempts to restart inter-party talks or even early discussions of the Framework Document.'

The Irish government clearly had a different agenda, based on the belief that the Adams leadership was sincerely interested in peace, in which both the Downing Street Declaration and the *Irish Press* leak of 19 November played a key part. It is a tribute, however, to British adroitness that they accommodated a highly persistent Irish strategy while retaining the support of the Molyneaux unionists. In part, this was achieved by allowing Molyneaux and other unionists to contribute to the text – indeed, in concert with Albert Reynolds, Archbishop Robin Eames helped to draft paragraphs 6 to 8 of the Declaration.

The Downing Street Declaration, when it appeared on 15 December, proved to be a document of considerable originality and sophistication. For unionists it formalised a distasteful message, albeit one already sent by Peter Brooke in 1990: 'The Prime Minister ... reiterates on behalf of the British government that they have no selfish strategic or economic interest in Northern Ireland.' In truth, though, only in the brief aftermath of the Second World War had the belief in a 'selfish strategic interest' really existed in Whitehall.

The real novelty of the Downing Street Declaration lay elsewhere. It is necessary at this point to consider the complex language of the Joint Declaration's fourth paragraph. After Downing Street the phraseology of the Hume-Adams talks continued to dominate the political scene, but its content was dramatically altered. One of the most effective slogans of Irish nationalism had been given a new, decidedly softer, conceptual content – and this had been done by a Fianna Fail government.

The self-determination of the Irish people was conceded by Britain, but solely on the basis that the Irish government only wished to operate that principle in favour of Irish unity with the support of a majority in the North.

Superficially, the rhetoric of the Hume-Adams process had been conceded but, in essence, the process had been stripped of its content in a quite dramatic way. The British, it is true, were now 'facilitators', but for an agreed Ireland rather than for Irish unity, and an 'agreed' Ireland, by definition, could not be a united Ireland until there was majority consent in the North. 'The role of the British government will be to encourage, facilitate and enable the achievement of such agreement over a period through a process of dialogue and co-operation based on full respect for the rights and identities of both traditions in Ireland.'

As Martin Mansergh was later to explain in the *Irish Times*, 'The British government wish to promote enough political agreement to prevent the two communities from fighting each other and harming British interests ... They had made it clear that they will not be persuaders for a united Ireland nor do they wish to see it come about.'

**19 December** In an interview with the *Sunday Life* John Major denies that the Downing Street Declaration is a move toward joint British-Irish authority over NI and says, 'It is about consent. It is about reconciliation. It is about co-operation between the two sides of the community, and between the North and South ... The Declaration recognises that both nationalists and unionists have every right to their point of view, to put it forward and have it heard. It acknowledges that they have a tradition of their own, and cultural and historical roots which deserve equal respect. And, yes, it also makes an important offer to Sinn Fein: an invitation to them to join in the debate on Northern Ireland's future, having shown that they have given up violence for good. Our invitation is clear and specific. Three months after a cessation of violence, the British government is ready to enter an exploratory dialogue with Sinn Fein.'
A 500 lb IRA landmine explodes in Derry injuring six people, three of them children.

**20 December** In a radio interview James Molyneaux rejects the proposition that the Downing Street Declaration represents a 'sell-out' of unionists.

**21 December** In the first SF press conference since the Downing Street Declaration Gerry Adams calls for 'direct and unconditional dialogue' with the British and Irish governments and says that, 'We have a document here which, in its ambiguity, in its lack of mechanisms and in its lack of a clear process, needs to be clarified.'
An Ulster Marketing Survey poll for ITN finds 56% support for the Downing Street Declaration in NI. 87% of nationalists support the Declaration but only 43% of unionists.

**22 December** During a visit to NI John Major says clarification of the Declaration is unnecessary and he will not be drawn into negotiations.

Albert Reynolds says the people of Ireland are 'impatient to move ahead'. In an interview with the *Irish Times* President Clinton says, 'US policy on NI is made in the context of the deep ties of friendship and history the American people enjoy with the peoples of *both* Ireland and Britain ... I am convinced the December 15th joint declaration of Prime Minister Reynolds and Prime Minister Major offers an historic opportunity to end the cycle of bloodshed. I think the best approach for the US now is to continue to encourage this courageous and visionary initiative.'

On the possibility of Gerry Adams being given a visa, he notes, 'As you know Gerry Adams was refused a US visa earlier this year. That decision followed a careful review of his case and was consistent with our own immigration laws regarding terrorist activity. We will, of course, keep the issue under review as the developing situation warrants.'

**23 December** The IRA announces a three-day ceasefire to begin at midnight.

450 paramilitary prisoners in NI are released on parole for Christmas.

Two members of the Royal Marines are acquitted of the murder of SF member Fergal Caraher in Cullyhanna, Co. Armagh, in December 1990.

**27 December** The three-day IRA ceasefire ends with a mortar attack on a police station in Fintona, Co. Tyrone.

**28 December** Some 400 republican activists meet in Loughmacrory, Co. Tyrone, to discuss the Downing Street Declaration. None of those present is believed to have supported the Declaration.

**29 December** In an end of year statement the IRA claims that the British government 'holds the key to peace'.

**30 December** A soldier is shot dead by an IRA sniper in Crossmaglen, Co. Armagh.

The UVF says that it will not support another 'publicity stunt' by Ian Paisley and that it does not feel threatened by the Declaration.

Deaths Arising from the Troubles: 84. Shootings: 476. Bombs Planted: 289. Incendiaries: 61. Weapons Found: 196. Explosives Found: 3.9 tonnes. Persons Charged with Terrorist Offences: 372.

# 1994

**1 January** IRA incendiary devices damage eleven stores in the Belfast area. The historic Linen Hall Library is also slightly damaged by an incendiary device.

A UFF statement says, 'So long as the pan-nationalist terror and political coercion continues, we retain the right to respond militarily in 1994.' On the Downing Street Declaration the organisation states, 'It is widely agreed that the declaration, despite its grand claims regarding consent freely given, is part of a wider agenda and once again ignores the reality that the status of Northern Ireland within the United Kingdom was dramatically changed with the imposition of the Anglo-Irish diktat.'

**2 January** In an interview with the *Sunday Business Post* Martin McGuinness says he would find anything short of a British withdrawal from NI unacceptable. He adds, 'If someone was to say to us that even five years [to leave NI] is difficult, it might take six or seven, then we are prepared to look at that.' McGuinness says that loyalist opposition to a British withdrawal would be 'very quickly smashed'. He also states that republicans would regard a three-month ceasefire as 'particularly long'.

The UFF fires up to 30 shots in an attack on the home of SF councillor Alex Maskey in West Belfast.

Albert Reynolds calls for 'demilitarisation' and claims that the British and Irish governments are 'persuaders' for agreement in Ireland.

**4 January** In a public statement John Hume says, 'The challenge that we now face is ... to remove the last remaining legacy of imperialism in Europe, the deep divisions among our island people, and to do so in a manner that respects our basic humanity and our basic diversity. It is an enormous challenge ... that, as I have said publicly, will require from the republican movement, given the experience that its members have been through, one of the greatest acts of moral courage of this century.'

In Dublin two bomb disposal experts are injured when one of two UVF parcel bombs sent to Sinn Fein and *An Phoblacht* explodes.

**5 January** It is revealed that Gerry Adams (as well as the other four main party leaders) has been invited to attend a New York conference organised by the National Committee on American Foreign Policy.
NIO Minister of State Robert Atkins is replaced by Under-Secretary Tim Smith. On 11 January the Earl of Arran is replaced by Baroness Denton, the first woman to serve as a minister in the NIO.

**7 January** Gerry Adams writes to John Major seeking clarification of the Downing Street Declaration, 'The opportunity for a real and lasting settlement has never been more realisable – your government holds the key in all of this. It is crucial, therefore, that you clarify these issues, urgently and effectively through direct dialogue. If peace is a realistic prospect, as you have asserted, then the opportunity should not be lost because of confusion occasioned by the absence of open and honest dialogue.'
Sir Patrick Mayhew says that clarification of the Declaration would inevitably lead to negotiation with SF.

**8 January** In an *Irish News* interview Gerry Adams criticises Sir Patrick Mayhew's post-Declaration statements that talks between SF and the government will concern the decommissioning of arms, 'Mr Mayhew goes on to say, "Well the exploratory dialogue will be so we can discuss with Sinn Fein how the IRA will hand over their weapons." So I say to myself: "This is what they want. They want the IRA to stop so that Sinn Fein can have the privilege twelve weeks later, having been properly sanitised and come out of quarantine, to have discussions with senior civil servants of how the IRA can hand over their weapons." I hear that reiterated again and again; by Douglas Hurd, by John Major, by Patrick Mayhew.'

**10 January** In a speech in Dublin Albert Reynolds says that with the Joint Declaration, 'British imperialist interest in Ireland is dead, even if we still have to resolve some of its legacy.' He also says that the Irish government will provide 'continuing clarification to the best of our ability' of the Downing Street Declaration.

**11 January** The Irish government announces that the order banning Sinn Fein from radio and television will not be renewed. The ban lapses at midnight on 19 January.

**13 January** In the Commons John Major says that, 'The joint declaration is not an invitation for renegotiation,' but adds, 'The Secretary of State for Northern Ireland and I have gone to great lengths in this House and beyond it to ensure that the joint declaration is fully understood.' The following day Major tells John Hume that the Declaration speaks for itself.

Veteran Irish political figure Brian Lenihan reveals that he has had talks with SF.

**15 January** In the US four Irish-American Senators, including Edward Kennedy, appeal to President Clinton to grant Gerry Adams a visa.

**16 January** A UDA plan for the repartition of NI followed by the 'ethnic cleansing' of Catholics from remaining areas is revealed by the *Sunday Independent*.

**17 January** At Westminster Sinn Fein chairman Tom Hartley presents a document contradicting the British government account of contacts with his party.

**18 January** Sinn Fein launches a 'peace commission'; the first session is held in Derry on 27 January.

**20 January** John Major's private secretary replies to Gerry Adams's letter of 7 January and states: 'Both the Prime Minister and Taoiseach have made clear that there can be no question of renegotiation of their Joint Declaration. It provides a balanced framework for peace and democracy which recognises the interests and aspirations of both main traditions that exist in Ireland. That text, and only that text, is what is at issue.'

In London Sir Patrick Mayhew says there could be clarification of how SF could enter the political process but not of the Declaration itself. On 21 January Adams says that it is 'absurd' to deny clarification.

In an important speech to the University College, Dublin, Law Society, Albert Reynolds says, 'Issues of sovereignty over any substantial territory ought not to be finally resolved by contending states over the heads of the inhabitants of the area in question without their consent.'

**23 January** Albert Reynolds says he will give clarification of the Downing Street Declaration to anyone who wants it.

SDLP MP Seamus Mallon reads out part of the Hume-Adams document concerning 'self-determination' on an RTE television programme. The document states: 'The Taoiseach accepts on behalf of the Irish government that the democratic right to self-determination by the people of the island of Ireland as a whole must be achieved and exercised with the agreement and consent of the people of the North of

Ireland.' Comparing it with paragraph 5 of the Downing Street Declaration he asks, 'Where is the difference to the peace declaration?'

**24 January** UFF incendiary devices are discovered at a school in Dundalk and in a Dublin sorting office.

**25 January** The CLMC says it will adopt a 'wait and see' attitude towards the Declaration.

**27 January** The UVF shoots dead a Catholic man and wounds his wife during an attack on their home in Ballymena, Co. Antrim. In Belfast another Catholic is murdered by the UFF at his home in the Ormeau Road area.
In London IRA incendiary devices detonate in three stores in Oxford Street. The following day a further firebomb explodes in the same area, while others are defused on 28 and 29 January.

**28 January** Following an Anglo-Irish Intergovernmental Conference meeting in Dublin Sir Patrick Mayhew says he will continue to make clear, through speeches, what the Declaration does: 'You can call it clarification or anything else you like.'

**29 January** President Clinton authorises a 'limited duration' visa for Gerry Adams to enter the US. Clinton says the 'difficult decision' will 'help advance the cause of peace in Northern Ireland'. The decision, supported by the National Security Council and Irish-American politicians, is taken against the advice of the State Department and the British government.
Albert Reynolds replies to a letter from Gerry Adams and details the political developments he would like to see after the end of the IRA campaign.

**31 January** In an *Irish Times* interview Gerry Adams says that clarification of the Declaration solely through speeches is not 'the fitting way'. Arriving in New York, Adams says that, 'This generation of young republicans will see peace in Ireland.'

**1 February** In New York the National Committee on American Foreign Policy is addressed by John Hume, Gerry Adams and Alliance leader John Alderdice. Unionist leaders boycott the conference because of Adams's presence. In the following days both President Clinton and Vice-President Gore urge Adams to support the Downing Street Declaration, but the visit is still viewed as a major publicity coup for Sinn Fein; the US *Daily News* comments that, 'Adams reaped more publicity in two days than in two decades of resisting British rule in Northern Ireland.'

**2 February** John Major condemns the 'smokescreen of evasions and falsehoods' surrounding Gerry Adams's visit to the US. UUP MP Ken Maginnis says, 'Already we are witnessing the growing disgust within the United Kingdom to the obscenity of violent republicanism being pandered to by Mr Clinton.'

Albert Reynolds says he has given an abundance of clarification on the Declaration, 'And the time is coming when I would expect to get some clarification in return.'

In a New York press release Gerry Adams states, 'It is nonsense to argue that the consent of a national minority within an undemocratic and artificially created state is necessary before any constitutional change could occur.'

**3 February** In Newtownards, Co. Down, a Catholic taxi driver is shot dead by the UFF. In West Belfast a UVF gun attack wounds the driver of a minibus used by relatives of republican prisoners and injures a woman passer-by.

Gerry Adams faces a protest from victims of IRA violence on his return to Dublin Airport.

**9 February** Gerry Adams says that he welcomes the clarification of the Declaration which he has received in a confidential letter from Albert Reynolds.

**10 February** Former INLA leader Dominic McGlinchey is shot dead in Drogheda. In June 1993 McGlinchey had been wounded in Dundalk during an attack by former IPLO members.

In London Pairic MacFhloinn, Denis and John Kinsella are jailed for a total of 80 years for their part in the bombing of Warrington gasworks in February 1993.

Sir Patrick Mayhew says that under the Joint Declaration the British and Irish governments are 'persuaders for agreement on the divided island of Ireland'.

**11 February** James Molyneaux says that the Declaration has failed and that the British government should proceed with a political settlement for NI alone.

The UFF attacks the homes of two SDLP members, wounding the son of an SDLP member in Belfast. The following day there is a UFF rocket attack on SF's Connolly House in Belfast.

**13 February** Interviewed on ITV, Gerry Adams says that the British government will have to convince unionists that their future lies 'with the rest of the Irish people'. Adams also says there can be no definitive response to the Declaration until it has been clarified.

Gardai find parts for a heavy machine-gun and 3,000 rounds of ammunition in Mullingar, Co. Westmeath. The following day a second heavy machine-gun and nearly 70 lb of semtex are also recovered.

**17 February** A police constable is killed and two other RUC officers injured in an IRA rocket attack on their Land Rover in the Markets area of Belfast.

In North Belfast Red Hand Commando gunmen wound Sean McParland while he is babysitting his four grandchildren. Mr McParland dies from his injuries a week later.

**18 February** Three workmen are wounded by UFF gunmen outside Sinn Fein's Andersonstown Road headquarters in Belfast.

**19 February** John Major and Albert Reynolds hold talks at Downing Street. After the meeting Major says that, 'No one should be able to veto progress on the talks. We have made clear what Sinn Fein need to do to join.'

**20 February** John Hume adds his support to the SF call for clarification of the Declaration. Dick Spring says that the required clarification has already been given.

Gardai recover a heavy machine-gun, two rifles and 500 rounds of ammunition in Newport, Co. Tipperary.

**21 February** In a BBC Panorama programme Sir Patrick Mayhew confirms that two 'unauthorised' meetings with IRA representatives took place in 1993, but says no official was authorised to say that Britain eventually intended to withdraw from NI. Panorama repeats the claim that in March 1993, three days after the Warrington bombing, a British government representative told Martin McGuinness and Gerry Kelly that eventually the 'island of Ireland would be one'.

An IRA mortar attack on a police station causes extensive damage to the village of Beragh, Co. Tyrone.

**23 February** In Birmingham Sir Patrick Mayhew says that Britain will not 'hang onto' NI but neither will it persuade people to go for one option or another.

**24 February** The INLA shoots dead a doorman outside a restaurant on the Lisburn Road in Belfast.

**26 February** At the Sinn Fein ard fheis in Tallaght, West Dublin, Gerry Adams says, 'That the declaration addresses the issue of Irish national self-determination at all is a significant departure from an attitude of the British towards Ireland which has endured for centuries. However, the serious flaw in the document is that, having declared that the Irish are entitled to exercise the right to self-determination without external influence, they then proceed, or so it seems to me, to interfere ... There can be no justification for trying to instruct the people whose right to self-determination you have just conceded how they are to use it.' Later, to loud applause, he adds, 'One also has to ask does anyone really expect the IRA to cease its activities so that British civil servants can discuss with Sinn Fein the surrender of IRA weapons after we have been "decontaminated".'

**28 February** The UUP reveals its plans for administrative devolution and says it will not take part in a resumption of the three-strand talks process. The following day Albert Reynolds describes the UUP proposals as 'a cul-de-sac in political terms'.

**1 March** John Major ends a two-day visit to Washington. The visit is widely viewed as an attempt to repair the damage caused to Anglo-American relations resulting from the decision of the US administration to grant a visa to Gerry Adams in the face of British objections.

**2 March** The European Commission announces that it will recommend the continuation of its 15 million ECU support for the International Fund for Ireland 'as an expression of practical support for the peace process'.

**4 March** Sir Hugh Annesley, Chief Constable of the RUC, is subpoenaed to produce the Stalker report to assist the inquest into those killed as a result of the alleged 'shoot to kill' policy.

**5 March** After a meeting with Sir Patrick Mayhew, Dick Spring says they are confident that the three-strand talks can be recommenced. The following day, however, James Molyneaux says his party will not return to 'the three-strand circus act'.

**6 March** A *Sunday Express* report claims that during a secret meeting between John Major and John Smith, the Labour leader, Smith had indicated that his party would support renewal of the Prevention of Terrorism Act provided the maximum seven-day detention period was reduced and exclusion orders were dropped.

**9 March** The House of Commons votes to establish a Select Committee on Northern Ireland Affairs. On 24 March six Conservative, two Labour, two UUP (Ken Maginnis and John Taylor), one DUP (Peter Robinson), one SDLP (Eddie McGrady) and UPUP MP James Kilfedder (later appointed chairman) are selected as committee members.

The Commons votes to renew the Prevention of Terrorism Act. The Labour Opposition votes against renewal.

IRA members fire five mortars, none of which explode, from cars parked near Heathrow Airport. On 11 March four more mortars hit Heathrow but fail to explode. An RAF VC10 with the Queen on board lands while the police are searching Terminal Four. In Dublin Gerry Adams comments, 'Every so often there will be something spectacular to remind the world the tragic signs of conflict are ongoing.' On 13 March Heathrow shuts down for two hours after a third IRA mortar attack.

**10 March** The IRA shoots dead an off-duty RUC officer in front of his wife at a greyhound track in North Belfast.

**11 March** A Catholic haulier is killed when a UVF bomb blows up his lorry in Portadown, Co. Armagh.

**13 March** A statement from the leadership of the IRA says that, 'Despite the negative attitude of the British government since [the Downing Street Declaration] and their refusal to build on the opportunity for peace, the IRA wish to publicly note that our positive and flexible attitude to the peace process is an abiding and enduring one. This is evident from our response to developments to date and in our continued willingness to be flexible and positive in exploring the potential for moving the situation forward.' Dick Spring says the IRA's statement is 'difficult to accept' and calls on its members to 'come to their senses'. He adds, 'They are endangering life yet again and as long as that continues they are not going to be part of the political process.'

**14 March** Sir Louis Blom-Cooper, the independent commissioner for RUC holding centres, calls for audio and visual taping of interrogations.

**16 March** NIO security minister Sir John Wheeler refuses a request from the Bloody Sunday Justice Group for a fresh inquiry into the January 1972 killings in Derry.

**17 March** In Belfast Gerry Adams says that each side in the conflict will have to accept 'democratic compromise'.

At a St Patrick's Day press conference in Washington President Clinton calls on the IRA to 'lay down their arms'. Albert Reynolds says it is time

for Gerry Adams's words to be translated into actions.
At Westminster Sir Patrick Mayhew says the Republic's claim to NI 'is an anachronism. I believe that to be essentially understood.'

**19 March** In a Radio Ulster interview Albert Reynolds says 'talk of an internal settlement' in NI is 'a waste of time'. John Bruton later accuses Reynolds of 'appeasing the terrorists'.
At the Ulster Unionist Council annual general meeting James Molyneaux rejects North-South institutions.

**20 March** An army helicopter is shot down by an IRA mortar in Crossmaglen, Co. Armagh.

**21 March** There are angry exchanges between John Major and Ian Paisley during what is described as a 'very rough' meeting at Downing Street. The DUP submission to the Prime Minister states, 'The joint authority which we have *de facto* in Northern Ireland ... has never been more explicit or evident ... Dublin interference is now such that the British government cannot and will not take any initiative except in partnership with, and with the agreement of, the Dublin government.'
SDLP MP Joe Hendron's car is set alight by loyalists outside his home in South Belfast.

**22 March** Gardai find a number of weapons and 1,300 rounds of ammunition at a secret IRA training camp in Co. Sligo.

**23 March** In a radio interview Martin McGuinness says that the situation could move 'quite dramatically' if British representatives met SF for face-to-face clarification.
Two IRA 'barrack-buster' bombs are defused in Milford, Co. Armagh, and Claudy, Co. Londonderry.

**24 March** SDLP councillor John Fee is severely beaten by republicans outside his home at Crossmaglen. The following day SF President Gerry Adams says the attack was 'unjustified and unwarranted'.

**25 March** Irish President Mary Robinson visits Newry, Craigavon and Derry during a visit to Northern Ireland.

**28 March** After Sir Patrick Mayhew says that he is confident that Ulster Unionists will rejoin the three-strand talks process. The UUP says Mayhew's confidence is 'very misplaced'.

**29 March** The UFF launches a rocket and gun attack on a SF office on

Belfast's Falls Road.
An FEC report suggests that Catholic under-representation in the workforce is 5% compared to 7% in 1990.

**30 March** The IRA announces a three-day ceasefire. An IRA statement says, 'Last year in an effort to enhance the success of proposed meetings between Sinn Fein and the British government we agreed to a British government proposal to suspend operations for two weeks. In the event the British government rejected this and in so doing closed down the potential opportunity for progress which this represented. Our statement of 13 March reiterates our continued willingness to be positive and flexible in exploring the potential for moving the situation forward. As further evidence of that we will unilaterally suspend offensive military actions for 72 hours from midnight Tuesday, 5 April, until Friday, 8 April. There are no conditions attached to this unilateral initiative but we hope that the British government will accept this further opportunity in the spirit in which it is offered and utilise it to the best advantage of the British and Irish people.'
While on a visit to NI John Major says, 'What people in Northern Ireland want is not a ceasefire over two or three days but a permanent end to violence … That is the message we wish to hear, not just a brief public relations gesture.' John Hume responds to the IRA statement by saying, 'I didn't go through any peace process to get a ceasefire. I'm interested in a total cessation of violence.'
NI Lord Chief Justice Sir Brian Hutton dismisses the appeal of Private Lee Clegg against his conviction for the murder of a joyrider in West Belfast in 1990.

**31 March** Two Catholic men are wounded in a UFF attack in East Belfast. Another Catholic man is injured in a UVF attack in Antrim.
Cardinal Cahal Daly says the forthcoming IRA ceasefire shows that republicans are sincere in the search for peace.

**1 April** Women members of the RUC are issued with guns for the first time.

**5 April** The IRA begins its three-day ceasefire. The following day Sir Patrick Mayhew, speaking in Montreal, describes the ceasefire as a 'three-day abstention'. John Hume says the Prime Minister should appoint a senior backbench MP to establish what clarification is required by Sinn Fein.

**6 April** Margaret Wright from Belfast is beaten and shot dead in a loyalist band hall in the Donegall Road area. It is thought that her loyalist

killers believed she was a Catholic. On 12 April UVF member Ian
Hamilton is shot dead by the organisation, which claims he had admitted
killing Margaret Wright.

**9 April** The IRA ceasefire ends with attacks on the security forces in
Newtownbutler, Co. Fermanagh, Aughnacloy, Co. Tyrone, and on the
Stewartstown Road in Belfast.

**10 April** Speaking to a Fianna Fail convention in Dublin, Albert
Reynolds says the time for deliberation by SF is over.
Work begins on a major refurbishment of the joint RUC/army base at
Crossmaglen, despite strong opposition from nationalist politicians.

**12 April** In New York Sir Patrick Mayhew says, 'The ending of the
armed conflict which has so afflicted the lives of so many in Northern
Ireland over the last 25 years … that's not going to require any
surrender.'
The *Belfast Telegraph* reports the Chief Constable of the RUC, Sir Hugh
Annesley, as saying at a private function that paramilitary violence will
end in three years. In an *Irish Times* article John Hume states, 'The basis
of the rule of law – agreement on how we are governed – has never
obtained since [1912] in Northern Ireland.'

**14 April** The NIO says that if SF asks for specific points concerning the
Declaration to be clarified it will consider the request.
Theresa Clinton, the wife of a former SF election candidate, is killed
when UFF terrorists spray her home with gunfire. Two Catholic men are
also wounded in a UFF attack on Belfast's Antrim Road on the same day.

**16 April** At a Fianna Fail conference in Co. Dublin Albert Reynolds
says he envisages 30% Northern representation in any united Ireland
government.

**17 April** The *Observer* quotes a UFF leader as saying that there could be
a loyalist 'assault on the South' if 'interference' from the Republic grew.

**20 April** An RUC constable is killed and two other officers injured in an
IRA mortar attack on their Land Rover in Derry.

**21 April** NI Lord Chief Justice Sir Brian Hutton quashes the conviction
of Paul Hill for the murder of a former British soldier in 1974. Sir Brian
declares the conviction 'unsafe and unsatisfactory' and says the 'inhuman
treatment' Hill had suffered at Guildford police station may have led him
to confess to the murder.

**24 April** The IRA murders two Protestant men in Garvagh, Co. Londonderry, saying they were UFF members. The claim is denied by the UFF.

**25 April** Sixteen alleged drug-dealers are kneecapped by the IRA. The following day the body of a Catholic man killed by the IRA because it said he was a drug-dealer (a claim denied by the man's family), is found in West Belfast.

**26 April** A Catholic man is murdered by the UFF at his home in the New Lodge area of Belfast.

**27 April** The murders of Gerry Evans by the INLA in Glengormley and Paul Thompson by the UFF in the Springfield Road area of Belfast brings to eight the number of people killed in the previous eight days.
Speaking in Washington, Cardinal Cahal Daly says that SF should be given clarification of the Downing Street Declaration if it spells out what it wants.

**28 April** The Iranian chargé d'affaires is summoned to the Foreign Office after the British government claims that Iran is planning to supply the IRA with money and arms.
SF chairman Mitchel McLaughlin is given a US visa to enable him to speak in Cleveland, Ohio.
A Catholic newsagent is shot dead by the UVF in the Docks area of Belfast and the IRA kills a former UDR member at his home near Armagh. On 29 April the IRA shoots dead a man it claims was an informer.

**1 May** In a speech in Killarney, Co.Kerry, Dick Spring says that any agreement must be based on the recognition that the rights and allegiances of both communities in NI are equally valid. 'It means that we in the Republic of Ireland must be prepared to recognise, and to preserve and protect, the rights of unionists as British subjects and citizens. It also means that the nationalist community in Northern Ireland must have the absolute assurance that there can never be a return to the days of intolerance and injustice in the administration of Northern Ireland.'

**4 May** A report by the independent assessor of military complaints procedures in NI reveals that only one soldier had been severely disciplined in 1993 as a result of 606 complaints received.

**8 May** Rose Ann Mallon, a 76-year-old Catholic from Co. Tyrone, is shot dead by the UVF at her home near Dungannon. On 27 July surveillance cameras are discovered near the house, leading the Mallon family to call for an inquiry.

**11 May** Following a meeting with SDLP representatives police agree to support the proposal to build a 20-foot high wall to separate the Springfield and Springmartin areas of Belfast. On 15 June the NIO confirms that the wall will be built.

**12 May** In Belfast 23-year-old Martin Bradley is shot dead by a UFF gunman while he is cradling his one-year-old baby nephew on his shoulder. Police say Mr Bradley was the victim of mistaken identity.

In a speech to the Irish Association in Dublin Sir Patrick Mayhew says the 'broad shape of a possible agreement' is emerging containing political structures with 'widespread support among both traditions'. He adds, 'We need to make progress on new arrangements for North/South relationships ... [but] there is no necessity for them to impinge upon sovereignty.' Mayhew says that stereotyped characterisation of unionism is unfair. 'It fails to recognise in unionism a historic political tradition that is authentically Irish ... Certainly unionists can sometimes be defensive, and inclined to see themselves as inhabiting an embattled enclave in these islands. But there is another, important side to unionism: the belief that all the different people of these two islands – English, Welsh, Scots and Irish too – share far more than divides them; a belief that there is as much value in their continued and various diversity as there is in their mutual conformity; a belief that in a democratically established union there is more strength to be found than in the sum of its constituent parts; and a belief, therefore, that all will gain from being freely associated together within an entity that is a union. These are political beliefs which, in their best and most inclusive form ... are far from unique to the north-east of this island. They form an important part of the British Conservative tradition. They are the foundation of the United States of America. We see them reflected on the other side of the world, in the hopes and aspirations of President Mandela for a genuinely inclusive and democratic new South Africa, accommodating the diversity of all its people.'

**13 May** The *Irish Times* reports that SF has submitted a written list of points it wants clarified. The list is to be forwarded to the British government.

Fred Anthony, who worked as a police station cleaner, is killed and his wife and two children injured when an IRA bomb explodes under their car in Lurgan, Co. Armagh.

**14 May** A Scottish soldier is killed when an IRA bomb explodes at a checkpoint in Keady, Co. Armagh.

**16 May** A Downing Street statement says full acceptance of the Joint Declaration is not a prerequisite for SF involvement in talks.

**17 May** Two Catholic workmen are shot dead by the UVF at a building site in the Tiger's Bay area of Belfast. The following day two more Catholic men are fatally wounded by loyalist gunmen at a taxi office in Armagh.
A review of the Emergency Provisions Act recommends that police interviews be taped. On 24 May Sir Patrick Mayhew rejects the proposal.

**19 May** The NIO issues a 21-page 'commentary' on the twenty questions submitted by SF via the Irish government. The commentary says that the British government's primary interest is 'to see peace, stability and reconciliation established by agreement among all the people' of the island. No political objective will be excluded from discussion in the talks process. The government accepts the validity of all electoral mandates, including that of Sinn Fein. However, 'All who join in political dialogue should demonstrate a commitment to exclusively peaceful methods and to the democratic process.' Britain will 'encourage, facilitate and enable ... a process of dialogue and co-operation based on full respect for the rights and identities of both traditions in Ireland'. It will also introduce legislation 'to give effect to any measure of agreement on future relationships which the people of Ireland may freely determine'. The commentary also reiterates the view that 'any change in the constitutional status of Northern Ireland would be subject to the consent of a majority of its people'.
After the release of the commentary Sir Patrick Mayhew says SF must decide whether it wants to join the political process or stand outside it: 'They've got the key, they can turn it.'
Albert Reynolds describes the British response as 'comprehensive and positive'. Dick Spring says the commentary 'is sufficient to end the clarification debate'. On 28 May, however, Gerry Adams says the British response has left 'disappointment and frustration'.

**20 May** There is rioting in Protestant areas of Belfast after a man appears at Belfast Magistrates' Court accused of 'directing the activities' of the UFF.

**21 May** IRA member Martin Doherty is shot dead by the UVF in an attack on a Dublin bar holding a republican function.

**23 May** A security guard is shot dead by the IRA in Belfast city centre.

A UVF bomb attack on the SF office in Belfast City Hall leaves two workmen injured.

**25 May** At the launch of the SF European election campaign Gerry Adams says Irish unification is 'not only inevitable but a prerequisite on the road to a durable peace'.

**27 May** Addressing the Oxford Union, Albert Reynolds says that the principle of consent for a united Ireland, which has been accepted by the Irish government as a condition for the establishment of a united Ireland, must also apply to any other constitutional arrangements for the North, 'including the existing ones'.

**30 May** At a Belfast press conference Ian Paisley says the Irish government is pushing for all-Ireland institutions to administer a wide range of social and economic functions with greater recognition of Irish language, symbols and culture in NI. 'The secretariat from Dublin will be not only an advisory body but a body almost with executive power to deal with all sections of matters relevant to Northern Ireland.' The DUP leader also describes James Molyneaux as 'a Judas Iscariot'. On 1 June the UUP leader says Paisley's remark is 'a shattering blow' to unionist unity.

**1 June** In the Dail Dick Spring states that the key to Sinn Fein joining political discussions is a permanent cessation of violence. 'There will have to be a verification of the handing over of arms. As I said publicly on many occasions, there is little point in attempting to bring people into political dialogue if they are doing so on the basis of giving it a try and if it does not work returning to the bomb and the bullet. It has to be permanent and there must be evidence of it ... There can be no participation by Sinn Fein-IRA in political discussions with either government until they have made a very firm commitment that the violence has ended.'

**2 June** A helicopter carrying 25 senior anti-terrorist experts crashes in dense fog on a hillside on the Mull of Kintyre, killing all those on board. The helicopter was travelling from Belfast to a conference in Inverness where, it has been suggested, they were to discuss the implications of a potential IRA ceasefire. Killed in the crash are six members of MI5 including the two most senior MI5 members in NI (one of them, John Deverell, a former deputy director-general), ten senior officers of RUC Special Branch, including Assistant Chief Constable Brian Fitzsimons of the RUC, and nine members of army intelligence, including Colonel Christopher Biles, Assistant Chief of Staff at army HQ in Northern

Ireland. Four RAF crew members are also killed. In June 1995 an RAF report claims pilot error was responsible for the crash but in March 1996 a fatal accident inquiry concludes that there is no evidence of pilot error.

**5 June** A report in the *Independent on Sunday* says that the European Commission on Human Rights has decided that the SAS soldiers responsible for killing three unarmed IRA members in Gibraltar in 1988 did not use excessive force. The case was nevertheless referred to the Court of Human Rights.

**8 June** After planting a series of incendiary devices in a number of towns in the Republic, the UFF issues a statement saying, 'Our war against the Irish will intensify the further they interfere with the internal affairs of our beloved Ulster.'

**9 June** A Catholic worker is shot dead by the UVF in the Harland and Wolff shipyard. The following day 2,000 shipyard workers walk out in protest at the killing.
In Germany Paul Hughes, Donna Maguire and Sean Hick are acquitted of the murder of a British army officer in Dortmund in 1990. Hick and Hughes are released while Maguire is held on further charges.

**13 June** Elections in Northern Ireland to the European Parliament (held on 9 June) return the three sitting MEPs. Ian Paisley receives 163,246 first preference votes (29.2%), John Hume 161,992 (28.9%) and both are elected on the first count. Ulster Unionist Jim Nicholson receives 133,459 votes (23.8%) and is elected on the second count. Three SF candidates receive 55,215 votes, 9.9% of first preference votes, and the Alliance Party receives 23,157 votes (4.1%). The turn-out in many unionist areas of the province is exceptionally low.

**15 June** Albert Reynolds sends a letter giving 'clarification' of the Downing Street Declaration to Gary McMichael of the UDP. On 24 June the *Belfast Telegraph* publishes Albert Reynolds's response to McMichael's questions. Reynolds's reply states, 'We do not seek to impose constitutional change by stealth or coercion, whether it be a united Ireland, or joint sovereignty or joint authority. What we seek is a new accommodation between the two traditions on this island.' He adds that, 'The Irish government have a strong moral duty towards the nationalist community in Northern Ireland, because of experience in the past, to ensure that the principles of equal citizenship, equality of treatment and parity of esteem are translated into practice.' Reynolds also says there is a need for strong North-South institutions to facilitate co-operation and joint action.

**16 June** UVF member David Hamilton and Colin Craig, who has loyalist connections, are fatally wounded and two other men injured in an INLA gun attack on the Shankill Road. On 9 July another UVF member, Trevor King, dies from wounds received in the attack. In the wake of the attack local DUP councillor Revd Eric Smyth says Protestants have to 'wake up to the fact that this is a war situation'.
UVF member Laurence Maguire is sentenced to 480 years' imprisonment for his involvement in five sectarian murders.

**17 June** The UVF murders a Catholic taxi driver in Carrickfergus. A Protestant building worker is killed in a separate UVF gun attack on a workmen's hut in Newtownabbey. The UVF believed it was attacking Catholic workmen. A second man, also a Protestant, dies from injuries received in the attack on 9 July.
Sir Patrick Mayhew says there is no prospect of a successful political settlement unless Articles 2 and 3 of the Irish constitution are amended. Dick Spring states that the Irish government would propose changes to the articles but would require Britain to make changes in Section 75 of the Government of Ireland Act in return.

**18 June** UVF gunmen murder six men and wound five others when they open fire on a group of people watching a Republic of Ireland soccer match at The Heights bar in Loughinisland, Co. Down. One of those killed, Barney Green, was 87 years old. Sir Patrick Mayhew says the 'moral squalor' of the killers is beyond description.

**21 June** In an interview with the *Irish Times* Albert Reynolds says cross-border institutions with executive powers are a quid pro quo for changes to Articles 2 and 3 of the Irish constitution and that, 'Institutional links between North and South will have executive powers. That's the type of overall framework we're looking to.'

**24 June** John Major and Albert Reynolds hold a meeting during a European Union conference in Corfu. Reynolds says that 'executive boards' might be a better description for the type of North-South bodies he has in mind. A British official says, 'There is no question of imposing a joint authority on some aspects of the government of Northern Ireland.' In what later becomes known among the Frameworks Documents negotiators as 'the Corfu test', John Major insists the document must contain the removal of the Republic's territorial claim and that Dublin must recognise the legitimacy of Northern Ireland. This 'test' is used by the negotiators on all proposals for changes to the Irish constitution. A British source, however, says, 'It was not a matter of life and death for us that we had to nail down what the constitution should actually say.'

SF publishes the report of its Peace Commission. The commission received 228 submissions, 85 of them saying that SF should encourage the IRA to call a ceasefire for at least three months to enter negotiations. The report claims that most who gave submissions believed the Declaration helped ensure unionists 'would remain inflexible and opposed to any change in the status quo'.

**30 June** Sir John May's report into the wrongful convictions of the Guildford Four says, 'The miscarriages of justice that occurred in this case were not due to any weakness or inherent fault in the criminal justice system or the trial procedures which were part of the system. They were the result of individual failings.'

The government announces that nearly 40 prisoners are to be transferred from jails in England to NI.

In the Dail Albert Reynolds says there is 'an important distinction' between joint authority and North-South institutions. 'Joint authority could be the joint exercise of power over Northern Ireland from above by the two governments, without there necessarily being full democratic participation by the Northern parties. For that reason, I can readily see why unionists should be opposed to it. Joint institutions, however, would represent freely entered into co-operation or pooled effort, in which people of both traditions would work together on the basis of common interests between North and South.'

**3 July** The *Sunday Tribune* reports that the IRA is considering a ceasefire.

**5 July** Alliance Party member and former Belfast Lord Mayor David Cook is appointed chairman of the NI Police Authority.

**6 July** Dick Spring says the Irish government is not seeking joint authority over NI: 'What we are seeking is, first, political arrangements for the government of Northern Ireland which would command the support of the great majority of both traditions in the divided community of Northern Ireland. Side by side with that, we want the closest possible links between a Northern Ireland administration and the Irish government in the interests of the people on the island as a whole.'

**7 July** Prince Charles faces protests during a visit to Derry. The Prince is Colonel in Chief of the Parachute Regiment, which was responsible for the deaths of those killed on Bloody Sunday in 1972.

**9 July** The UFF murders a Catholic man in Cookstown, Co. Tyrone.

**10 July** The IRA fires 40 shots into the home of DUP MP Revd William McCrea in Magherafelt, Co. Londonderry.

**11 July** UDP spokesman Ray Smallwoods is shot dead by the IRA at his home in Lisburn. On 14 July Peter Robinson and Sammy Wilson of the DUP help carry the coffin at his funeral.
Belfast High Court rules that the coroner investigating the deaths of those killed by the RUC in 1982 in the 'shoot to kill' controversy cannot demand access to the Stalker report.

**12 July** A lorry with two tons of explosives hidden in false compartments is seized at the port of Heysham, Lancashire. It is believed that the IRA planned to use the explosives in London.
In the US Albert Reynolds says that 'enduring peace' would bring 'complete demilitarisation on all sides'. He adds, 'We will aim to reopen every single cross-border road within a relatively short period. The North-South electricity interconnector will be restored. We can expect obtrusive security installations along the border to fall into disuse and be dismantled. Northern nationalists will be seeking a restructured police force that is acceptable throughout the community and drawn from all parts of it ... In the event of an overall settlement, a balanced constitutional accommodation will require the principle of consent to be formally enshrined in the constitutional law of both countries. It is the people of Ireland, North and South, who will be sovereign in Ireland, both separately and together.'
At an Orange demonstration in Moira, Co. Down, James Molyneaux attacks Reynolds's view and says North-South institutions with executive powers would be 'stepping stones to his recently stated goal of Irish unity'.

**14 July** A CLMC statement says that if the IRA ends its campaign it will respond in order to allow 'magnanimous dialogue'.

**16 July** Crumlin Road prison in Belfast is extensively damaged after nearly 100 loyalist prisoners go on a rampage through the jail.

**17 July** The body of Caroline Moreland, murdered by the IRA because it claimed she was an informer, is found near Rosslea, Co. Fermanagh.

**18 July** In a *Daily Telegraph* interview Sir Patrick Mayhew says there must be a clear abandonment of the Republic's claim to NI: 'The Irish government realises the central importance to unionists of the territorial claim ... There has got to be, in my view, something much more positive than a broad assertion ... if unionists are going to have their fears allayed.'

**19 July** Following a Downing Street meeting with John Major, James Molyneaux says North-South bodies with executive powers are 'unreal'.

**22 July** A Catholic publican is shot dead by the UFF in Rathcoole, north of Belfast. Dick Spring says a three-month IRA ceasefire would be 'totally unacceptable', but if there was no IRA violence for six to twelve months it might help push the process forward.

**24 July** At a special Sinn Fein ard fheis in Letterkenny, Co. Donegal, Gerry Adams says, 'The declaration was the response by the two governments to the developing Irish Peace Initiative. From their perspective the declaration was an important development. From our perspective it marked a stage in the evolving peace process. In its positive elements it suggests a potentially significant change in the approach of the governments to resolving the conflict in Ireland and we welcome this. But it does not deal adequately with some of the core issues and this is crucial.'

**28 July** Two men are arrested after Gardai discover an IRA arms cache in Co. Meath. 24 Kalashnikov rifles, a flame-thrower, two machine-guns, a rocket launcher, a mortar, 30,000 rounds of ammunition, 300 magazines, timers and detonators are recovered.

**29 July** Over 40 people are injured in an IRA mortar attack on a police station in Newry, Co. Down.

**31 July** Two leading UDA men are shot dead by the IRA on Belfast's Ormeau Road.

**1 August** An *Irish Times* report says that there are strong indications that a temporary IRA ceasefire will be called within a month.

**3 August** After confirming that he had met the leadership of the IRA to discuss a ceasefire, Gerry Adams says he is 'guardedly optimistic' on the prospects for peace.

**5 August** The body of a Protestant man, alleged by the UVF to be an informer, is found in North Belfast.

**7 August** Kathleen O'Hagan is shot dead in front of her children by the UVF in Co. Tyrone. Mrs O'Hagan was pregnant at the time she was murdered.

**8 August** Trelford Withers, a part-time member of the Royal Irish

Regiment is shot dead by the IRA in Crossgar, Co. Down.

An *Irish Press* report claims that a joint UVF/UFF meeting held on 2 August had decided to continue the loyalist terrorist campaign whether the IRA called a ceasefire or not.

**10 August** A Catholic security guard is shot dead by the UFF at his place of work in East Belfast. The following day a Catholic printing worker is murdered at work by the UFF in Lurgan. The UFF says it launched the attack because the company printed *An Phoblacht*. The company denies this claim.

**11 August** RUC Chief Constable Sir Hugh Annesley says the number of troops on patrol will be reduced if there is a prolonged IRA ceasefire.

**12 August** Albert Reynolds tells Sean Duignan, his press officer, that he told the IRA, 'If they don't do this right, they can shag off; I don't want to hear … conditional stuff … just that it's over – period – full stop. Otherwise, I'll walk away. I'll go off down that three-strand talks framework document road with John Major, and they can detour away for another 25 years of killing and being killed – for what? Because, at the end of that 25 years, they'll be back where they are right now, with damn all to show for it, except thousands more dead, and for nothing.'

**13 August** An IRA explosive device planted in the pannier of a mountain bike causes damage to shops in Bognor Regis. A similar device is defused in Brighton.

James Molyneaux tells a Royal Black Institution rally in Glasgow, 'Adams, minus the adoration of the news industry, could never have by himself sold the product labelled "peace process" more successfully than Dr Goebbels, who used the same terms while herding Jews into gas chambers.'

**14 August** On the 25th anniversary of the deployment of troops on the streets of Belfast Gerry Adams states that he is confident that the peace process can move towards the goal of a negotiated political settlement.

A Catholic man is abducted and murdered by the UFF in Belfast.

**15 August** John Bruton says SF cannot be involved in political negotiations until the IRA calls a total cessation of violence and that 'the worst possible scenario' would be if the government initially set strict terms but was forced to relax them under threat of a resumption of violence.

Sammy Wilson of the DUP says unionists should distance themselves from the 'treacherous Tories' and begin making overtures to the Labour Party.

**17 August** An IRA bomb destroys a Protestant bar on Belfast's York Road and another IRA bomb in a bar on the Shankill Road is defused. The following day an IRA incendiary device explodes in a Protestant bar on the Ormeau Road.

In a letter to the Secretary of State Ian Paisley says his party will not be involved in a fresh round of political talks.

**18 August** A man alleged to have strong criminal connections is shot dead by the IRA in Dublin.

Seamus Mallon says the republican movement has a 'clear and unambiguous choice' between ending violence 'totally and permanently' or being removed from involvement in the peace process.

**19 August** An *Irish Times* report claims that the framework document which is being drawn up by the British and Irish governments will propose an 85-member NI Assembly with a three-member executive to oversee its activities. North-South structures would have 'practical and political power' which would be agreed by the government and accepted by the NI assembly. Relations between Britain and the Republic would operate through a revised Anglo-Irish Agreement in which unionists would participate in an Anglo-Irish parliamentary tier. Articles 2 and 3 of the Irish constitution would be amended to include a consent clause while the British government would amend the 1920 Government of Ireland Act. The Irish referendum on Articles 2 and 3 would not be held, however, until all other new political structures were agreed.

**20 August** An estimated 10,000 people take part in a republican 'Time for Peace – Time to Go' rally in Dublin.

There is a loyalist bomb attack on a bar in the Markets area of Belfast.

**21 August** In a radio interview NIO Minister Michael Ancram says, 'We are not prepared to enter into any form of dialogue, including exploratory dialogue, with those who support violence until there has been a permanent renunciation and cessation of violence on a credible basis.'

Albert Reynolds says that he had never suggested that 'a temporary ceasefire of three months or six months would provide a seat at the conference table for Sinn Fein'. Irish government sources add that, 'In order to address the long-term historical problem of Northern Ireland and to involve Sinn Fein in political structures what is required is for Sinn Fein-IRA to call a permanent cessation of violence.'

**25 August** An Irish-American delegation led by former Congressman Bruce Morrison arrives in Dublin. The delegation holds a three-hour meeting with SF in Belfast the following day.

Following a statement by John Bruton on 15 August saying that an IRA ceasefire was only 'the tactical laying aside of arms, with an implied threat of resumption, and it would be an appalling development if Sinn Fein was able to use the situation to garner political advantage', *An Phoblacht* criticises Bruton as being 'more unionist than (some) unionists'.

**26 August** Ten people are injured in an IRA mortar attack in Downpatrick, Co. Down.

**27 August** An NIO statement says that the 1973 NI Constitution Act is now the primary piece of legislation underwriting the status of NI as part of the UK. What remained of the 1920 Act was 'regarded as a largely redundant piece of legislation'. The spokesman adds that existing laws provide for a change in the status of Northern Ireland only with the consent of a majority of the population.

**28 August** Gerry Adams and John Hume issue a joint statement which notes, 'Last Easter we indicated that we were investigating the possibility of developing an overall political strategy to establish justice and peace in Ireland. We are presently addressing this area in particular and we believe that the essential ingredients of such a strategy may now be available.

'A just and lasting peace in Ireland will only be achieved if it is based on democratic principles. It is clear that an internal settlement is not a solution. Both governments and all parties have already agreed that all relationships must be settled. All that has been tried before has failed to satisfactorily resolve the conflict or remove the political conditions which give rise to it. If a lasting settlement is to be found there must be fundamental and thorough-going change, based on the right of the Irish people as a whole to national self-determination.

'The exercise of this right is, of course, a matter for agreement between all the people of Ireland and we reiterate that such a new agreement is only viable if it enjoys the allegiance of the different traditions on this island by accommodating diversity and providing for national reconciliation.'

The *Sunday Independent* publishes what it claims is the proposed new wording of Section 75 of the Government of Ireland Act 1920. While the original version of the Act states that, 'The supreme authority of the parliament of the United Kingdom shall remain unaffected and undiminished over all persons, matters and things in Northern Ireland,' the revised version says that, 'It is for the people of the island of Ireland alone, by agreement between the two parts respectively, to express their right of self-determination on the basis of consent, freely and concurrently given, North and South, to bring about a united Ireland, if that is their wish.

'Northern Ireland shall remain under the jurisdiction of the parliament of the United Kingdom so long, and only so long, as it is the democratic wish of a greater number of people on the issue of whether they prefer to support the union or a sovereign united Ireland, expressed freely and democratically without fear, intimidation or coercion, on the basis that such authority will be exercised upholding and applying to each community the principles of equality of opportunity and treatment and parity of esteem and recognition of the equal validity of their identity.'

**29 August** Gerry Adams says he has met the IRA Army Council and has told it that he believes that the conditions now exist to move the peace process forward.

**30 August** In an RTE interview Gerry Adams calls for the 'immediate recognition' of Sinn Fein's political mandate.

**31 August** A statement from the IRA announces: 'Recognising the potential of the current situation and in order to enhance the democratic peace process and underline our definitive commitment to its success the leadership of Oglaigh na hEireann have decided that as of midnight, Wednesday, 31 August, there will be a complete cessation of military operations. All our units have been instructed accordingly …

'Our struggle has seen many gains and advances made by nationalists and for the democratic position. We believe that an opportunity to create a just and lasting settlement has been created. We are therefore entering into a new situation in a spirit of determination and confidence: determined that the injustices which created the conflict will be removed and confident in the strength and justice of our struggle to achieve this.

'We note that the Downing Street Declaration is not a solution, nor was it presented as such by its authors. A solution will only be found as a result of inclusive negotiations. Others, not least the British government, have a duty to face up to their responsibilities. It is our desire to significantly contribute to the creation of a climate which will encourage this. We urge everyone to approach this new situation with energy, determination and patience.'

The announcement is greeted by triumphant celebrations in nationalist areas of Belfast and Derry.

The British government remains sceptical of the IRA's intentions as its statement does not refer to a 'permanent' cessation. As a result John Major says, 'We need to be sure the cessation of violence isn't temporary; that it isn't for one week or one month, but a permanent cessation of violence.' Albert Reynolds, however, accepts the IRA statement as implying a permanent ceasefire and notes, 'As far as we are concerned the long nightmare is over.'

Unionists remain highly sceptical and a statement from the CLMC calls on James Molyneaux and Ian Paisley to meet John Major in order to find out 'if the constitution is being tampered with' and 'what deals have been done'. PUP spokesman David Ervine says there is 'deep anger' among loyalists over signals that a deal has been done covertly.

Ian Paisley notes that the IRA have not declared a permanent cessation of violence and adds, 'The only way that you could prove that there would be a permanent cessation is by the surrender of their killing machine, their semtex stores, their guns, their mortars and their equipment.' After a meeting with John Major in London, James Molyneaux says, 'I'm very glad that there has been a halt to the killing in Northern Ireland and throughout the United Kingdom and I hope that those who have influence with the IRA will now be able to persuade them to take the next decisive step and make the halt permanent.'

At a rally in West Belfast Gerry Adams says, 'I want to say a word or two about the volunteer soldiers of the Irish Republican Army. This is a generation of men and women who have fought the British for the last 25 years and who are undefeated by the British. We have waited for too long for our freedom. We are demanding of Mr Major's government that he takes decisive steps now to move the situation forward in a fundamental way and that means fundamental political and constitutional change, it means a demilitarisation of the situation, it means our prisoners home from England and home with their families from prisons in Ireland.

'I want to salute the courage of the IRA leadership and the historic and bold and decisive initiative that they have taken and which they announced this morning. They have created, if you like, a crucial moment, a decisive moment in the history of this island and of Anglo-Irish relationships and I ... also applaud and commend you people here today, and others who could not be here, because you also are undefeated by 25 years.'

On the question of the permanency of the ceasefire Adams says, 'I don't think there is any confusion about it at all. I think the people who wrote the statement wrote what they wanted to say and what they said was "a complete cessation of military operations", they never mentioned violence. "A complete cessation of military operations", that's what they said and that's what they mean ... Let's look at it from the Sinn Fein perspective, we want to see a permanent peace, there needs to be a process of demilitarisation.'

John Major says, 'I am greatly encouraged but we need to be clear this is intended to be a permanent renunciation of violence. If it is, then many options are open. If they are genuinely and irrevocably committed to peaceful and democratic methods then we shall respond positively. Let words now be reflected in deeds.'

Speaking to the press in Downing Street, Sir Patrick Mayhew

emphasises the need to clarify whether the ceasefire is permanent. 'This is not just a piece of pedantry or nitpicking about a particular word. What lies behind it is the absolute essential importance that such talks and negotiations as may take place in future shall not take place under the implied threat that violence, which after all has gone on for so long, could be taken up again and renewed and resumed if people didn't behave during those discussions in a way which was congenial to the IRA.'

John Hume says he is 'very, very happy' to hear the IRA has announced a complete cessation of its campaign. He adds, 'As I said with Gerry Adams, as we said together throughout, our objective at the end of the day was a total cessation of violence. I am very glad that that has been announced today and now let's look forward to … what our primary challenge is, which will be reaching agreement among our divided people and I hope that all resources will now be devoted to that in a totally peaceful atmosphere.'

SDLP vice-chairman Jonathan Stephenson says Major, Mayhew and some unionists are engaging in 'Jesuitical nit-picking' over the fact that the IRA statement had not used the word 'permanent' and adds, 'The Collins National Dictionary defines the word "complete" as, "entire, finished, perfect, with no part lacking". I wouldn't expect people to welcome the statement from the IRA unreservedly, but I would expect the reasonable application of common sense.'

Alliance leader John Alderdice states, 'It's the announcement that the people of Northern Ireland have been waiting for for nearly 25 years now. Of course we'll all want to judge the IRA by their actions and not by their words.'

In Antrim a Catholic man is abducted and shot dead by the UVF.

Four IRA prisoners are transferred from Britain to jails in NI.

The *Belfast Telegraph* headlines its evening edition 'It's Over' and comments, 'Today could be one of the most significant days in the history of Northern Ireland – if not the island of Ireland. It could be the day when the Provisional IRA announced that after nearly 25 years they were abandoning politically-motivated murder and mayhem in favour of politics, pure and simple. Or it could be another false dawn to add to all the rest. The answer will only become gradually apparent, over the next few weeks and months.'

**1 September** Gerry Adams says in the *Irish Times* that the Irish and US governments have responded 'positively and correctly' to the IRA announcement. In a BBC radio interview Martin McGuinness says he 'took it at face value that it does mean a complete cessation of military operations under all circumstances … The British government should not be getting themselves on hooks over one particular word.'

The *Times* comments, 'The IRA ceasefire which began at midnight should not be greeted with euphoria or with cynicism but with the caution made necessary by 25 years of appalling bloodshed. Yesterday's brief statement by the republican leadership may perhaps be remembered by future historians as the first momentous step towards peace. But little is yet known about the terms, significance and likely duration of the ceasefire.'

The *Irish Times*, referring to 'this day of promise', says, 'There must be a welcome. And there must be caution. It may not yet be the day to hang out the flags and colours to mark a full and final peace. But with the IRA ceasefire since midnight, it becomes possible to hope that such a happy condition is now within measurable reach.'

The *Irish News* calls it 'a new era' and notes, 'The IRA ceasefire is not the end of something, it is the beginning. From today the future of Ireland is in the hands of its people – nationalist and unionist, Catholic and Protestant. We must seize the day and build for peace.'

The *News Letter* takes a more cynical approach and comments, 'The long-awaited IRA ceasefire announcement has come and gone and while initially some encouragement could be taken from the terse 146-word Provo statement, the real intent of the republican leadership became depressingly evident within a few hours of the signal to the world that peace was in the air. Firstly, Sinn Fein chairman Mitchel McLaughlin dropped the mask with his demands that Britain must now withdraw "psychological, political and military support" from the unionists and begin a process of "demilitarisation" in Northern Ireland immediately. His "Brits Out" demands were sinisterly couched with a threatening addendum that if the British government responded in "a negative or hostile way" to these demands the ceasefire was "doomed" and that would have implications for the future.'

A Catholic man is killed by the UFF in North Belfast.

## The IRA Ceasefire

Was there a secret deal between the British government and the IRA to bring about the ceasefire, as so many loyalists alleged? There is no doubt that the republican leadership was, rhetorically at least, principally motivated by the idea of a gesture to 'nationalist Ireland' – the Fianna Fail government, the SDLP and Irish America. Great emphasis was laid on the ability of this coalition to achieve results. There is, however, also little doubt that the republicans felt that a new agreement was about to dock, and it was one which might exclude them if they remained committed to violence. Albert Reynolds had encouraged this perception, especially in his discussions with them in early August. It seems likely that the republican leadership was aware of the broad contents of the Frameworks Documents – its key concepts were, after all, widely bruited in the media in mid-August. Ian Paisley pointed out that, 'Mr Mallon [of the SDLP] ... said that the IRA had received a preview of the Framework Document. There we see something of the promises that were being made to the IRA.'

On the other hand, if there was an understanding between the Provisionals and the British government, it was inevitably an imperfect one. The British in their private communications had refused all talk of withdrawal. They had also made it absolutely clear publicly that the IRA would have to decommission its arms before Sinn Fein's admissions to all-party talks – as Gerry Adams fully admitted in his interview with Tom Collins in the *Irish News* in January 1994. There was, therefore, no truth in the claim made later by Garret FitzGerald in the *Irish Times* in July 1995 and by others that the British had slurred over this matter. Even in the Frameworks Documents, the understanding was imperfect, for the British withheld their internal government proposals for Northern Ireland from the Irish government, let alone the republican movement, until February 1995. It is also doubtful whether the British government had shared with Adams its commitment to a referendum as was announced by Major in September. All in all, the caginess and even surprise which characterised British reaction to the IRA ceasefire announcement probably reflected genuine emotion.

In a way the ceasefire was above all a footnote to the Anglo-Irish Agreement, which was now working in a way that no one had intended. It had given the Irish government a prestigious role in the North and this allowed it to act as a broker for a ceasefire in a way which was inconceivable a decade earlier. This allowed the republican movement to dilute its cardinal principle which had been so forcefully articulated in the 1986 Sinn Fein ard fheis by Martin McGuinness: 'Our position is clear and it will never, never, never, change. The war against British rule must continue until freedom is achieved.' But still the question remained: what did the republican movement expect to get out of the peace process? Throughout the whole Hume-Adams process and the secret contacts with the government it had sought a commitment from the British government that it would act as a 'persuader' for Irish unity. Yet at no point does the British government appear to have given such a commitment; still less had it responded to Adams's support for joint authority.

**2 September** An opinion poll in the *Belfast Telegraph* suggests that 56% believe that the IRA ceasefire has come about as a result of a secret deal. Only 30% believe the ceasefire is permanent.
Ian Paisley says he will invite other unionist organisations to join the DUP in a pan-unionist forum.

**4 September** Local people re-open several roads closed by the army along the Fermanagh and Tyrone border. The unofficial re-opening of border roads continues in the following weeks.

A UVF car bomb explodes at a SF office in West Belfast.

**6 September** In Dublin Albert Reynolds meets and shakes hands publicly with Gerry Adams and John Hume. A joint statement says, 'We are at the beginning of a new era in which we are totally and absolutely committed to democratic and peaceful methods of resolving our political problems. We reiterate that our objective is an equitable and lasting agreement that can command the allegiance of all.' Andrew Hunter MP, chairman of the Conservative Committee on NI, says he speaks for his colleagues when he describes the meeting as a 'disastrous miscalculation' by Reynolds with 'potentially the most damaging consequences'. UUP secretary Jim Wilson calls the meeting 'outrageous' and says it is 'deeply insensitive and offensive in that murderers not yet apprehended continue to roam our streets'.

John Major throws Ian Paisley and other DUP members out of his office after Paisley refuses to accept Major's word that he had not done a secret deal with the IRA. Paisley later comments, 'By demanding an assurance that his word must be trusted, the Prime Minister was asking something that he had no right to ask. That is why he was so deeply stung when I said to him: "No other Prime Minister in the long line of British Prime Ministers has ever demanded from any Opposition MP such blind trust in his word." He shouted in response: "Then I shall be the first." '

**7 September** Vice-President Gore meets Albert Reynolds at Shannon Airport and says that the IRA statement speaks for itself.

Speaking to members of an Orange Lodge in Comber, Co. Down, Sir Patrick Mayhew says there is no reason why cross-border bodies could not have executive functions.

**8 September** The CLMC sets out a list of issues on which it requires assurances before it is prepared to call a ceasefire: '1. We have to ascertain the bona fides of the permanence of the IRA ceasefire. 2. The intent of the INLA has yet to be established. 3. To be convinced that no secret deals have been concocted between HMG and the IRA. 4. That our constitutional position as a partner within the United Kingdom is assured. 5. To assess the implications of the joint governmental "Framework Document" as soon as possible. 6. It is incumbent upon the British government to ensure that there is no "change" or "erosion" within Northern Ireland to facilitate the illusion of an IRA victory. Change, if any, can only be honourable after dialogue and agreement.'

British army soldiers begin wearing berets instead of helmets while on patrol in NI.

The Belfast coroner abandons the inquests into the six men killed by the RUC in Armagh in 1982 because of the refusal of the Chief Constable to provide the inquest with the Stalker report.

**9 September** UUP MP for Strangford, John Taylor, says he believes the IRA ceasefire is 'for real'.

**10 September** There is an attempted escape by six IRA prisoners in Whitemoor jail in Cambridgeshire. On 22 September semtex and detonators are found at the prison.

**12 September** Two people are injured when the detonator of a 3 lb UVF bomb explodes on a Belfast-to-Dublin train.

**13 September** Sectarian clashes occur at Crumlin Road courthouse in Belfast. Rioting takes place in Protestant areas of Belfast that night with shots being fired at the police.

**14 September** John Major says, 'The IRA were conducting intolerable outrages for 25 years. I hope they have now given up those outrages for good. They certainly seem to be indicating that. They haven't expressly said so. I hope they will expressly say so.'

**16 September** During a visit to Belfast John Major says that any political agreement will be subject to the approval of the people of NI through a referendum. In his statement Major says, 'The referendum means that it will be your choice whether to accept the outcome. My commitment means that no one can go behind your backs. Not today. Not tomorrow. Not at any time. It will be for you to decide.' Major also announces the end of the broadcasting ban on proscribed organisations. Albert Reynolds says that a referendum on the outcome of political talks will also be held in the Republic.

Sir Patrick Mayhew says that ten border roads will be re-opened. On 22 September he announces the re-opening of six more roads.

It is reported that the US administration has decided to end the ban on official contacts with Sinn Fein.

**17 September** There are clashes between nationalists and the RUC in the Ballymurphy area of Belfast.

**18 September** In an interview with the *Observer* Albert Reynolds says the unification of Ireland will not come about 'in this generation'. The statement is generally welcomed by unionists but Martin McGuinness says nationalists expect that, 'This problem can be solved an awful lot quicker than that.'

**20 September** John Hume meets President Clinton and Vice-President Gore in Washington.

**21 September** The European Commission increases its contribution to the International Fund for Ireland over the next three years by a third to £47 million.

**22 September** Vice-President Gore meets a UUP delegation in Washington.

**23 September** John Major says that exploratory talks with SF could begin by Christmas if it indicated that it intended to give up violence for good.
The US administration grants a visa to Gerry Adams enabling him to make a second trip to the United States. Former NIO Minister Michael Mates also flies to the US in an unsuccessful attempt to counter the publicity surrounding Adams's visit.

**25 September** Gerry Adams receives an enthusiastic reception as he begins a tour of the US. Addressing a gathering in Detroit, he says, 'We have to use our undoubted influence and send a very clear message to Britain. It's time for peace. It's time for them to go!'
A *Sunday Tribune* report claims that the Irish government first established contacts with SF via priests in West Belfast in 1986.

**26 September** Interviewed by the *Boston Herald*, Adams states, 'None of us can say two or three years up the road that if the causes of conflict aren't resolved that another IRA leadership won't come along because this has always happened.' In New York British Foreign Secretary Douglas Hurd says, 'We know ... exactly what support Gerry Adams and Sinn Fein have in Northern Ireland. It's 10 per cent. He's Mr Ten Per Cent. He's a minority within the minority in Northern Ireland.'

**27 September** The European Parliament passes a motion calling for an all-round paramilitary ceasefire in NI. John Hume receives a standing ovation and, two days later, is nominated for the Nobel peace prize by the Socialist group of the parliament.
Three men in Bangor, Co. Down, and another in East Belfast are shot in the legs by loyalist paramilitaries in punishment attacks.

**30 September** Speaking to the Centre for National Policy in Washington, Dick Spring says, 'The issue of permanence is beyond the capacity of any individual to guarantee.'

**3 October** Following a telephone call from Vice-President Gore to Gerry Adams, the SF leader receives a letter from National Security Adviser Anthony Lake saying that the US administration is ending its policy of prohibiting contact with SF. A statement from the British Embassy says that the decision is 'a matter for the Americans'. The following day a SF delegation led by Adams meets senior US government officials, including National Security Council adviser Nancy Soderberg, in Washington. Adams later participates in a television debate with UUP MP Ken Maginnis.

**6 October** In Philadelphia Albert Reynolds says that among the problems to be resolved in NI are the 'early withdrawal to barracks of British forces', the phased release of prisoners and the establishment of 'an acceptable system of policing that removes any excuse for vigilantism'.

**8 October** In a *News Letter* interview James Molyneaux says cross-border institutions with executive functions are 'out the window'. On 12 October the UUP leader repeats that there is 'no question' of such bodies operating. On 14 October Albert Reynolds insists that cross-border bodies must have executive powers.

**9 October** On Radio Ulster Dick Spring says, 'There are a lot of matters which have arisen in the past five weeks in terms of what is going to happen to prisoners, in terms of what is going to happen to the arms, but I think quite frankly they are issues to be discussed down the line. Let's start working on the political side of this.'

**10 October** Loyalist leaders are given permission to enter the Maze prison by the NIO to discuss a ceasefire with loyalist prisoners.

**11 October** Police officers begin patrolling West Belfast without army support.

**13 October** A statement from the Combined Loyalist Military Command announces: 'After a widespread consultative process initiated by representations from the Ulster Democratic and Progressive Unionist parties, and after having received confirmation and guarantees in relation to Northern Ireland's constitutional position within the United Kingdom, as well as other assurances, and, in the belief that the democratically expressed wishes of the greater number of people in Northern Ireland will be respected and upheld, the CLMC will universally cease all operational hostilities as from 12 midnight on Thursday the 13th October 1994.

'The permanence of our ceasefire will be completely dependent upon the continued cessation of all nationalist/republican violence; the sole responsibility for a return to war lies with them.

'In the genuine hope that this peace will be permanent, we take the opportunity to pay homage to all our fighters, commandos and volunteers who have paid the supreme sacrifice. They did not die in vain. The union is safe ...

'In all sincerity, we offer to the loved ones of all innocent victims over the past 25 years, abject and true remorse. No words of ours will compensate for the intolerable suffering they have undergone during this conflict.

'Let us firmly resolve to respect our differing views of freedom, culture and aspiration and never again permit our political circumstances to degenerate into bloody warfare.'

Reacting to the announcement of the ceasefire, John Major says it is 'another very important part of the jigsaw falling into place'. In the Dail Albert Reynolds says, 'This decision effectively signifies the end of 25 years of violence, and the closure of a tragic chapter in our history.'

## The Loyalist Ceasefire

The announcement of a ceasefire by the Combined Loyalist Military Command demonstrated a new confidence among loyalist paramilitaries. But while murders committed by the UVF, UFF, Red Hand Commando and others in the early 1990s had shown that loyalist paramilitaries could be as ruthless as their republican counterparts (in 1993, for the first time since 1975, loyalists murdered more people than republicans), a new generation of more politically astute spokesmen were beginning to emerge from the parties associated with the loyalist paramilitaries.

The loyalist ceasefire statement of October 1994 went beyond the IRA's in two significant areas. Firstly, the CLMC stated that its ceasefire was dependent upon the continued cessation of IRA violence, a position clarified and strengthened in August the following year when the CLMC said there would be no 'first strike' by loyalists; secondly, it offered an apology 'to the loved ones of all innocent victims over the past 25 years'. The significance of this newly discovered open-mindedness and 'abject and true remorse' would, of course, be determined by the loyalists' future actions.

The reason why the loyalists could afford to be magnanimous was clear; as self-appointed defenders of the constitutional status quo their aim was to oppose moves which might lead towards a united Ireland, unlike the IRA whose objective was continually to exert pressure in order to erode the position of Northern Ireland within the United Kingdom. Thus it was that, in the wake of the IRA ceasefire, loyalists sought assurances that no secret deal had been done by the two governments with the republicans which would weaken the province's position within the UK. Having been reassured on this point, the CLMC statement could announce that, 'The union is safe.'

The new generation of loyalist political leaders, David Ervine, Billy Hutchinson, Gary McMichael as well as Ray Smallwoods (killed by the IRA in July), had, however, gone some way in moving loyalist pronouncements away from the traditional 'not an inch, no surrender' stance toward a more sophisticated view of Northern Ireland's place within the union. Crucially, the loyalist ceasefire statement noted that they had been assured that, 'The democratically expressed wishes of the greater number of people in Northern Ireland will be respected and upheld.'

Not unlike Gerry Adams in America, loyalist leaders would now achieve near celebrity status in the Republic. Progressive Unionist and Ulster Democratic Party members entered the bastion of their traditional enemies, Dublin, for political discussions as well as for social events – the following year PUP spokesman David Ervine would be feted at the opening of the Abbey Theatre's production of Frank McGuinness's play *Observe the Sons of Ulster Marching Toward the Somme*.

Despite these beneficial developments, however, there remained an underlying loyalist suspicion of the Republic. In June Albert Reynolds, in his 'clarification' of the Downing Street Declaration to the UDP's Gary McMichael, noted that the Irish government had 'a strong moral duty towards the nationalist community in Northern Ireland, because of experience in the past, to ensure that the principles of equal citizenship, equality of treatment and parity of esteem are translated into practice'. Reynolds, rather than taking the traditional nationalist view, might, perhaps, have shown the courage he had demonstrated in other areas of the peace process and proclaimed the Irish government to be the defenders of the civil rights of all of the citizens of Northern Ireland. In the event Reynolds's standing among loyalists would be undermined in September 1995 after he rejected David Ervine's claim that he had told loyalist representatives, prior to their ceasefire, that weapons of an offensive nature would have to be decommissioned. Although relations between loyalists and the South might be showing the first signs of a thaw, confidence-building between loyalists and the Irish government clearly still had some way to go.

**14 October** Following a statement in the Dail by Albert

Reynolds three days earlier that Britain should 'accelerate' its response to the IRA ceasefire, John Major tells the Conservative Party conference that he will pursue the peace process in his own time.

**18 October** In the House of Commons John Major says, 'Armaments – especially semtex and detonators, perhaps more than guns – are a crucial issue that will have to be dealt with as we advance the process.'
The Police Authority for NI says that the Chief Constable must provide detailed written information on the measures being taken to redress religious and gender imbalances in the force within 30 days.

**20 October** NIO Minister Tim Smith resigns in the wake of the controversy surrounding the paying of MPs by political lobbyists to ask specific questions in the House of Commons. Smith is replaced by Malcolm Moss.
Marjorie Mowlam replaces Kevin McNamara as Labour spokesperson on NI.

**21 October** On a two-day visit to Belfast John Major announces that talks between government representatives and Sinn Fein could begin soon. He also announces the lifting of exclusion orders on Gerry Adams and Martin McGuinness and the removal of roadblocks on all unapproved roads between NI and the Republic. Major says he will make a 'working assumption' that the IRA ceasefire is permanent and preliminary talks with SF will begin before Christmas. He promises to review the role of the army, establish an Assembly in NI and calls an investment conference for December.
Albert Reynolds agrees to increase the representation of the Alliance Party at the Irish Forum for Peace and Reconciliation to three members after the party complained that it had only been allowed two delegates.

**23 October** During a visit to London Martin McGuinness states that IRA violence could return if a satisfactory outcome is not produced by the peace process.

**24 October** For the first time in 25 years troops stop patrolling the streets of Derry. RUC officers in Belfast begin patrolling without flak jackets.
In the US a six-man loyalist delegation led by Gary McMichael of the UDP and David Ervine of the PUP address the National Committee on American Foreign Policy.

**25 October** In the Dail Albert Reynolds says that, 'The question of the safe and permanent disposal of weapons and explosives is essential to the creation of a totally demilitarised situation and to the consolidation of peace.' He also notes that, 'North-South institutions form part of the recognition of the nationalist identity; like the unionists they are entitled to have their identity recognised.'

In the Commons John Major remarks, 'I do believe that we have now entered a fresh phase of the peace process in Northern Ireland ... there is greater hope that peace may now be permanently achievable than we have seen at any time in the last quarter of a century.'

**27 October** SF chairman Mitchel McLaughlin says any insistence that arms be handed over before political talks begin will 'invite this very fragile consensus to collapse'.

The European Parliament proposes that the European Union contribute £40 million (an increase of £28 million) to the International Fund for Ireland in the coming year.

**28 October** In Dublin Albert Reynolds opens the Forum for Peace and Reconciliation stating, 'Today's inaugural meeting within a few weeks of the two ceasefires represents a further important step on the road to a just and a lasting peace. No one should be in any doubt about the value of this forum or of the importance of its work.' The British ambassador does not attend the opening because of the presence of SF representatives.

A ceasefire is announced by the republican splinter group, the Catholic Reaction Force.

**30 October** In Dublin Gerry Adams says there are 'clear efforts' by the British government to reduce the momentum of the peace process.

In Belfast police and local residents are involved in scuffles on the Ormeau Road during a protest against the passing of an Orange parade through the area.

The *Sunday Business Post* quotes an Irish government official as saying that John Major is 'inherently opposed to doing anything that smacks of a diminution of sovereignty and to date the demands made on him by the Irish government in relation to substantial, independent, North-South bodies, have been resisted on that basis. But keeping Jim Molyneaux on side is important nonetheless. The [Irish] government now accepts that Major hardly sneezes in the direction of the North without first seeking Molyneaux's approval.'

**1 November** President Clinton announces that he intends to host a conference on trade and investment in Ireland to be held in Philadelphia in spring 1995; the conference is later relocated to Washington. The US government also says that it will increase its contribution to the International Fund for Ireland from $20 million to $30 million a year over the next two years.

**3 November** In Dublin Albert Reynolds says that there will be no change in the status of Northern Ireland without the consent of a majority of its people. He adds, 'We are aware of the fears of the unionist community, so we are prepared to insert the principle of consent in the Irish constitution.'

**4 November** Seamus Mallon calls for the RUC to be split into four local police forces. Chief Constable Sir Hugh Annesley dismisses this suggestion on 10 November.

**8 November** At the Old Bailey university lecturer Feilim O Hadhmaill is sentenced to 25 years' imprisonment for conspiring to cause explosions in Britain.

**10 November** Frank Kerr is murdered by the IRA during the robbery of a postal sorting office in Newry, Co. Down. Mr Kerr's killing is subsequently condemned by both Gerry Adams and Martin McGuinness. As a consequence of the murder the Irish government suspends the release of nine republican prisoners due the following day. On 12 November an IRA statement says, 'The IRA cessation of military operations is a complete one and covers any use of arms. The IRA leadership has granted no one permission to use arms since August 31st.' The IRA admits killing Frank Kerr on 20 November but says the action 'was not sanctioned by the IRA leadership'.

**14 November** At the Lord Mayor's banquet in London John Major says talks with loyalist political representatives will begin before Christmas.

**17 November** Albert Reynolds resigns as Taoiseach following controversy surrounding the appointment of Harry Whelehan to the position of President of the Irish Supreme Court. The Irish Labour Party had opposed Whelehan's appointment because of his involvement, as Attorney-General, in delaying the extradition of a paedophile priest, Brendan Smyth, to face charges in NI. On 16 November Labour leader Dick Spring said that information concerning an earlier case, which could have led to Smyth's early extradition, was withheld from his party and that Labour ministers were therefore resigning from the government.
During a two-day visit to Britain Gerry Adams says his commitment to the peace process is absolute irrespective of who is in power in Dublin.

**19 November** Fianna Fail elects Bertie Ahern as the new party leader.

**22 November** In the Dail Dick Spring says that, 'Peace can only come from decommissioning all the means of destruction and commissioning new arrangements, structures and relationships.'

**23 November** An army statement says that 150 soldiers involved in guarding the Maze prison are to be withdrawn.

**24 November** A joint tourism marketing initiative is launched by the ministers responsible for tourism in NI and the Republic.

**29 November** It becomes known that SF is to be excluded from the investment conference to be held in Belfast in December. On 1 December Sir Patrick Mayhew says Belfast and Derry City councillors will be invited to the conference and that this might include SF representatives.

**30 November** John Hume and Gerry Adams meet and issue a statement which reads, 'It is essential that the British government adopt a constructive approach by responding positively and enthusiastically to the new situation which has been created. The demilitarisation process should be accelerated and inclusive negotiations, aimed at securing agreement and an overall settlement, should begin without further delay. The British government has a key role to play in this. They can and should be persuaders for agreement between the Irish people.'

**1 December** President Clinton appoints former Senate majority leader George Mitchell to be a special economic adviser on Ireland from January 1995.

**3 December** Ian Paisley says the intention of his party will be to wreck any new assembly.

**5 December** In Washington Gerry Adams meets US ambassador to Dublin Jean Kennedy-Smith as well as State Department officials and insists that his party receive equal treatment at the NI investment conference to be held in Belfast. Adams again raises the issue during a meeting with National Security Adviser Anthony Lake at the White House the following day. On 8 December US Commerce Secretary Ron Brown says it is a mistake to exclude SF from the conference.

**7 December** The European Commission agrees a £230 million aid programme for NI and border counties in the Republic over the next three years.

**9 December** British civil servants meet Sinn Fein representatives at

Stormont in the first formal meeting of the two groups in more than two decades. One of the main issues for discussion on the British side is the question of the handing in of weapons while SF push for 'parity of esteem' for their party. Michael Ancram, the NIO minister responsible for political talks (who is not directly involved in the meeting), notes that failure to resolve the arms issue would create 'a substantial barrier' to the full involvement of Sinn Fein in political discussions. DUP MP Peter Robinson criticises the meeting and claims, 'It represents a triumph of terror over the democratic process.'

**11 December** UDP councillor Gary McMichael says it is unrealistic to expect paramilitaries to hand over weapons at this stage.

**12 December** Acting Taoiseach Albert Reynolds says it is not a 'sensible precondition' to require the IRA to hand in weapons before multilateral talks begin.

**13 December** A two-day investment conference, attended by 300 delegates, begins in Belfast. The conference is addressed by John Major and US Commerce Secretary Ron Brown. The economic forum is picketed by republicans in protest at the exclusion of SF representatives.

**14 December** In Belfast John Major announces a £73 million investment package for NI. He also says that 'huge progress' will have to be made toward the destruction of IRA arms before talks with SF could be formalised.

**15 December** In Dublin Fine Gael leader John Bruton, widely regarded as a strong critic of the IRA, is elected Taoiseach. Bruton leads a coalition government which also includes Labour and the Democratic Left. Labour leader Dick Spring retains his positions as Deputy Prime Minister and Foreign Minister. The following day the new Taoiseach shakes hands with Gerry Adams at the Forum for Peace and Reconciliation.
British officials hold exploratory talks with UDP and PUP representatives at Stormont.

**17 December** Unionists react angrily to a claim by former Taoiseach Albert Reynolds that all-Ireland bodies with executive powers have been agreed between the British and Irish governments.

**18 December** In a *Sunday Tribune* interview John Bruton warns that the peace process should 'not get into a stand-off' on the decommissioning of arms.

**19 December** A 2 lb semtex bomb is defused at a shop in Enniskillen, Co. Fermanagh. The IRA denies responsibility for the device.

**20 December** John Major meets John Bruton in London. Major later says that 'substantive progress' is required on the decommissioning of arms.
Government officials and SF representatives hold a second meeting at Stormont.
Gerry Adams and John Hume issue a joint statement calling for inclusive negotiations without delay.

**21 December** John Bruton meets Gerry Adams in Dublin.

**22 December** A Catholic student at Queen's University is found beaten to death in the Donegall Road area of Belfast, apparently as the result of a sectarian killing.
The government releases 97 paramilitary prisoners on Christmas parole; 30 are granted parole in the Republic while nine IRA prisoners are given early releases.

**23 December** Sir Patrick Mayhew says RUC numbers might eventually be reduced to 3,500.
Civil servants again meet loyalist representatives for talks at Stormont.

**28 December** In an interview in the magazine *Decision Maker*, UUP MP John Taylor says there is greater scope for co-operation between Northern Ireland and the Republic than there had been since 1921. Taylor calls for improved transport and communications between North and South and the introduction of a common currency for the British Isles and says he can envisage local cross-border bodies with executive powers, though not all-Ireland bodies.

**29 December** The SDLP accepts a UDP request for a meeting.

**30 December** In a radio interview John Major repeats that there must be 'significant progress' on the question of arms before the government and other parties would join SF in round-table talks.

Deaths Arising from the Troubles: 61. Shootings: 348. Bombs Planted: 222. Incendiaries: 115. Weapons Found: 178. Explosives Found: 1.3 tonnes. Persons Charged with Terrorist Offences: 349.

# 1995

**2 January** The old Commons chamber at Stormont is gutted by an electrical fire.

**8 January** The *Observer* quotes Sir Patrick Mayhew as having told sixth-form students in London that unless the government could help Gerry Adams he would be 'replaced by someone much harder'.
Writing in the *Sunday Press*, African National Congress activist Gavin Evans notes that, 'Between John Hume and the IRA, the nationalists have sewn up the massive and lucrative US Irish constituency, and American public opinion more generally. Yet their political efforts on the British mainland have been pathetic, despite repeated polls showing declining support for the union. Far more significant is the lack of any real political engagement with the Protestant community. The absence of debate is partly a consequence of war, but it is also a result of a tribal conservatism and a deficiency in political imagination.'

**10 January** Gary McMichael of the UDP calls for a phased release of prisoners if the ceasefires continue.

**12 January** It is announced that troops will end patrols on the streets of Belfast during daylight hours from the following weekend. On 25 January it is reported that daytime patrols are also to end along part of the border in counties Down and Armagh.

**13 January** John Bruton says the decommissioning of arms 'isn't the only item on the agenda and it shouldn't be a blocking item for dealing with others'.

**15 January** The government announces that the ban on contacts between ministers and SF, the UDP and the PUP is to end.

**16 January** Speaking of the forthcoming Frameworks Documents, John Major says, 'There's no question of joint authority with Dublin … we have not got joint authority in the document. The document itself is for consultation.' Major adds that the document will have to be approved by political parties in NI and then by the people, 'So they have a triple lock on their own future.'

SF representatives meet government officials at Stormont and accept that the party has an 'influence' on paramilitary weapons. NIO Minister Michael Ancram later says that the decommissioning of weapons is not a precondition of SF's entry into substantive talks.

**18 January** The Irish government says that nine republican prisoners released on parole at Christmas will be freed permanently.

**19 January** The Law Lords dismiss an appeal by Lee Clegg against his conviction for the murder of a joyrider in 1990.

An article in the *Times* on the Frameworks Documents notes that, 'The latest indications suggest that this document will be considerably more green than the Ulster Unionists have expected, apparently vindicating Ian Paisley's more pessimistic predictions.'

**20 January** At the Old Bailey Robert Fryers from Belfast is jailed for 25 years for plotting bomb attacks in England. In April Fryers is transferred to a prison in NI; he is the eleventh IRA man to be transferred in order to make visiting easier for their families.

**22 January** Dick Spring says that the decommissioning of arms should not be allowed to become an obstacle to talks on the future of the North. He also says that 'steady progress' is being made toward the inclusion of SF in negotiations.

**24 January** The Boundary Commission proposes that NI have an additional Westminster seat, to be known as West Tyrone.

The CLMC warns that there is 'fear and apprehension' over cross-border institutions.

**27 January** John Bruton and Dick Spring hold their first formal meeting with SF representatives.

Sean Kelly from Belfast is sentenced to nine terms of life imprisonment for his involvement in the Shankill Road bombing of October 1993.

**30 January** In a BBC Panorama programme former NI Secretary of State Peter Brooke describes Gerry Adams as 'a brave and courageous man'.

Fianna Fail leader Bertie Ahern meets Ulster Unionists at the party's Glengall Street headquarters. The Fianna Fail delegation also meets SF and SDLP members during the one-day visit to Belfast.

**1 February** Extracts from the Frameworks Documents are published in the *Times*. The newspaper claims that, 'The British and Irish governments have drawn up a document that brings the prospect of a united Ireland closer than it has been at any time since partition in 1920 … Today's disclosures will alarm many Unionists who were promised by Mr Major last week that the draft would contain "no proposals" for joint authority.' John Major later makes a television broadcast to appeal for support for his policies. James Molyneaux claims that officials have 'run amok without ministerial supervision'.
Five people are injured as the result of a series of punishment beatings carried out by loyalists and republicans.

**2 February** The results of the 1993 Labour Force Survey show that Catholics are still twice as likely to be unemployed as Protestants. The reasons for higher Catholic unemployment, variously attributed to demographic, geographical and other factors or to discrimination, remains a highly contentious area of debate.
An Ulster Unionist wins a council by-election in Newtownabbey, with the UDP candidate coming second from last.

**3 February** The Irish government releases a further five IRA prisoners.

**5 February** A *Sunday Times* report claims that, in the wake of the *Times* story of four days earlier, Major had offered to show James Molyneaux the document from which the leaks came. Molyneaux declined the offer because he believed the document was fatally flawed and he wanted nothing to do with it. The newspaper comments: 'What is clear is that he [Molyneaux] had made his reservations known publicly and privately and the British and Irish governments appeared not to be listening.' A senior British source is quoted as saying, 'We have to make it clear to the Unionists that what they see in the final framework plan is what they will get – if they agree to it.'

**7 February** John Bruton's proposal that the state of emergency first declared in the South in 1939 and renewed in 1976 be lifted is accepted by the Dail.
8,000 rounds of ammunition are recovered by the Gardai at Oldcastle, Co. Meath. Two mortar tubes and more ammunition are recovered the following day.
Following further talks between SF representatives and British

government officials, civil servants say that NIO ministers will join the talks if they continue to make progress.

A semtex device is defused in Newry, Co. Down. The IRA later denies responsibility for planting the bomb.

**8 February** Private Andrew Clarke is sentenced to ten years' imprisonment for the attempted murder of republican Eddie Copeland outside the home of Shankill bomber Thomas Begley in October 1993.

**9 February** A meeting between SF and NIO officials is called off after SF representatives claim the room is bugged.

**14 February** Following a meeting with John Major in London the delegation of UUP MPs write to him saying that they will not take part in all-party talks based on a document believed to have a 'nationalist agenda'. On 17 February Major replies that the Frameworks proposals will be 'neither a unionist agenda nor a nationalist agenda'.

**17 February** Sir Patrick Mayhew ends ten exclusion orders.

**19 February** A *Sunday Telegraph* report gives some indication of the executive functions of the North-South body to be proposed by the Frameworks Documents by stating that, 'This may include the management of rivers and loughs, heritage protection measures and mapping.'

**20 February** Seven SF members are arrested and there are clashes between republicans and RUC officers following a police operation at the party's Derry offices.

James Molyneaux, John Hume and Ian Paisley meet for discussions at Westminster.

**22 February** The documents Frameworks for the Future are released. Introducing the proposals in Belfast, John Major notes that, 'The process would have three strands. It would seek a new beginning for relationships within Northern Ireland, relations between the North and the South of the island of Ireland and relations between the United Kingdom and the Republic. We agreed that it was only by addressing all these relationships together that agreement would be found across the community in Northern Ireland.'

Part I of Frameworks for the Future suggests 'A Framework for Accountable Government in Northern Ireland'. The document proposes a single chamber assembly of about 90 members elected by PR and serving for a fixed four- or five-year term. All-party assembly committees would oversee the work of NI departments. The work of the assembly would, in turn, be overseen by a directly elected panel of three individuals.

Part II deals more directly with the contentious issue of North-South relations. 'A New Framework for Agreement' states that the guiding principles for achieving co-operation in the search for overall agreement are: '(i) the principle of self-determination, as set out in the Joint Declaration; (ii) that the consent of the governed is an essential ingredient for stability in any political arrangement; (iii) that agreement must be pursued and established by exclusively democratic, peaceful means, without resort to violence or coercion; (iv) that any new political arrangements must be based on full respect for, and protection and expression of, the rights and identities of both traditions in Ireland and even-handedly afford both communities in Northern Ireland parity of esteem and treatment, including equality of opportunity and advantage.' (para. 10)

North-South institutions are to 'promote agreement among the people of the island of Ireland; to carry out on a democratically accountable basis delegated executive, harmonising and consultative functions over a range of designated matters to be agreed; and to serve to acknowledge and reconcile the rights, identities and aspirations of the two major traditions'. (para. 13b) Such institutions should be created to 'cater adequately for present and future political, social and economic inter-connections on the island of Ireland, enabling representatives of the main traditions, North and South, to enter agreed dynamic, new, co-operative and constructive relationships'. (para. 24) Membership would consist of department heads from the NI assembly and the Republic and areas where harmonisation would take place would include: agriculture and fisheries; industrial development; consumer affairs; transport; energy; trade; health; social welfare; education and economic policy. The overall objective of the new North-South body will be to 'provide a forum for acknowledging the respective identities and requirements of the two major traditions; express and enlarge the mutual acceptance of the validity of those traditions; and promote understanding and agreement among the people and institutions in both parts of the island. The remit of the body should be dynamic, enabling progressive extension by agreement of its functions to new areas. Its role should develop to keep pace with the growth of harmonisation and with greater integration between the two economies.' (para. 38)

The Irish government also says it will introduce and support proposals for change in the Irish constitution. These changes 'will fully reflect the principle of consent in Northern Ireland and demonstrably be such that no territorial claim of right to jurisdiction over Northern Ireland contrary to the will of a majority of its people is asserted'. (para. 21)

In the Commons John Major makes a statement, primarily aimed at reassuring unionists, in which he says, 'I am a unionist who wants peace for all the people of the union. I have no intention whatsoever of letting that role change, unless it is the democratic wish of the people of Northern Ireland to do so.' Discussing the terms of the Documents he notes, 'One crucial component is that, as part of an overall settlement, the Irish government have committed themselves to introducing and to supporting proposals to amend article 2 and article 3 of their constitution. Those amendments would fully reflect the principle of consent in Northern Ireland.' On the question of the proposed North-South body he declares, 'It would not have free-standing authority: it would be accountable to the Northern Ireland Assembly and to the Irish parliament respectively … It would discharge or oversee only such functions as were designed for it. There is no predetermined list of those functions: that would be decided only after discussion and agreement with the political parties in Northern Ireland. It would be for the Northern Ireland Assembly and the Irish Parliament to decide whether any additional functions should subsequently be designated.' Major also adds, 'There is a triple safeguard against any proposals being imposed on Northern Ireland: first, any proposals must command the support of the political parties in Northern Ireland; secondly, any proposals must then be approved by the people of Northern Ireland in a referendum; and thirdly, any necessary legislation must be passed by this Parliament. That provides a triple lock designed to ensure that nothing is implemented without consent.' Unionists, nevertheless, remain highly sceptical of the Documents. UUP MP Ken Maginnis, referring to Margaret Thatcher's comment in her autobiography that the Anglo-Irish Agreement had been a disappointment, asks, 'When the Prime Minister comes to write his memoirs, does he believe that, like his predecessor, he will regret his part in driving Northern Ireland back at least ten years by promoting this dishonourable blueprint for a united Ireland?' John Hume, however, comments that, 'When all the words have been taken away from the document published today, the fundamental message is that the problem we must solve in Ireland is not that we are a divided piece of earth but that we are a divided people.'

In the Dail John Bruton says, 'This document is the contribution of two governments together. It aims at a balance between aspirations that are, if put within a traditional, absolutist and territorial matrix, basically irreconcilable. However, the document does more than just attempt to balance two irreconcilable aspirations. It is the beginning of work towards a wholly new form of expression of traditional aspirations, focusing on individuals and communities rather than on territory. By expressing aspirations in this new way, we hope that the two otherwise irreconcilable sets of aspirations can, in fact, be reconciled.' In a statement that goes beyond paragraph 21 of the Frameworks Documents, he says that more time is required for consultation and consideration before amendments to the constitution are tabled, but adds that, 'The principles and immutable political commitments underlying the changes to our constitution will be to remove any jurisdictional or territorial claim of legal right over the territory of Northern Ireland contrary to the will of the people of Northern Ireland.'

The *Belfast Telegraph* comments on the Frameworks Documents, 'There is something for everyone, of all shades of unionist or nationalist opinion, and not enough for anyone to wholeheartedly endorse. Unionists can, if they want, regard the strong North-South dimension as a slippery slope to Irish unity. Republicans, on the other hand, may see the emphasis on agreement and consent as a means of copper-fastening partition for generations to come.'

**23 February** The *Times* notes that the Frameworks Documents are substantially the same as the draft version it had reported on three weeks earlier and comments, 'Peace plans generate distrust as readily as they generate hope. There is already considerable opposition to the long-awaited proposals, Frameworks for the Future, and the Prime Minister and Taoiseach can be sure that there will be more.'

The *News Letter*, while recognising that the document cannot be fully understood at a glance, says, 'There are clear signs that large parts of the Document have a distinctive nationalist agenda which would be totally contrary to the views, aspirations and the citizenship of the unionist majority community in Northern Ireland. Permanent peace, we are assured, is the objective of the whole exercise, but on whose terms?'

The *Irish Times* notes unionist scepticism and opposition to the Documents and states, 'What the document does not do is give grounds for either side to claim a victory. If it formed a blue-print for action, as unionists claim is the intention, it would mean the abandonment, for the foreseeable future, of nationalist demands for a united Ireland and the acceptance of the consent principle. In counter-balance, it demands that unionists should give up the exclusivity of power within the North which they claim as the majority. Neither tradition offers a full solution and both, if the outline of the document were to be adopted, would be expected to accept compromise.'

The *Irish News* comments, 'There are many areas in the document which people on both sides of our community will, no doubt, be unhappy with. But it should be clearly recognised that this is a starting point for politicians to discuss and hammer out a future where our people can live in harmony and peace.'

## The Frameworks Documents

The fall-out from the Frameworks Documents was entirely predictable – unionists engaged in self-pity while nationalists and, in particular, republicans engaged in self-deception.

The Frameworks Documents met none of Sinn Fein's demands for a timetable for withdrawal, yet most unionists were angry and the impression persisted that the government may have miscalculated. How had this happened? The core belief of Ulster unionism was clear: it is better to be separated from the rest of Ireland than from Great Britain. This belief carries with it the definite implication that unionist politicians are unlikely to make major sacrifices to bring about a local assembly if the price is to give Dublin an unacceptably large role in Northern affairs. The proposal for a Northern assembly did not, in itself, therefore calm unionist fears about the content of the Documents.

Let us begin with the genuine causes for unionist complaint. Unionists felt that they had an understanding with the British government that any new 'Irish dimension' would emerge from a Northern assembly. Now they were told that the legislation establishing the North-South body would emerge from Westminster and Dail legislation, though in a late softening of the text this would require 'agreement of the parties' (para. 25).

Furthermore, there was as yet no hard evidence that unionist politicians were out of touch with their community. Most unionists gave power-sharing as a preferred option, but only 12% opted for power-sharing plus an Irish dimension. Both governments would hope for a shift.

The key problem was the nature of the proposed Irish dimension. The Frameworks Documents proposed a new North-South body that would have executive functions at the outset in, for example, the areas of EU programmes and initiatives, marketing and promotion activities abroad and culture and heritage. The appearance of the last item indicated the depth of change since the Sunningdale experiment in 1974. Then, as the documentation showed, a senior UK official insisted privately, 'For a government to hand over its functions in respect of ... culture to some international authority would be to abdicate its basic responsibility.'

But behind these executive functions was a range of functions subject to harmonisation, defined as 'both sides using their best endeavours to reach agreement on a common policy'. These included aspects of agriculture and fisheries, industrial development, consumer affairs, transport, energy, trade, health, social welfare, education and economic policy – sensitive matters for middle-class and working-class unionist opinion alike. In addition, further areas were subject to consultation.

This looked like a bureaucratic fantasia designed to appeal to a Sinn

Fein leadership anxious to begin a long march through the institutions towards a united Ireland, yet it may well be that some very modest realities lurked behind the apparently all-embracing scenario outlined in the text.

The last time harmonisation of social welfare had been seriously suggested was in 1984 when Clive Soley MP, then a Labour Party spokesman on Ulster, called for pensions and other social welfare entitlements for Northern Ireland citizens to be mailed from Dublin but paid for by the British Exchequer. The Dublin postmark was seen as a means of breaking down working-class unionist prejudice against the Southern neighbour.

Were we to believe that anything like this was intended this time? Certainly not. After the leak to the *Times*, it became clear that abstract concepts like 'harmonisation' needed to be clarified. In a very significant late presentational change, paragraph 33 offered a vitally important translation of that term. Harmonisation in education, for example, was reduced to 'mutual recognition of teacher qualifications, co-operative ventures in higher education, in teacher training, in education for mutual understanding and in education for specialised needs'. All perfectly sensible, but hardly very exciting.

It was, however, clear that all was not well on another decisive front: the dropping of the Irish territorial claim. Public comments by the Irish government displayed an increasing and telling unease on this topic. In July 1994 Sir Patrick Mayhew said, 'What unionists are looking for in order to gain more confidence is an abandonment of the territorial claim to the North expressed in terms that don't need a constitutional lawyer to tease out the meaning and intent.' John Major took a similar line, but in the end the matter was fudged.

The Irish government *did* move significantly by offering to incorporate the principle of Northern consent into the Irish constitution, but it refused to drop the words, 'The national territory consists of the whole island of Ireland,' on which a unanimous Irish Supreme Court had founded the 'territorial claim' as recently as March 1990. The quid pro quo for unionist participation in North-South institutions had thus been diluted and the whole matter was left in the air.

**24 February** Four members of the UFF are each given eight life sentences for their involvement in the October 1993 Greysteel murders. One of the defendants also admits to the murders of four Catholic workmen at Castlerock in March 1993.

**25 February** The Sinn Fein ard fheis meets at the Mansion House in Dublin for the first time in four years. At the conference, which appears to be buoyed up by the Frameworks Documents, Gerry Adams says,

'Our principles have not and must not change but our strategic objectives, our strategy and our tactics must be rooted in objective reality … Our struggle has not ended. We are in another phase – a new phase of struggle which needs new thinking and new tactics … The achievement of equality of treatment for nationalists in the North will erode the very reason for the existence of that statelet. The unionist leaders know this. That is why they so dogmatically turn their faces against change. Unionists traditionally support the union because it enables them to be "top of the heap" in the six counties. A level playing field will make this impossible for them in practice and much of unionism will be left without any rational basis.' The following day Martin McGuinness says of talks with government officials, 'We have told them, just in case the reality has escaped them, that the British government and the British army has not defeated the IRA; that the IRA has not surrendered; that the British government could not even remotely expect Sinn Fein to deliver that surrender for them.' McGuinness adds that the question of the decommissioning of arms is 'an excuse to delay all party peace talks'.

**27 February** During a visit to Japan Irish President Mary Robinson expresses concern at the 'genuine fears' of unionists toward the Frameworks Documents. Mrs Robinson says, 'The fear of the ground shifting, the fear of a takeover, is undermining a sense of identity. If somebody tried to undermine our sense of identity, if somebody said to us that Ireland should join the Commonwealth tomorrow, think of the ripples of fear that that would produce.'

**1 March** The army ends patrols in East Belfast and the city centre.
Speaking in London, Gerry Adams says the decommissioning of arms will happen at the end of negotiations, not the beginning.
In Washington Dick Spring says, 'If we make the attitude that nothing will happen unless there is a surrender or decommissioning of arms, then I think that is a policy for disaster.'

**2 March** Former RUC constable James Seymour dies from injuries which he sustained in an IRA attack on Coalisland police station nearly 22 years earlier. Mr Seymour had been paralysed and partly comatose since the attack.

**4 March** Mitchel McLaughlin tells a conference at the University of North London, 'Sinn Fein have yet to formally pronounce on the Framework Document, yet one aspect is clear to all. John Major, by the very act of publishing the Framework Document in the teeth of opposition from right-wing Conservatives and the Unionist leaderships, has demonstrated that his government is not totally hostage to the mathematics of Westminster.'

**5 March** The *Independent on Sunday* reports that UUP MP Ken Maginnis has presented a plan to John Major suggesting that an international disarmament commission oversee the decommissioning of paramilitary weapons.

The *Sunday Tribune* says that during negotiations on the Frameworks Documents the previous autumn Fianna Fail proposed specific changes to the wording of Articles 2 and 3 of the Irish constitution. The party suggested that Article 2 state: 'The national territory consists of the whole island of Ireland, its islands and the territorial seas, and is the shared inheritance of all the people of Ireland, their diverse identities and traditions.' Article 3.1 would state: 'The re-integration of the national territory, which is a primary, legitimate objective of the Irish people, shall be pursued only by peaceful and constitutional means, and shall be achieved in a spirit of concord and reconciliation only with the consent freely and concurrently given of a majority of the Irish people in each of the jurisdictions which exist within that territory.'

At a SF rally in Pomeroy, Co. Tyrone, Martin McGuinness says, 'When we go to the negotiating table … we go to end British rule in this country.'

**6 March** The UUP releases the text of a plan drawn up by Ken Maginnis for a seven-member, internationally led disarmament commission which the party had presented to John Major in January. The proposal is rejected by Sinn Fein and the UDP.

**7 March** Speaking in Washington, Sir Patrick Mayhew outlines a three-point plan for the decommissioning of IRA weapons that would allow Sinn Fein to join political negotiations in NI. He says that there must be a 'willingness in principle to disarm progressively', agreement on the method of decommissioning and, thirdly, a start to the process of decommissioning as a 'tangible confidence-building measure'. The proposal that only a beginning be made to decommissioning before talks commence is attacked by unionists as capitulating to the IRA.

**8 March** Home Secretary Michael Howard lifts sixteen exclusion orders made under the Prevention of Terrorism Act. The NIO announces that security barriers in Belfast are to be removed.

In the Dail John Bruton says it is important that the arms issue be dealt with seriously and notes that, 'The British government want to exercise the maximum legitimate leverage to have the question of arms dealt with, not only from the point of view of its own prospective but from the point of view of the understandable perspective of those in the Unionist community who see themselves as having been victims of IRA violence over a long period. Those perspectives cannot be ignored or swept aside. It cannot be said that they do not count; they do count but so also do the concerns which are felt strongly in the nationalist community about loyalist arms. They, too, are legitimate concerns.'

**9 March** The White House announces that Gerry Adams has been invited to the President's St Patrick's Day reception and will also be allowed to raise funds in the US. The decision is strongly criticised in Britain.
During a one-day visit to NI the Queen meets Catholic Primate Cahal Daly.

**10 March** The UUP says it rejects the Frameworks Documents proposals in their entirety.

**12 March** At a rally in New York Gerry Adams calls for the permanent withdrawal of British troops from NI. The following day he says, 'John Major has responsibility for 30,000 troops in a part of my country. When we talk about arms we must talk about all arms.'

**14 March** 150 UVF prisoners in the Maze riot after warders carry out searches for 'illicit material'. During the following week there are a number of loyalist attacks on the homes of prison officers.
It is announced that the 5th Regiment, Royal Artillery, will not be replaced at the end of its current tour of duty in NI. The removal of this battalion will leave seventeen major units in the Province; six battalions on two-year tours, five on six-month tours and six battalions of the Royal Irish Regiment, a total of approximately 18,000 soldiers.
It is revealed that the case of paratrooper Lee Clegg is to be reviewed in June. After the Law Lords rejected his appeal for a reduction of his sentence to manslaughter, a petition of support for Clegg was signed by two million people. The Northern Ireland Life Sentence Review Board would not usually consider a case until the prisoner had served ten years, however prison authorities say there are 'exceptional mitigating' factors in the Clegg case.
Speaking at Dublin Airport before flying to the US, John Bruton says that some method will have to be devised whereby arms can be decommissioned before political talks in NI can proceed: 'You won't see Ian Paisley or Jim Molyneaux sitting down with Gerry Adams until this issue is dealt with. If you are pursuing the democratic road you don't need arms. These arms are now redundant. It is a question now of how they are to be dealt with.'

**15 March** Press interest in Gerry Adams's visit to the US is such that a fund-raising event in New York is relocated to a larger venue. At the same time relations between Britain and the US over Northern Ireland appear to reach a new low point. John Major does not speak to the President about the issue for several days despite Clinton's efforts to contact him. In the course of a BBC television interview several weeks later Major comments, 'I think it was a mistake that Mr Adams was received as he was in the United States, and I made that very clear to the United States.'

It emerges that members of the UDP will attend a St Patrick's Day reception at the White House despite the presence of Gerry Adams. A UDP spokesman says, 'It would be wrong to let Gerry Adams put forward republican propaganda unchallenged. The party believes it is important for the loyalist analysis to be heard.'

**16 March** In Newry, Co. Down, an improvised semtex explosive device partially detonates while being defused by army technical officers. Sinn Fein denies any republican involvement. John Bruton says that whoever planted the device was 'out to wreck the peace process'. Gerry Adams says the incident is a 'British dirty trick'.

**17 March** On St Patrick's Day President Clinton says he wishes to take the opportunity 'to urge all the parties to look carefully at the Framework Document, to accept it as the basis for moving forward … To those who have laid down their arms, I ask you now to take the next step and begin to seriously discuss getting rid of these weapons so that they may never be used again and violence will never again return to the land.'

UDP representatives including Gary McMichael meet US National Security Adviser Anthony Lake and later NSC staff director Nancy Soderberg. The UDP delegation also meets Senator Edward Kennedy.

**18 March** The Ulster Unionist Council re-elects James Molyneaux as Unionist Party leader. Leadership challenger, 21 year-old-student Lee Reynolds, receives 88 votes to Molyneaux's 521 with ten spoiled votes. Molyneaux claims that the 15% who voted against him were 'taking a kick at John Major through me'.

**20 March** North Down MP Sir James Kilfedder dies of a heart attack in London. Sir James was chairman of the Northern Ireland Select Committee at Westminster.

**22 March** NIO Minister Michael Ancram participates in a meeting between civil servants and members of the loyalist UDP and PUP. An NIO statement says that the meeting took place after the two parties confirmed that, 'They will engage in constructive discussion of the key issues, including the decommissioning of arms.' The NIO says it has not had the same 'clarity of response' from Sinn Fein.

**23 March** It emerges that discussions between NIO ministers and Sinn Fein had been delayed because Sinn Fein had declared that it wished to discuss the issue of 'demilitarisation' rather than the 'decommissioning' of arms. The term used by Sinn Fein implied a discussion of legally held arms and not merely the disposal of paramilitary held weapons as sought by the government.

A statement issued by UFF prisoners expresses support for the ceasefire and the policies being pursued by the UDP. The statement also warns that 'appropriate action' will be taken against scaremongers.

The Boundary Commission says that it will continue with its revised plan for electoral boundaries. The most significant changes to the existing situation are the addition of an extra seat, West Tyrone, centred on the Strabane and Omagh council areas and the extension outward of the four Belfast seats.

The Ulster Unionists win a council by-election in North Down; the result does not suggest that the UUP stand on the Frameworks Documents is unpopular.

**24 March** Routine army patrols throughout the greater Belfast area are suspended at midnight. The decision is attacked by DUP MP Peter Robinson who asks, 'What kind of world do we live in where terrorists keep their organisations intact, they hold onto their arms and their ammunition and their explosives and Her Majesty's Government instructs the army to demilitarise?'

The UUP issues a statement rejecting the proposals of the Frameworks Documents and stating, 'In the coming weeks great efforts will be made to persuade you that the benefits of a continuing ceasefire are a fair price to pay for the sacrifice of your British identity. A ceasefire with the terrorists retaining their weapons and bombs is not peace ... These papers cannot be considered as a basis for discussion, only rejected in their entirety.'

**27 March** In a speech to the Irish Association in Dublin, UUP MP John Taylor rejects the idea of powerful cross-border executive bodies, but says that the opportunity exists for 'new and well-founded relations to be established'. While describing the Forum as 'the political equivalent of Alcoholics Anonymous for Sinn Fein-IRA, its purpose being for nationalists to wean them off violence for good', he also notes that Sinn Fein has 'considerable talent' in the economic sphere. He adds, 'With my experience of the European Union my preference would be for comparable committee-based arrangements at Stormont. Membership of committees would be proportional to party strengths as would chairmanships of those committees. This poses a significant challenge to Unionists, but perhaps the inclusion of Democratic Left in the Rainbow Coalition provides a role model. Having been on the receiving end of the IRA campaign, I know this will be a "bitter pill" for Unionists to swallow, but their effectiveness and ingenuity cannot be denied.'

**28 March** John Bruton and Dick Spring meet a Sinn Fein delegation for talks in Dublin. The decommissioning of arms is discussed in detail during the meeting.

**29 March** NIO Minister Michael Ancram has a second meeting with UDP and PUP members. The meeting takes place at a time of continuing tension between prison authorities and loyalist prisoners. Six attacks have been made on the homes of prison officers over the last two days. UDP spokesman Gary McMichael condemns the attacks, but Billy Hutchinson of the PUP says he will not intervene to stop the attacks. On the issue of policing the loyalist groups call for the RUC to be made more accountable but reject SF's demand for the force to be disbanded. The loyalist groups do, however, call for the abolition of the Prevention of Terrorism Act and non-jury Diplock courts.

**30 March** The annual report of the Fair Employment Commission notes that 62.7% of the workforce in NI is Protestant and 37.3% Catholic, compared with 65.1% and 34.9% in 1990. It is estimated that Catholics, make up 40% of those available for work.

**31 March** Official statistics show that republicans have been responsible for 51 punishment beatings since the ceasefires began. In the same period loyalists carried out 39 attacks on individuals. After one such incident in North Belfast a twenty-year-old man was found impaled on railings, his fingers broken and his face battered.
Senior DUP and UUP members meet in Belfast. It is the highest level of contact between the two parties since the disputes which followed the Downing Street Declaration.

**1 April** NIO officials hold an unscheduled meeting with a SF delegation led by Martin McGuinness in an attempt to break the deadlock surrounding the agenda on which Sinn Fein and NIO ministers would meet for discussions.
Bomb disposal experts defuse an incendiary device in a Belfast grocery store. It is the third such device to be found in Belfast in a week.

**4 April** Bill Clinton and John Major meet for discussions in Washington. At the end of three hours of talks the two leaders appeared to have patched up differences which had arisen over the US decision to invite Gerry Adams to the White House reception on St Patrick's Day. President Clinton praises Major's 'vision and courage' and states, 'I was very clear when the Adams visa was granted with permission to fund-raise that there must be an agreement, a commitment in good faith, to seriously and quickly discuss arms decommissioning. Without a serious approach to arms decommissioning there will never be a resolution to this conflict.'

Four men believed to have links with the INLA are arrested by Gardai near Balbriggan as they drive north from Dublin. Twenty handguns, six rifles and 2,500 rounds of ammunition are also recovered. The following day UDP spokesman Gary McMichael says the arms find 'firmly reinforces the unease within the loyalist community toward the commitment of elements in the republican movement to the peace process'.

**11 April** The Irish government announces that seven more IRA prisoners are to be granted early releases. 21 IRA prisoners have so far been released since the ceasefire was announced.

**12 April** Leaders of the SDLP meet with UUP and DUP leaders in preparation for a renewed round of political talks. In the evening, during a speech to the CBI at Cultra, Co. Down, Sir Patrick Mayhew formally announces that the three parties as well as Alliance are to be invited to participate in separate bilateral talks. He adds, 'I hope that our intensive and ongoing communications with Sinn Fein will shortly make it possible to add them to the numbers.'

The NIO announces that a further 400 troops, members of the 40th Regiment, Royal Artillery, are to be withdrawn from NI; the troops leave on 21 April. Criticising the move, DUP MP Peter Robinson says the decision is 'solely politically motivated. Before the IRA stand down; before they hand over one gun or bullet, the government is not only pulling down its defences but unilaterally decommissioning weapons.'

The seasonally adjusted NI unemployment figure for March is announced as 89,600, the lowest since 1981.

**14 April** Three people are arrested after police discover 40 weapons and hundreds of rounds of ammunition at Holywood, Co. Down. The guns are believed to have been held for the UVF. Another arms cache, which includes five sub-machine-guns, is subsequently found by police at Chester-le-Street in Co. Durham.

**15 April** Speaking on Radio Ulster, Gerry Adams appears to rule out the idea of a decommissioning of weapons by the IRA. Asked about the perception that there was no prospect that the IRA would ever hand over its weapons, Adams says, 'I think that is a sensible view of the situation.' He also says that his party has exhausted all efforts to facilitate talks with government ministers and it was now the duty of the Irish government to exert pressure on John Major to begin round table talks involving Sinn Fein.

**16 April** In Dublin Gerry Adams says that, 'If the British won't listen to reasoned and reasonable argument then let them listen to the sound of marching feet and angry voices. We cannot accept the exclusion of the Sinn Fein electorate from the dialogue and negotiations which will shape the future of Ireland and the Irish people.'
A *Sunday Life* report claims that individual IRA members have been involved in the theft of a number of legally held weapons over the previous weeks. The report claims that the weapons have been stolen because the IRA quartermaster general has ordered guns and explosives moved to new arms dumps to prevent the weapons falling into the hands of potential breakaway units.

**17 April** Police re-route an Apprentice Boys of Derry parade away from the lower Ormeau Road area of Belfast. 200 locals and SF members protested against Orange parades passing through a nationalist area. On 23 April a crowd of almost 500 protesters demonstrate against a second Orange parade in the area. This parade is also re-routed by police.

**18 April** Nationalists criticise the continuing government policy of ministers refusing to meet Sinn Fein until they are prepared to discuss the decommissioning of arms. While SF accuses the British of 'stalling', SDLP leader John Hume says there is 'no excuse' for a further delay. Addressing the Fermanagh Unionist Association in Enniskillen, Sir Patrick Mayhew says that the decommissioning of arms cannot be equated with 'demilitarisation' involving the army and RUC. He adds, 'We won't negotiate on the political structures of Northern Ireland with people who imply by their prevarication that if they don't get what they want at the table they will go outside and cause guns to be picked up again.' He also says that the Conservative Party is more unionist than at any time in its history.

**20 April** As the deadlock over talks between SF and government ministers continues, John Bruton says he fully understands the 'exasperation' felt by many that they had not yet begun.

**23 April** The *Sunday Tribune* publishes what it claims is an IRA document circulated on the eve of the ceasefire. The newspaper states that the letters 'TUAS' contained in the document stand for 'Total Unarmed Struggle', but others, later including the *Sunday Tribune* itself, more realistically believe the letters refer to the 'Tactical Use of the Armed Struggle'. The document says that the IRA alone does not have the strength to achieve Irish unity but this objective might be achieved by allying with other groups to construct 'an Irish nationalist consensus'. The document states, 'After prolonged discussion and assessment the leadership decided that if it could get agreement with the Dublin government, the SDLP and the IA [Irish-American] lobby on basic republican principles which would be enough to create the dynamic that would considerably advance the struggle then it would be prepared to use the TUAS option ... Contact with the other parties involved has been in that context. There are of course differences of opinion on how a number of these principles are interpreted or applied ... Nevertheless, differences aside, the leadership believes there is enough in common to create a substantial political momentum which will considerably advance the struggle at this time.' 'Substantial contributing factors' pointing toward this being the time for an initiative were John Hume being 'the only SDLP person on the horizon strong enough to face the challenge', the Dublin government being 'the strongest government in 25 years or more' and President Clinton being 'the first US President in decades' to be substantially influenced by the Irish-American lobby. 'These combined circumstances are unlikely to gel again in the foreseeable future. The leadership has now decided that there is enough agreement to proceed with the TUAS option.'

In an interview with the *Observer* Albert Reynolds says that 'British intransigence' over talks with SF could provoke a split in the IRA and wreck the ceasefire. Reynolds comments, 'The British may have miscalculated that they can sit back and do nothing. But if they [the IRA] went back to the armed conflict people won't blame them because they have shown good faith.'

**24 April** In a widely welcomed statement the NIO announces that, 'Following intensive exchanges with Sinn Fein, the government believes that a sufficient basis now exists for the entry of ministers into the exploratory dialogue with Sinn Fein.' Martin McGuinness predicts that all-party round table talks could take place before the summer. The question of the decommissioning of arms remains a point of dispute, however, with the British saying that it must be the first item for discussion, while SF argues that it will be only one of a number of issues discussed.

**25 April** Four men from NI appear at a Special Criminal Court in Dublin charged with possession of arms at Balbriggan, Co. Dublin, on 4 April. During their court appearance their solicitor reads a statement claiming that the men were a delegation appointed by the IRSP. The statement says: 'For the last eighteen months we have been involved in discussions with relevant individuals and groups. We concluded some time ago that a new non-violent approach was needed to address and overcome problems relating to Irish unity. In keeping with this point of view, we were able to influence the Irish National Liberation Army to suspend its military operations in July 1994.' On 1 May, however, the INLA states that, 'The suspension of military operations is not as has been quoted a permanent ceasefire. This tactical cessation is still ongoing and will remain under constant review.'

A Catholic taxi driver is shot and seriously wounded in an apparently sectarian attack near Lurgan, Co. Armagh.

**26 April** The *Irish News* claims that secret talks have taken place between the government and the IRSP over the previous months. The NIO denies the claims but accepts that there has been contact with the IRSP over prison matters.

A report by the Independent Commission for Police Complaints for Northern Ireland shows complaints against RUC officers reached record levels in 1994. The total of 2,803 complaints was an increase of 16% over 1993 figures.

**27 April** The first report of the Commons Select Committee on NI is published. The committee's report on job creation warns against premature cutbacks in the law-and-order budget but notes that, in the event of a permanent peace, many of the 20,000 security-related jobs in the province are likely to disappear.

An RUC spokesman warns that loyalist paramilitaries have moved away from terrorism and into the drugs trade.

**28 April** Following an Anglo-Irish Intergovernmental Conference meeting in Dublin Sir Patrick Mayhew says that in talks with SF substantial progress will have to be made on the decommissioning of weapons and evidence of 'making arms no longer available for use and doing that on a permanent basis'. He adds that, 'Although the decommissioning of arms is a very important element to be discussed, it is only one of a number of matters. This is not the sole issue.' Gerry Adams rejects the view that the statement implies a softening of the government's attitude and says that Sir Patrick 'says different things in different cities'.

A Dublin ceremony held to pay tribute to the memory of all Irishmen who died during the two world wars as well as those who died in the Holocaust is attended by John Bruton, Sir Patrick Mayhew, UUP MP Ken Maginnis, Tom Hartley of SF and Alliance Party leader John Alderdice.

Police suggest that the murder of a man in a Belfast city centre bar may have been connected to paramilitary involvement in selling drugs. Initial investigations indicate the possibility of republican involvement in the killing.

A German federal court rejects an appeal by the prosecution against the June 1994 acquittal of Donna Maguire, Sean Hick and Paul Hughes of the murder of Major Michael Dillon-Lee in Dortmund in 1990. Hick and Hughes were freed in 1994 but Maguire remains in custody awaiting trial with three others for the bombing of a British barracks in 1989.

**29 April** Four vehicles are hijacked and set on fire in the Shankill area of Belfast. The trouble comes several days after police had closed down an illegal drinking establishment in the area.

**1 May** It is announced that an official meeting for bilateral talks between Sinn Fein and government representatives, including an NIO minister for the first time, will take place on 10 May.

**3 May** Approximately 100 republicans are involved in a riot in Derry in protest at John Major's visit to the city. During the one-day visit to the province Major meets a number of church leaders and community groups. Despite the disturbances, the first official talks between SF and a government minister in recent years is set to take place on 10 May. The following day in the Commons, however, Major says, 'Sinn Fein's mask slipped yesterday,' but adds, 'As we have come this far, the wider interests of the people of Northern Ireland should not be abandoned without holding Sinn Fein's feet to the fire in face-to-face negotiations.' He also says, 'I have no illusions about the people with whom we are dealing. I say again that peaceful democratic parties do not act in the way that Sinn Fein supporters acted yesterday. They do not act as front organisations for heavily-armed paramilitaries; they do not intimidate and threaten the population; they do not break the legs of teenagers with baseball bats.' At a Westminster press conference Gerry Adams blames the riot on the RUC and says SF has 'nothing to apologise for and no one to apologise to'.

**4 May** Up to 200 loyalists are involved in a riot in the Newtownards Road area of Belfast. Seventeen RUC officers are injured and ten arrests made. Trouble began when nationalists in the Short Strand area clashed with Orangemen returning from a service in the city centre marking the end of the Second World War in Europe. When police intervened to separate the two sides loyalists began attacking the police. Further rioting takes place in the same area the following night.

**5 May** At the Forum for Peace and Reconciliation in Dublin Fianna Fail leader Bertie Ahern says that a constitutional understanding which maintains the core principles of Irish nationalism, while removing what causes most offence to unionists, can be achieved by removing the territorial claim of right by the Irish state to jurisdiction over NI with or without the consent of its people. John Bruton says, 'The principles and immutable political commitments underlying the changes which we will propose in the Irish constitution will remove any jurisdictional or territorial claim of legal right over the territory of Northern Ireland contrary to the wishes of the people of Northern Ireland.'

**7 May** As controversy over marches continues, a republican parade is re-routed by police away from the Protestant Suffolk estate in West Belfast.
Gerry Adams leaves on a three-week tour of the US saying that the trip shows there is no risk of a split in republican ranks and that the ceasefire is secure.

**9 May** After a meeting with Sir Patrick Mayhew, James Molyneaux claims there is 'sufficient daylight' between the government's exploratory talks with SF and substantive discussions with other parties. Later, however, Mayhew says, 'There is a programme of bilateral talks in train. They take a different nature and character depending upon and reflecting the different nature of the parties. Some are further down the track than others but those others can catch up.'

**10 May** A SF delegation led by Martin McGuinness, and including noted republican Gerry Kelly, meets NIO Minister Michael Ancram at Stormont. While the government seeks movement on the issue of the decommissioning of IRA weapons, the SF delegation looks for the release of prisoners, the disbandment of the RUC and access to the Secretary of State for talks. Before the meeting McGuinness states, 'We are hoping to move forward on the basis of equality of treatment into an inclusive peace process and all party peace talks.'
In Portland, Maine, Gerry Adams says, 'The British have to understand that we are going into these talks in a generous mood, but against the background of them refusing to recognise our mandate.' John Major replies, 'Sinn Fein say they want to move forward with a democratic mandate. You cannot move forward with a democratic mandate with a gun in your hand. The reality is that in the discussions the gun is going to have to come out of Irish politics.'

**11 May** Loyalist paramilitary leaders warn that they will take action against any UDA or UVF members found to be dealing in drugs.

Asked in a BBC interview if he believes evidence of decommissioning of IRA arms is needed before SF can enter inclusive talks, Dick Spring replies, 'Anything we can do in relation to removing illegal arms from Northern Ireland from all sides obviously would be helpful, but we've got to move the process on as best we can.'

**13 May** A *Belfast Telegraph* report claims that an internal Irish government memo has proposed that VAT in Northern Ireland be increased to 25% as a way of harmonising the Northern economy with the Republic's.

**14 May** In an interview with the *Sunday Business Post* Conservative MP Peter Temple-Morris, co-chairman of the British-Irish interparliamentary body, says that republican frustration with the progress of talks might lead to a return to violence: 'There could be an escalation of demonstrations which others, including sections of the security forces, could provoke. Then the IRA might resume a mainland campaign with a thumping blow in the City [of London] and that would put back the process for years.'

**15 May** Fianna Fail leader Bertie Ahern meets members of the UDP and PUP for talks in Belfast. Seamus Mallon of the SDLP and Gary McMichael of the UDP also hold discussions.

In the US the International Relations Committee rules that the MacBride principles on fair employment must be applied when deciding how the $30 million aid package to the International Fund for Ireland is used.

Senior SF member Jim Gibney says republicans must be prepared to examine compromise solutions for a new Ireland: 'Republicans have a vision of an island where all the Irish people are living in peace and harmony, where the spectre of a cyclical return to armed conflict has been permanently ended. This we believe can best be achieved in a united Ireland, that is our preferred option. But if there are other options then we will examine them carefully. We will consider any political models designed to accommodate the special characteristics of the Irish people which history had handed down to us.' He urges nationalists to reassess their attitudes to unionists, saying it is time to adopt 'the language of invitation' and adds, 'As we move forward in [the] search for an all-embracing solution, nationalists must rediscover those positive aspects of Britishness of a sizeable section of Irish people, and I'm not just referring to those who live in the six counties.'

**16 May** In Derry NIO Minister Malcolm Moss and Mitchel McLaughlin of SF shake hands during the minister's visit to open a shopping complex in the Creggan.

**17 May** NI's unemployment figure of 88,700 (11.8%) for April is the lowest for thirteen years.

**18 May** A joint UUP and SDLP delegation meets John Major at Downing Street to discuss economic and social matters. Shortly after the meeting ends an NIO statement is released saying that Sir Patrick Mayhew will seek to meet Gerry Adams informally during the forthcoming investment conference on NI to be held in Washington. James Molyneaux decides not to attend the conference as a result of this decision.

**19 May** In what many see as the most important exchange in the Forum at Dublin Castle, Seamus Mallon of the SDLP criticises Jim Gibney of SF. Gibney appears to support imposed all-Ireland institutions with no necessary basis in a democratic structure in the North; Mallon, in opposition, defends the model proposed in the Frameworks Documents.

**22 May** UUP MP Ken Maginnis criticises the Secretary of State's decision to meet Gerry Adams saying, 'The general consensus, not only in Northern Ireland, but in Dublin, is that Sir Patrick has made an absolute idiot of himself by agreeing to turn an economic investment conference into a high-profile propaganda platform for Sinn Fein.'

**23 May** In Boston Sir Patrick Mayhew says that, 'The government cannot and therefore will not fudge the issue of arms and explosives. We do not ask for everything all at once. But if Sinn Fein and the other parties associated with paramilitaries have truly given up justifying violence then there is no longer any need for paramilitary weapons.' Gerry Adams says his meeting with the Secretary of State must be more than symbolic.

**24 May** A major investment conference on NI, attended by nearly 1,300 delegates, opens in Washington. Addressing delegates attending a gala dinner, Vice-President Gore calls for an end to all political violence and punishment beatings.
The Police Authority for Northern Ireland rejects the Chief Constable's annual report saying that the report failed to meet the requested standards of public accountability. In December 1994 the Authority's chairman, David Cook, had written to Sir Hugh Annesley requesting changes to the format used in the report for 1993. The Chief Constable

says the criticisms are 'not valid'.

Michael Ancram meets a SF delegation at Stormont for further exploratory discussions.

In Washington Sir Patrick Mayhew and Gerry Adams meet privately for 35 minutes. Adams describes the meeting as substantive and says there was 'a frank and friendly and positive exchange of views ... I think that tonight's meeting has helped to bridge the gap between Sinn Fein and the British government.' The Secretary of State says he asked for progress on the decommissioning of arms: 'I left Mr Adams in no doubt of the importance that the government attaches to substantial progress being made by the Provisional IRA in the decommissioning of arms. That means getting rid of them so that they can never be used again, ever.'

**25 May** In his keynote address to the NI investment conference in Washington President Clinton calls for an end to violence, punishment beatings and intimidation and adds, 'To all who are observing the ceasefire I appeal to you to take the next step and begin to discuss serious decommissioning of weapons. Paramilitaries on both sides must get rid of their bombs and guns for good and the spectre of violence that has haunted Ireland must be banished, once and for all.' Clinton also announces a number of economic initiatives during his speech. The White House later confirms that the President hopes to visit NI in the autumn.

**28 May** Seventeen RUC officers are injured during rioting on the Shankill Road. It is claimed that a shot was fired at police officers. The rioting is condemned by the PUP.

**31 May** Prince Charles begins a two-day official visit to the Republic of Ireland. A huge security operation is mounted but there are only limited protests against the visit by republicans.

**1 June** SDLP councillor Alasdair McDonnell is elected Deputy Lord Mayor of Belfast; he is the first nationalist councillor to hold the position. Belfast SDLP councillors had been divided on whether to accept the position, with the majority rejecting the offer because UUP members refused to guarantee that an SDLP candidate would become Lord Mayor the following year. Despite this councillor McDonnell accepts the offer, stating, 'Having stood for office over the past eighteen years and having been refused office all that time, to have rejected a position when one is offered would have been very childish.' On 8 June the SDLP temporarily withdraws the party whip from councillors McDonnell and Mary Muldoon, who supported the decision to accept the position of Deputy Lord Mayor.

**2 June** Nine UDA prisoners are transferred from the Maze to Maghaberry jail following political disputes with senior UDA members at the Maze.

**3 June** In a *Belfast Telegraph* interview Gerry Adams insists that, 'The process of decontamination of Sinn Fein is over – we now need to engage on the same basis as all of the other parties.'

**6 June** NIO Minister Michael Ancram and Gerry Adams shake hands publicly at an international conference on peace and reconciliation held at Belfast's Europa Hotel.

At the NI Police Federation's annual conference Sir Patrick Mayhew says, 'Future policing in Northern Ireland does rest with the RUC ... I will go further. It will be an RUC whose Chief Constable continues to provide one pillar of a tripartite structure for its control and administration, and his operational independence will continue to be assured ... We want no repetition of the kind of broken promises that would make us the embarrassing victims of political expediency.' He also says, 'The ceasefires provide the first opportunity for many years to take account of the community's own views on its police service's priorities and needs without an ever present fear arising from terrorism. I believe we have a uniquely favourable opportunity to review policing needs, to reassess strategies and to build a police service for Northern Ireland for the 21st century.' On the question of the decommissioning of arms Mayhew notes, 'Democracy and violence cannot be reconciled. Parity of esteem at a conference table depends on no one participant implying a readiness to get his associates once more to resort to violence if others at the table don't agree with him.' SDLP chairman Mark Durkan later describes Mayhew's remarks as 'the RUC, the whole RUC and nothing but the RUC. That is neither reasonable nor responsible.'

**9 June** Speaking in Paris, John Bruton warns that the early release of Lee Clegg might damage the peace process unless there were also moves to release republican and loyalist prisoners at an early date by increasing remission on sentences from 33% to 50%. An NIO statement responds by saying there is no link between the Clegg case and those of paramilitary prisoners. The statement also comments, 'Decisions on changes to remission rates for prisoners in Northern Ireland or anywhere else in the UK are a matter solely for the British government.'

**12 June** Anti-terrorist laws are renewed at Westminster despite the paramilitary ceasefires. Sir Patrick Mayhew announces plans to set up an independent review into NI's emergency powers. He also says that rules allowing prisoners compassionate home leave will be relaxed.

**13 June** Leading North Down by-election candidate Robert McCartney says that, if elected, he will consider taking the Labour whip and says of the party's new leader Tony Blair that he 'has done the sort of things with the Labour Party that I would like to do for Northern Ireland'.

**14 June** Following a meeting with loyalist representatives at Stormont, Political Development Minister Michael Ancram says, 'If there is a decommissioning of weapons, then obviously that will have an impact on the level of risk in Northern Ireland and that will, in turn, have an impact on prison policy. This would not be a trade-off, but a natural progression.'
In an interview with the *Irish Times* Gerry Adams says that, 'The demand for the surrender of IRA weapons as a precondition to negotiations was never mentioned by the British government before August 31 [1994] ... In my view, had a surrender of IRA weapons been imposed as a precondition to peace negotiations prior to the cessation, it is possible there would have been no IRA cessation on 1 September last year.' Adams adds that by asking the IRA to hand over weapons, 'The British government is not simply interested in a gesture. It is, in reality, demanding the start of a surrender process as a precondition to all-party talks.'

**15 June** In a record low turn-out for a parliamentary by-election in NI (38.8%), UK Unionist Robert McCartney (10,124 votes) wins the North Down by-election; the UUP candidate finishes second and Alliance third. A Conservative candidate receives 583 votes. In the wake of the poll James Molyneaux causes controversy among unionists by stating that North Down had 'suffered least from terrorist savagery and can afford to forget people in the frontier counties'.

**17 June** Gerry Adams says that as far as his party is concerned exploratory talks with the government had run their course and were now over.

**18 June** Police again redirect an Orange march away from the lower Ormeau Road area of Belfast in an attempt to avoid a conflict between marchers and local nationalists. On 22 June a CLMC statement says it does not agree with the Orange Order's failure to challenge the RUC's re-routing decision.

**20 June** After Sir Patrick Mayhew says that SF can not become involved in full talks until the decommissioning of weapons begins, Martin McGuinness says that, 'In reality there is not a snowball's chance in hell of any weapons being decommissioned this side of a negotiated settlement.'

**21 June** UDP member John White says that, 'The arms issues should not impede progress on either the prisoners or the political processes.' He also claims that the perception in loyalist communities is that republicans were being given concessions by the government while loyalists had gained nothing.

**22 June** In a letter to the *Times* Sir Patrick Mayhew praises John Major's 'commitment to a just settlement in Northern Ireland' and warns that internal Conservative Party opposition to John Major's leadership could put the peace process at risk. Later in the day, in a bid to see off opposition to his leadership within the party, Major resigns as Conservative leader but says he will contest the resulting leadership contest.

**23 June** Prince Charles meets members of the PUP during a visit to the Shankill Road in Belfast.
Members of the UUP launch a Unionist Labour Group which is supported by the Labour MP for Falkirk, Michael Connarty.

**24 June** Police and SF supporters clash during a protest against an Orange march in the Springfield Road area of Belfast.

**25 June** The *Sunday Independent* claims that an arrangement has been reached whereby the Irish government will act as a decommissioning agent for IRA weapons. John Bruton says there has been no such proposal.
It is reported that the UUP and SDLP have agreed on the division of committee chairmanships for the coming year in Belfast City Council. A DUP member is, however, quoted as saying, 'The Unionist Party is building bridges with the SDLP and we are the group that is losing out. This is a party that is intent on destroying Northern Ireland.'

**26 June** The High Court awards compensation to the mother of Karen Reilly, shot dead by Lee Clegg during a joyriding incident in 1990.

**27 June** At a European summit meeting in Cannes, John Bruton and John Major agree to ask officials to study ways in which progress can be made on the issue of decommissioning weapons.
Veteran peace campaigner Senator Gordon Wilson dies in Enniskillen aged 68.

**28 June** Sir Patrick Mayhew says that if the IRA and loyalist paramilitaries are not prepared to decommission weapons then political talks will have to proceed without Sinn Fein and fringe loyalist parties.
In Germany Donna Maguire is sentenced to nine years' imprisonment for involvement in the bombing of a British army barracks in Osnabruck in

1989 but is later released because she had been held on remand for almost four years.

A statement from the Mid-Ulster UVF warns that if loss of life or serious injury occurs as a result of nationalist demonstrations against Orange marches, 'These hate-filled people ... will be held responsible ... These people give an insight into life in a nationalist regime and only serve to strengthen our determination to resist them.'

**29 June** UUP MP Ken Maginnis claims that the IRA's senior command has ordered a 'rolling resumption' of violence.

**3 July** The release of Private Lee Clegg, after four years in custody, leads to widespread rioting in nationalist areas of the North. Breidge Gadd, chief probation officer for NI, resigns from the Life Sentence Review Board in protest at the decision. John Bruton says he expects British authorities to apply the same rules 'to all other similar prisoner cases', while Sinn Fein and loyalist paramilitary representatives demand the immediate release of all 'political prisoners'.

**4 July** John Major retains the leadership of the Conservative Party, receiving the votes of 218 Conservative MPs to challenger John Redwood's 89; twenty Conservative MPs abstain or spoil their votes. Sir Patrick Mayhew rejects claims that Lee Clegg's release was linked to the Tory leadership contest as 'outrageous'.

Rioting continues in nationalist areas of the North. Cardinal Daly describes Clegg's release as 'a grave blunder in substance and it was a grave blunder in timing'.

**5 July** Gerry Adams rejects claims by John Major that SF has orchestrated rioting over the previous two days. Ulster Unionist MP David Trimble calls on the government to end contacts with Sinn Fein because of the rioting.

Confrontations between loyalists and the RUC occur in the Ormeau Road area of Belfast and with nationalists in Bellaghy, Co. Londonderry, as a result of protests involving Orange marches. There are also scuffles between SF protesters and loyalists outside the Maze prison.

**6 July** The *Belfast Telegraph* claims that 'senior IRA figures' are organising rioting in nationalist areas of NI.

A White House statement says that President Clinton will visit London, Belfast and Dublin between 29 November and 2 December.

In Dublin Senator George Mitchell says he believes the riots are a 'temporary phase' in the peace process, adding, 'Obviously no one can foresee the future but, provided there are no deaths, it should be just a minor bump on the road to peace.'

**7 July** As nationalist protests following the release of Lee Clegg continue, a CLMC statement warns, 'Republicans are playing a game of the highest stakes and appear prepared to test the peace process to its very limits.'

**8 July** Lisburn SDLP councillor Hugh Lewsley is attacked and beaten by a gang of eight men outside a Belfast pub. Councillor Lewsley, who had criticised IRA punishment beatings in the previous weeks, claims that he was attacked by republicans. Sinn Fein denies any involvement in the attack.

**9 July** The RUC and Orange marchers become involved in a stand-off (later referred to as the 'siege of Drumcree') after police prevent Orangemen from marching along the nationalist Garvaghy Road in Portadown on their return from a church service. Orangemen, who say they would have been prevented from marching along the road for the first time in nearly 200 years, refuse to accept the decision. Ian Paisley, UUP MP David Trimble and local negotiators later attempt, but fail, to achieve a compromise and the RUC and Orangemen confront each other overnight.

**10 July** The Garvaghy Road confrontation continues in Portadown with 1,000 RUC officers confronting some 10,000 Orange supporters. Intermittent clashes occur with the protesters throwing bricks, stones and bottles and police firing plastic baton rounds. Early the following morning, however, a compromise is reached and later that day 500 Orangemen march along the road (despite protests from local nationalists), but unaccompanied by loyalist bands.

During the course of the confrontation trouble occurs in loyalist areas of Derry, Newtownabbey, Greyabbey, Crumlin, Ahoghill, Bushmills and in Protestant areas of East and West Belfast. Larne Harbour is also brought to a standstill by loyalists supporting the Portadown Orangemen. Ian Paisley is criticised by a number a sources (including the UDP) for making a speech during the course of the confrontation in which he said, 'If we don't win this battle all is lost, it is a matter of life or death. It is a matter of Ulster or Irish Republic, it is a matter of freedom or slavery.' Paisley is later defended by several members of the UUP; William Ross MP says the criticism is 'misplaced' while UUP honorary secretary Jeffrey Donaldson says Paisley was a 'calming influence' during the confrontation.

## The 'Siege' of Drumcree

While few ambitious Protestant professionals still joined the Orange Order in the mid-1990s, it remained the embodiment of the resistance of many ordinary unionists to the claims of Irish nationalism. Since the implementation of Direct Rule in 1972, and with it the end of the era of mainly Orange governments in Belfast, educated Irish Protestants had become increasingly cool about Orangeism. Yet the fact remained that for tens of thousands in the Protestant lower-middle and working classes Orangeism was still the most dramatic and defiant expression of their identity.

The events at Drumcree again brought the Order centre-stage, thus posing a problem for moderate unionists who wished to advance a rational, non-sectarian case for the union.

Although the crisis had been defused, at least temporarily, by the art of compromise, the 'Siege of Drumcree', coming after the nationalist rioting which followed the release of Lee Clegg, was a shocking development. While the British government could hardly have been surprised by the reaction to Clegg's release, it seemed to be taken aback by the seriousness and scale of the Orange protests.

One of the most striking features of recent developments had been the Orange Order's mastery of the concept of 'parity of esteem' for the two traditions – a phrase which had underpinned much recent government policy. The head of the Orange Order, the Revd Martin Smyth noted, 'The nationalists who keep calling for parity of esteem are not prepared to give us that.' Related to this was another problem – Ulster's unionists were now officially encouraged to believe that they constituted a local 'cultural tradition'. This was the language of Northern Ireland's semi-official cultural traditions industry and of many pronouncements by both governments. Being redefined in this way, unionists of the Orange tradition felt all the more impelled to defend their long-established customs – including those of marching against what they perceived to be the threat of extinction by an insatiable Catholic nationalism.

The confrontation in Portadown was the product of a general unionist lack of faith in British intentions. This insecurity was intensified with the publication of the Frameworks Documents in February. Ian Paisley firmly believed that Gerry Adams had been given a preview of the Documents the previous summer. David Trimble equally believed that when his party leader, James Molyneaux, asked for a similar preview in September, he had been rebuffed by Sir Patrick Mayhew.

This was a striking example of the British government marginalising the leadership of majority opinion in Northern Ireland. These snubs were, unfortunately, all too visible to ordinary unionists who had little interest in mastering the nuances of the Frameworks Documents or of the tortuous peace process. Furthermore, the British had lapsed into unbecoming silence over one of their announced objectives, persuading the Irish government to end the territorial claim to the province.

Nevertheless the degree of unionist pessimism was not justified. The republican movement had, for the moment, stopped trying to coerce unionists into a united Ireland and both British and Irish governments were genuinely committed to the principle of majority consent. The problems arose not from a back-door pursuit of Irish unity, but from the two governments' rather clumsy approach to a balanced settlement. Unionist suspicions had been generated by the partial Irish amnesia concerning the original insistence of both governments that arms be decommissioned. Unionist fears over the Frameworks Documents were also somewhat exaggerated. Even in some of their key elements the Documents were something of a paper tiger: behind some of their more ambitious rhetoric lay rather more prosaic projects.

The British government now needed to cultivate intelligent unionism. Failure to do so had led to the build-up of resentments which threatened the peace. Those resentments might have been reduced by some frank and expansive explanation and by a tacit pruning of the nationalist sub-text of the Frameworks Documents. But the modernising unionists also needed to reorganise; it was pointless piously to conjure up a new vision of the union without indicating to nationalists where a realistic compromise might be reached.

The immobility of unionist political leaders also needed to change. It was essential that the initiative be regained by political leaders and taken away from those who preferred confrontation on the streets. Modernising unionists had enjoyed some minor triumphs in the previous weeks: the deal at Belfast City Hall which saw the appointment of an SDLP Deputy Lord Mayor, the election of Robert McCartney in North Down and a 'Visions of the Union' conference at the Ulster Hall. Other questions remained to be dealt with, however, and the role of the Orange Order in the organisation of the Ulster Unionist Party in particular was a key issue which could no longer be avoided.

**12 July** Orange marches take place across NI. In Portadown a confrontation is avoided when Orangemen agree not to march along the Garvaghy Road. In the lower Ormeau Road area of Belfast, however, a heavy police presence prevents nationalist protesters from stopping an Orange march. The Irish government subsequently accuses the RUC of bias in favour of the marchers and lodges a complaint with the Anglo-Irish Secretariat at Maryfield. The homes of several Protestant and Catholic families are attacked and there are arson attacks on five Orange Halls.

**14 July** In an *Irish Times* article Gerry Adams claims the British government knew the IRA would not call a ceasefire if the question of arms had been a major issue. He also says that the government reassured republicans that the way would be clear for all-party talks when violence ended.

SF says it will hold a special conference to discuss the peace process in September or October.

After a meeting in Dublin, John Bruton, Dick Spring, John Hume and Gerry Adams issue a joint statement calling for all-party talks as soon as possible.

**15 July** SDLP leader John Hume says that the IRA will 'get rid' of its arms if republicans are included in political talks.

**16 July** Orangemen picket a mass at a Catholic church in North Belfast following a series of sectarian attacks on Protestant homes, businesses and Orange halls in the area. The following morning a fire is started in a Catholic primary school on Belfast's Shore Road. Sectarian attacks on both Protestant and Catholic premises continue in the following weeks.

**18 July** Sir Patrick Mayhew and Michael Ancram meet Gerry Adams and Martin McGuinness secretly in Derry for talks on the peace process. John Major had personally authorised the British ministers to take part in the meeting. The talks are severely criticised by both the UUP and DUP. It later emerges that another meeting between the two sides had taken place earlier.

**20 July** Three republican prisoners are transferred from prisons in England to NI. Four other republican prisoners continue a 'dirty protest' at Whitemoor prison.

**22 July** Senior Conservative MP Peter Temple-Morris praises Sinn Fein's role in bringing about the IRA ceasefire by saying, 'I think we have to more openly and overtly acknowledge the fact that we are enjoying, and the long-suffering people of Northern Ireland are enjoying, the peace now ... because it has been delivered by Sinn Fein-IRA.'

**23 July** In Scotland three loyalists are held under the Prevention of Terrorism Act and a number of guns recovered. One of those held in a series of subsequent arrests in Scotland and Liverpool is PUP member Lindsay Robb, who had participated in political talks with Michael Ancram in June.

**24 July** Sir Patrick Mayhew says there is a 'fair hope' of progress on the issue of the decommissioning of IRA arms. Gerry Adams says that he told Mayhew at their 18 July meeting that, 'The IRA were not going to surrender its weapons, were not going to disarm, were not going to decommission, unilaterally, at any time, or as part of a precondition.'

**26 July** In the Dail Dick Spring says the Irish government attaches 'primary importance' to getting all-party political talks under way in NI at the earliest opportunity.

**27 July** A *Belfast Telegraph* report claims that a senior NIO official has held several secret meetings with leading loyalists who have no political connections. The meetings were sanctioned by Sir Patrick Mayhew.

**28 July** The Irish government gives early releases to twelve republican prisoners; a total of 33 republican prisoners have been released since the IRA ceasefire. Three republican prisoners involved in a 'dirty' protest at Whitemoor jail in Cambridgeshire are transferred to NI prisons. 21 prisoners convicted of terrorist offences have now been moved from Britain to NI jails since the IRA ceasefire began.
Sir Patrick Mayhew lifts a ban, imposed ten years earlier, on funding organisations which are suspected of having paramilitary links.

**30 July** Police halt a 500-strong Sinn Fein march into Lurgan town centre to prevent a clash with up to 1,500 loyalists in a counter-demonstration. The loyalist protesters are addressed by Peter Robinson and David Trimble who call on the crowd to hold their ground in order to halt the SF march. Three RUC officers and one civilian are injured in a subsequent confrontation between the police and loyalists. A dispute later occurs between UUP MPs David Trimble and Ken Maginnis after Maginnis criticises the actions of the loyalist protesters.

**3 August** In an interview with the *Irish Times* President Clinton says he 'would be pleased if talks were under way by the time I visit Northern Ireland [on 30 November]'. Clinton's apparent support for all-party talks is welcomed by SF, but DUP member Sammy Wilson criticises the statement by saying, 'Bill Clinton may not have inhaled the IRA propaganda drug but he cannot deny that he has partaken of it.'

**8 August** Members of the Apprentice Boys of Derry threaten to blockade chapels if Orange marches in Belfast and Derry are re-routed. The secretary of the Co. Down Committee of the Apprentice Boys states, 'Our parading is part of our religious worship. If people of other religions say we cannot practise our faith, then we will say that we will do the same thing to you.'

**9 August** Albert Reynolds claims that the issue of the decommissioning of paramilitary arms was not an issue in the talks leading to the Downing Street Declaration and that if it had been he would not have signed the Joint Declaration. NIO Minister Baroness Denton says Reynolds's memory 'seems to have slipped' and reminds him that on 16 December 1993 Sir Patrick Mayhew had said that the issue of dealing with illegal arms would be discussed in any exploratory talks. On 12 August Reynolds reiterates his position and claims that the British government had changed its position on the arms issue after November 1994.

**12 August** A confrontation between police and republicans protesting against an Apprentice Boys' march in the lower Ormeau Road area leads to 22 people being injured. In Derry the Apprentice Boys march around the city walls for the first time in 25 years. Republicans conducting a sit-down protest against the march are removed by RUC officers. Rioting later breaks out in Derry city centre. Sectarian clashes also occur at Dunloy and Rasharkin in Co. Antrim.

**13 August** Gerry Adams is widely criticised after he tells a republican demonstration at Belfast City Hall that the IRA 'haven't gone away'. The government and unionists say the statement underscores the need for IRA weapons to be decommissioned.

**14 August** Dublin government sources suggest that John Major convene all-party talks to draw up an agenda for full negotiations.

**15 August** In a *Belfast Telegraph* interview a leading loyalist claims that the approach of the Irish government 'has not been balanced. It has broken its word. We could not have sold the ceasefire on the basis of the Framework Document.' He adds that, 'Dublin must stop dancing to Sinn Fein's tune.'
SDLP MP Seamus Mallon criticises a statement by Martin McGuinness that nationalists have 'nothing to give' at the negotiating table by saying, 'On the contrary, the nationalist community on this island alone can and must give unionists the real sense of security which comes from knowing that they belong in this island and are an essential and valued part of the present and future.'

**17 August** Gerry Adams says republicans are ready to make 'critical compromises' to attain peace and appeals to unionists to enter all-party talks. Adams also says that a number of 'significant meetings' between Sinn Fein and members of the unionist community have taken place over recent weeks.

**18 August** RUC Chief Constable Sir Hugh Annesley says that, although he is aware that IRA units are active behind the scenes, he believes the IRA ceasefire will hold.

**22 August** A poll conducted for the *Irish News* finds 52% support for the setting of a date for all-party talks by the government irrespective of weapons being decommissioned. While 86% of Catholics questioned support the proposition, only 26% of Protestants do so. The same poll finds 54% of Catholics interviewed support the early release of paramilitary prisoners compared to 20% of Protestants. 71% of Protestants believe the RUC have done a good job in handling recent parades, but only 25% of Catholics hold the same opinion.

**25 August** In a speech at Queen's University, Belfast, Sir Patrick Mayhew announces that the government will produce a White Paper on the reform of policing structures, an independent review of emergency legislation and that remission on the sentences of those convicted of terrorist related crimes will be returned to 50%. Loyalist spokesmen welcome the return of 50% remission but Pat McGeown of SF says the 'derisory increase is an insult to our community'.

A statement from the CLMC says that, provided the rights of the people of NI are upheld, they 'will not initiate a return to war. There will be no first strike.' The statement also notes, 'It is inconceivable for the Combined Loyalist Military Command to decommission weapons with a fully operational, heavily armed republican war machine intact and refusing to relinquish their arsenals.'

**26 August** Dublin government sources cast doubt on whether a summit meeting, proposed for 6 September, between John Major and John Bruton will take place as a result of the increasing differences between the two governments on the issue of decommissioning arms.

Marches by the (Orange) Royal Black Preceptory pass off relatively peacefully, although scuffles between republican protestors and police take place in Bellaghy, Co. Londonderry.

Sinn Fein says it does not rule out agreeing to an international commission to oversee the decommissioning of weapons. SF chairman Mitchel McLaughlin says that if a practical progamme were announced, 'We will look very, very carefully and seriously at it.'

**27 August** At a peace forum in Killala, Co. Mayo, also attended by Gerry Adams and John Hume, Albert Reynolds suggests that, 'Decommissioning can be made a condition of agreement at the end of the day rather than a precondition for starting the talks.' An NIO statement replies that, 'Substantive political dialogue cannot take place until there is confidence that those with whom we have been negotiating are committed to exclusively peaceful methods, and have demonstrated their good faith in that regard by the beginning of a credible process of decommissioning of illegally-held arms. To proceed on any other basis would not be sustainable in democratic or constitutional terms.'

**28 August** James Molyneaux announces his resignation from the leadership of the Ulster Unionist Party.

A meeting between the Irish government and Sinn Fein ends with a statement that, 'The clear priority now is a comprehensive and inclusive all-party talks process.' The following day a joint SF-SDLP statement says that, 'The people of Ireland as a whole have a right to national self-determination,' and calls for all-party talks with all issues on the table for discussion.

### Molyneaux Resigns as Unionist Leader

James Molyneaux, the Ulster Unionist leader, had, politically, been living on borrowed time since February 1995, when John Major discounted his advice on the Frameworks Documents. Like an earlier leader of his party, Brian Faulkner in 1974, Molyneaux had put his trust in a Tory Prime Minister and had been sacrificed. Indeed, in Molyneaux's case this had happened twice: first with Margaret Thatcher and the Anglo-Irish Agreement of 1985 and then with John Major over the Frameworks Documents.

In March, Lee Reynolds, an unknown 21-year-old student, had obtained 15% of the vote in an audacious leadership challenge against Molyneaux. In the summer the party lost the by-election in North Down, a prime Unionist seat, to an arch Molyneaux critic, Robert McCartney QC. In the aftermath of the Downing Street Declaration, when James Molyneaux's Ulster Unionists tacitly accepted its terms, McCartney sharply attacked both Molyneaux's stand and the soft green rhetoric of the Declaration, but he was then an isolated and marginalised figure. After his by-election victory, however, McCartney was at the centre of the stage and in the wake of the North Down result the Unionist leader found life increasingly uncomfortable in the Glengall Street head-quarters as activists and party officers made known their criticisms of his leadership.

There was no mystery about the timing of James Molyneaux's resignation as leader of the Ulster Unionists. His 75th birthday on 27 August was always a likely date, but there was another factor. Ever since his humiliation in February, he had been looking for a chance to make a dignified exit, and Sir Patrick Mayhew's speech on 25 August gave it to him. The speech was billed as a balancing exercise, designed to reassure unionists that the government would not pay too high a price for peace, while offering reforms intended to appeal to nationalists. But because the government maintained that IRA arms must be handed in before Sinn Fein could be admitted to all-party talks, the speech appealed more to unionists than might have been expected.

When Molyneaux handed over the leadership of the Unionist Party, at least British policy was not obviously anti-unionist. This, however, was a small victory and would not placate those who believed that the Molyneaux years had been wasted, but then Molyneaux's career had been built around small victories.

What did Molyneaux really believe in? Where did he stand in the debate which divided Ulster Unionism? As his biographer, Ann Purdy, made clear, Molyneaux was at heart an integrationist rather than a devolutionist. He told her that Stormont – 'a puppet parliament' as he called it – had not strengthened the union even when it was dominated by Unionists from 1921 to 1968; hardly surprisingly, he felt in the 1970s and 1980s that 'devolution was not worth the candle' if it also involved accepting both the Anglo-Irish Agreement and power-sharing.

Who were his likely successors? On 28 August, when David Trimble appeared to rule himself out of the race, the leadership contenders were John Taylor, William Ross, Martin Smyth and Ken Maginnis. All the remaining candidates had flaws. Ross was a respected figure on the right of the party, but the previous weekend had received a mere 3% approval rating in an opinion poll. On the left the liberal security spokesman Ken Maginnis was boosted by a 39% poll rating; arguably the most decent and affable man in Northern Irish politics, he had been criticised for being less than incisive. This would worry some of the 800 or so Unionist Council delegates who would make the leadership choice. It was in any case doubtful whether a naturally conservative party could be led from the left.

This left two more centrist candidates. The Revd Martin Smyth was the leading Ulster Orangeman and enjoyed some support, but he was in many ways closely linked with the Molyneaux leadership. Those looking for a more distinctive message might turn to John Taylor, the MP for Strangford who had considerable experience and was also the survivor of an IRA assassination attempt. His political career stretched back to ministerial office at Stormont, but he had been the most unpredictable of unionist politicians. In recent months he had made a point of making frequent and well-received visits to the Irish Republic while still maintaining a firm unionist line.

None of these contenders showed any interest in all-party negotiations, but John Taylor would appeal to the energetic, modernising wing of the party. All these calculations, however, were to be upset by David Trimble's late and ultimately successful entry into the leadership race. Molyneaux's bravery in going to Dublin for talks in 1992 had created a precedent; the new leader might well wish to talk to a new Irish government which was a much paler shade of green.

**30 August** On the eve of the first anniversary of the IRA ceasefire President Clinton issues a statement in which he urges republicans and loyalists to 'seriously address the issue of decommissioning paramilitary arms'. He also urges the parties to 'sit down together to discuss their aspirations for the future, as well as their fears and differences'.

**31 August** On the first anniversary of the IRA ceasefire Gerry Adams says his party will look constructively at any proposal addressing the issue of decommissioning of arms. In London Martin McGuinness rules out decommissioning of any weapons as a way of breaking the deadlock in the peace process, saying the IRA would regard this as an act of surrender. The anniversary is marked by a number of republican pickets and vigils calling for all-party talks.

Gary McMichael of the UDP says loyalists are ready to decommission their arms if the IRA will do the same.

**1 September** Newspaper reports suggest that former US Senator George Mitchell will be asked by the British and Irish governments to chair an international commission on the decommissioning of paramilitary weapons. It is believed that the forthcoming summit meeting between Major and Bruton will also announce the start of trilateral talks with the British and Irish governments meeting all of the Northern parties.

A senior IRA spokesman says, 'There is absolutely no question of any IRA decommissioning at all, either through the back door or the front door.'

**3 September** Dublin Sunday newspapers report officially inspired leaks suggesting a British climb-down on the question of arms. Such leaks, while bitterly resented by London, have worked for Dublin in the past, but on this occasion merely serve to stiffen British resolve in negotiations in the following week's Anglo-Irish discussions.

**4 September** A two-hour meeting between Sir Patrick Mayhew and Gerry Adams at Stormont fails to break the deadlock over the issues of all-party talks and the decommissioning of paramilitary weapons. Adams comments, 'What they are actually saying is that before there can be all-party talks there has to be a beginning of the IRA surrendering its weapons. We can't deliver that. What we can deliver is republicans to the table, as others should deliver their particular constituencies, to work out our future and deal with all the issues, including demilitarisation and disarmament.' Mayhew responds by saying he is 'not prepared to destroy the political process by calling talks where there will be a large number of empty chairs'.

**5 September** The Irish government calls off the summit meeting between John Bruton and John Major scheduled for the following day after officials fail to reach agreement on the concept of a body to oversee the decommissioning of arms. A British official in Belfast reacts angrily to the cancellation of the meeting by stating, 'Sinn Fein have seen the entire package in advance and rattled the cage. If the reality is that they are threatening to return to violence unless they get their way politically, then we have trouble.' Another British source says, 'We thought it was in the bag but the rats got at it.' Major later sends a letter to Bruton asking for his views on how to proceed.

A man, said by Families Against Intimidation and Terror to be on an IRA death list because of alleged drug-dealing activities, is shot dead after attending a funeral in Belfast.

**6 September** PUP spokesman David Ervine claims that, in secret talks with loyalists before their ceasefire, the then Taoiseach Albert Reynolds said the IRA would have to decommission its 'offensive' weapons. Ervine says the Irish government has moved to a 'republican agenda' on the issue of all-party talks and that this is the most damaging thing to happen since the ceasefires. He warns that when the CLMC stated it would not fire the first shot in any new conflict this was only on the proviso that 'the democratic rights of the people of Northern Ireland were upheld. That is subtly different from saying you will not fire the first shot under any circumstances.' The following day Albert Reynolds says, 'No such preconditions on the prior decommissioning of IRA heavy weapons as alleged *vis-à-vis* Sinn Fein's right to attend all-party talks was ever communicated by the then Taoiseach to loyalist leaders.'

UFF member Johnny Adair is sentenced to sixteen years' imprisonment for directing loyalist paramilitary activities.

**7 September** In a speech at Dublin Castle John Bruton says the Irish government's acceptance that the IRA cessation of violence is irreversible is 'an act of faith'. He adds that, 'Unionists feel that … a public insistence on retaining arms implies the possibility that they might be used in the future and they have a problem negotiating with Sinn Fein on that basis.'

**8 September** David Trimble is elected leader of the Ulster Unionist Party, defeating pre-election favourite John Taylor on the third count. Trimble is perceived as being on the right of the party.

At the British Irish Association conference in Cambridge Dick Spring says that the decommissioning of paramilitary weapons should not be a precondition for all-party talks. Sir Patrick Mayhew, on the other hand, draws an explicit analogy with the late 1930s and says the British people have learnt the lesson of appeasement.

**9 September** David Trimble says there is no evidence that the IRA is committed to exclusively peaceful methods: 'The private army is being maintained, the weapons are still there, the punishment beatings continue, murders are occurring. The political representatives of this body are using language which is wholly inconsistent with a commitment to peaceful methods, because implicit in their language is the threat of a resumption of violence.'

**10 September** Newspaper reports claim that, at a meeting in Belfast at the beginning of September, Irish government officials were told by Sinn Fein representatives that there would be 'bodies in the streets' if plans for an international body to oversee decommissioning of weapons went ahead. The reports also claim that the hostile SF reaction to the proposal led John Bruton to cancel the proposed summit with John Major. SF later denies that any such threat was made.
Four police officers and a number of civilians are injured during a clash between GAA supporters and Orange marchers in Dunloy, Co. Antrim.

**11 September** David Trimble meets Irish Social Welfare Minister Proinsias de Rossa at the UUP's Belfast headquarters.

**12 September** Sir Patrick Mayhew holds his first formal talks with representatives of the loyalist UDP and PUP.
The RUC confirms that certificates have been issued blaming an 'unlawful association' for causing damage to Orange halls in Newcastle and Banbridge. The decision leads unionists to claim that the IRA has breached its ceasefire.

**14 September** John Hume and David Trimble hold an hour-long meeting in Derry and agree that co-operation between their parties on economic matters should continue.
A fourteen-member 'Unionist Commission' holds its inaugural meeting in Belfast. While the commission involves a broad range of unionist opinion, the UUP is represented by only two councillors sitting on the commission in a personal capacity.
Former Labour spokesman on NI Kevin McNamara resigns as Opposition spokesman on the civil service, giving one of his reasons for doing so as Labour 'slavishly' following the government's policy on NI.

**16 September** Gerry Adams ends a week-long visit to the US during which he met Vice-President Gore and National Security Adviser Anthony Lake. Adams says he is not bringing back any proposals from the US government concerning the deadlock over decommissioning of weapons. During the visit it is revealed in the US that Friends of Sinn Fein raised almost $900,000 between 24 February and the end of June. The largest single donation, $65,000, comes from Irish-American businessman Charles Feeney.

**18 September** Sinn Fein and UDP spokesmen share a public platform for the first time when Mitchel McLaughlin and Gary McMichael take part in a debate during the Liberal Democrat conference in Glasgow.

**19 September** A four-man UDP delegation meets John Bruton and Dick Spring for talks in Dublin. The following day Bruton meets a delegation from the PUP.
In London David Trimble has his first meeting as UUP leader with John Major and later with Opposition leader Tony Blair.

**20 September** At a meeting of the British-Irish inter-parliamentary body in Cardiff former NIO Minister Michael Mates says the British and Irish governments should be ready to 'call the bluff' of Sinn Fein and the IRA over decommissioning even if this meant contemplating 'a short-term return to violence'.
In a speech to the National Press Club in Australia Sir Patrick Mayhew says, 'Sinn Fein wish to start all-party talks before even giving any commitment on how weapons could be decommissioned, let alone that there should be a start to decommissioning in order to signal the start of the process … We are speaking crucially of a start being made, not of a complete disposal. The only people who speak of this being a surrender are the IRA and Sinn Fein. It is of course no such thing.'

**21 September** Speaking in London John Major says he has no wish to 'humiliate' Sinn Fein by forcing the IRA to surrender weapons to the British. He insists, however, that a 'credible and verifiable' decommissioning of IRA arms must begin before SF can enter all-party talks. Gerry Adams responds by stating, 'The placing of preconditions on the road to dialogue is indeed a formula for disaster and the British government have shown no willingness at all to lift that new precondition. It is my view that if the British government stick to their position, as it appears they will, then the peace process, or this phase of the peace process, is doomed to collapse.'
Government figures indicate that, by the end of March 1995, £1,119,585,000 had been paid in compensation as a result of the Troubles. The bulk of the compensation paid by the Exchequer resulted from damage to property (£300,516,000) or personal injury (£814,219,000).

**22 September** At a reception to mark the 90th anniversary of the Ulster Unionist Council David Trimble proposes that a new NI Assembly be established. The idea is generally welcomed by unionists and loyalists but rejected by Sinn Fein and the SDLP.

Police clash with loyalists in Downpatrick after a parade had been re-routed by the RUC in an attempt to prevent serious public disorder.

**23 September** John Bruton and John Major meet for discussions while attending a European Union meeting in Majorca. Major criticises Gerry Adams's statement that the peace process might be doomed by asking, 'Who is going to be violent? That is a matter that is in Mr Adams's hands.' Bruton says that Adams's statement is not particularly helpful. Adams later issues a statement rejecting the accusation that his statement is a threat and says he is only stating 'the reality'.

**26 September** John Major meets SDLP and later DUP leaders in London for political discussions.

Speaking in Australia, Sir Patrick Mayhew says 'it would be an advance' if republicans gave a declaration, similar to that given by loyalists, that they would not resort to violence first.

**27 September** The European Court of Human Rights at Strasbourg rules that the shooting of three unarmed IRA members in Gibraltar in March 1988 breached the Human Rights Convention. The ten votes to nine decision against the British government overturns all previous findings that the killings were not unlawful. The government is ordered to pay the legal costs of the case but no damages are awarded. While a senior Downing Street source condemns the decision as 'completely daft', the families of the three IRA members call for a full judicial inquiry into the killings.

In a speech to the United Nations in New York, Dick Spring says that, 'To make the decommissioning of weapons a precondition for entry into negotiation, as opposed to an important goal to be realised in that process, ignores the psychology and motivation of those on both sides in Ireland who have resorted to violence and the lessons of conflict resolution elsewhere.'

**28 September** Michael Ancram and Martin McGuinness meet at SF's request to discuss the current political situation and agree that they will meet again for further discussions.

After a loyalist is shot dead in Bangor, Co. Down, reports suggest that his murder is connected to the killing of Margaret Wright in March 1994.

**29 September** On the eve of a Sinn Fein delegate conference in Dublin an IRA statement says, 'There is no possibility of disarmament except as part of a negotiated settlement. … The demand for an IRA handover of weapons is ludicrous.'

At the Forum for Peace and Reconciliation John Bruton says they are 'tantalisingly close' to the objective of all-party talks. He adds, 'We accept that the unionist and loyalist community in particular requires convincing evidence of the IRA's commitment to decommissioning of arms and to non-recourse to arms at any time. Equally we have accepted that the IRA, whose weapons have thankfully been silent for 400 days now, is not in a position to offer a physical decommissioning of arms gesture as a precondition to the start of all-party round table talks.' John Major comments, 'If they are seriously seeking peace then there can be no question of the IRA returning to violence. If there is no question of them returning to violence then there is no need for them not to make this start on decommissioning their weapons.'

**30 September** At the end of a special one-day conference on the peace process attended by nearly 800 SF activists Gerry Adams says, 'Nearly all the speakers expressed both concern and some anger at the British government's response.' While some speakers were unhappy with the party's strategy, Adams says there was no personal criticism: 'We aren't leading sheep and this party is not, and never has been, a monolith.'

**1 October** Five people are arrested in Glasgow after bottles are thrown by loyalists protesting against Gerry Adams's first visit to Scotland.

**2 October** In an interview with the *Irish Times* David Trimble says Dick Spring is 'wobbling out on a limb' on the issue of decommissioning paramilitary weapons before talks begin. He calls for the establishment of a new NI assembly and says that if SF took their seats in this assembly, 'We would be obliged to recognise their position and could debate with them across the floor, and thus talk to them at a time when they would not have fulfilled all the requirements of the Declaration and therefore not as yet be able to move into formal inter-party talks.' Trimble later meets John Bruton for talks at Government Buildings in Dublin. Bruton says that they are 'moving inexorably' towards all-inclusive dialogue, but Trimble says the prospect of all-party talks by the end of the year is not realistic.

At a fringe meeting at the Labour Party's annual conference in Brighton SF chairman Mitchel McLaughlin says the IRA has 'effectively decommissioned' its arms and that its weaponry is out of circulation. He adds, 'When the Royal Navy takes its warships out of commission, do they surrender them to someone, or do they simply take them out of active service?' He points out, however, that weapons could be 'recommissioned' if the conditions of conflict re-emerged. The following day Sir Patrick Mayhew says McLaughlin has made a 'spurious comparison' and says decommissioning involves 'making no longer available to those who at present hold them, arms that are illegally held at present'.

**3 October** At the Labour Party conference Tony Blair states that his party will 'play a supportive role' to government policy in NI and adds, 'I believe that peace is too important to us to play politics with.'

**4 October** In Belfast the US ambassador to the UK, Admiral William Crowe, and Assistant National Security Adviser Nancy Soderberg hold discussions with leading members of the UUP, DUP, SDLP, SF and the Alliance Party.

**5 October** It is announced that the 1995 Nobel prize for literature has been awarded to Northern Irish poet Seamus Heaney.

**6 October** Speaking in New York, John Bruton says he believes sufficient common ground will soon exist to enable the British and Irish governments to establish an international commission to oversee the handing in of terrorist arms. He also says that, side by side with this, is the requirement to move forward in creating the basis for all-party round table talks.

**9 October** Gerry Adams says that statements by his party have shown it is committed to 'the democratic and peaceful process'. He adds that, 'It is self-evident that threats of any description from any quarter have no role in any such process. They are certainly no part of any talks process in which we will engage.' On 11 October John Bruton tells the Dail this statement and others shows a 'significant and important new commitment on the part of Sinn Fein'. He adds that he believes SF have satisfied the conditions of paragraph 10 of the Joint Declaration (a commitment to exclusively peaceful methods) and that all-party talks should begin as soon as possible.

**10 October** Speaking on the issue of decommissioning weapons, Dick Spring says, 'The crucial point is that the guns are silent. The total cessation of violence was the critical point at which political engagement with Sinn Fein on the one hand, and the loyalist parties on the other, became possible. Permanent peace is guaranteed only by a transformation in the hearts and minds of those who might use the weapons. We must therefore create the conditions where those who hold arms are motivated to take them out of the equation for ever.'

**11 October** In the Dail John Bruton says there is increasing movement toward agreement between the two governments on the concept of an international body being established to oversee the decommissioning of paramilitary weapons. He notes, however, that differences between the British and Irish governments on the issue still remain.

**12 October** At the Conservative Party conference Sir Patrick Mayhew says both governments are willing to invite an international commission to examine the question of illegally held arms and advise how weapons might be decommissioned. At the same time preliminary talks would take place which would later lead to all-party negotiations.

**13 October** John Major at the Conservative Party conference states that NI will continue at the top of his priorities. He says that, 'A just peace and one that is fair to all sides ... must be a peace that is constructed away from the shadow of the gun.'

On the anniversary of the loyalist paramilitaries' ceasefire a spokesman says, 'Sinn Fein should forget about putting pressure on the British government to call all-party talks. It is the unionist and loyalist people they have to convince. Republicans must answer the question everyone wants answered – is the war really over for good? Loyalists will not initiate a return to war, but if there is a war we are fully prepared to fight it.' Later, at a loyalist rally in Belfast, PUP spokesman David Ervine says the attitude of republicans is the obstacle to all-party talks and the release of prisoners. He also calls on the government to set a date for Assembly elections. UDP councillor Gary McMichael accuses republicans of trying to 'push the peace process to the edge', adding, 'Either the war is truly over or it is not. That is what the IRA must decide.' The City Hall rally is attended by a crowd variously estimated at between 12,000 and 25,000 people.

**14 October** The last 'Peace Train' runs from Dublin to Belfast. The Peace Train campaign began in 1989 in protest against repeated IRA attacks on the rail link.

Police and republicans are involved in scuffles in Lurgan after SF supporters attempt to hold a demonstration in the town centre. Police had also prevented a SF march through the town earlier in the week.

**15 October** PUP spokesman Billy Hutchinson says that, 'Political parties will be forced to talk to Sinn Fein in the not too distant future. We have to consult with our constituency but I expect we will be moving towards talks with Sinn Fein based on bilateral and multi-lateral dialogue.'

**16 October** John Hume and David Trimble hold separate meetings with US National Security Adviser Anthony Lake in London. The following day Lake meets Sir Patrick Mayhew and Michael Ancram.

**17 October** After an Anglo-Irish Intergovernmental Conference meeting in Belfast Sir Patrick Mayhew says the British government would consider an acceptable alternative to the decommissioning of IRA arms which would allow Sinn Fein to join all-party talks. He adds, however, that he can see no suitable alternative at this stage. SF gives a guarded welcome to the government 'possibly' taking a more 'flexible and pragmatic approach'.
It is revealed that a Catholic member of the UUP, and former assistant to James Molyneaux, has lodged a case against the party with the FEC claiming she was not fairly considered for the post of party public relations officer because of her religion.

**18 October** Sir Patrick Mayhew and Michael Ancram deny there has been any shift by the government on the issue of decommissioning arms, but despite this denial the NIO ministers are criticised by unionists and by Conservative backbenchers. David Trimble says that the proposed international body cannot be a substitute for decommissioning.

**19 October** John Major meets SDLP leaders John Hume and Seamus Mallon for talks at Downing Street. The previous night Major met Alliance leader John Alderdice.

**21 October** At the Ulster Unionist annual conference in Portrush David Trimble outlines plans to loosen the party's links with the Orange Order by ending the Order's right to appoint delegates directly to the Ulster Unionist Council. Trimble adds, however, that this does not mean expelling Orange delegates or cutting the link with the Orange Order.
Figures for RUC recruitment since the ceasefires indicate that Catholics accounted for 21.5% of 2,381 applicants but 16.5% of 121 people accepted by the force. The proportion of Catholics applying to join the Home Services Battalions of the Royal Irish Regiment also increased from 3% to 6% in the first six months of the ceasefires.

**23 October** In Belfast Dick Spring meets David Trimble for talks at the UUP's headquarters. Although they fail to agree on the decommissioning issue, the meeting is described as 'useful'. Spring also meets a PUP delegation led by former UVF leader Gusty Spence. Speaking to students at Methodist College, Belfast, Spring says that decommissioning of arms 'will be possible only within the context of full negotiations'.
Following threats from the UVF and attacks on two houses, several alleged drug-dealers are forced to leave Ballymena, Co. Antrim. A UVF

statement telephoned to a newspaper says, 'Ceasefire or not, if these people do not get out, we will take them out.'

**25 October** A man on trial in the Republic for attempted murder appears in the dock at Enniskillen courthouse. It is the first occasion on which evidence is taken in Northern Ireland for a trial in the South.

In London the Queen and President Mary Robinson share their first public engagement, celebrating the 150th anniversary of the foundation of Queen's University, Belfast, University College, Cork, and University College, Galway.

In the Dail John Bruton says he will meet John Hume and Gerry Adams whenever they wish. Bruton is criticised by Fianna Fail leader Bertie Ahern for having refused to meet the SDLP and SF leaders together to discuss their proposals for the peace process earlier in the month.

**26 October** An announcement by the NIO that the oath of allegiance to the monarch made by Queen's Counsels in Northern Ireland is to be replaced is criticised by unionists. The decision leads to the withdrawal of a case by more than 20 barristers who had campaigned for the oath to be removed as it did not apply elsewhere in the UK.

**27 October** Alliance leader John Alderdice announces that he is withdrawing temporarily from the Irish Forum for Peace and Reconciliation and criticises SF and SDLP leaders for not taking the Forum more seriously. The criticism is rejected by these two parties' leaders.

Ian Paisley and Peter Robinson of the DUP meet US Vice-President Gore and National Security Adviser Anthony Lake at the White House and accuse the Clinton administration of 'a gross imbalance in favour of the minority point of view'. A White House official later says that the US is neutral in the peace process.

**31 October** Michael Ancram and Martin McGuinness hold a three-hour meeting. McGuinness later says there are 'major difficulties' preventing agreement on decommissioning and all-party talks but that SF has been attempting 'to salvage the peace process'.

**1 November** David Trimble meets President Clinton for talks in Washington. White House Press Secretary Mike McCurry later says the peace process is 'at a fairly critical stage'.

Belfast City Council passes a motion condemning SF councillors who attended a memorial parade for IRA man Thomas Begley on the second anniversary of the Shankill bombing.

SF vice-president Pat Doherty rejects a proposal by David Trimble for a date to be set for Assembly elections saying, 'Such a proposal outlined by Mr Trimble cannot bring peace. What is required is a new democratic accommodation involving all the people of Ireland.' Gerry Adams, meanwhile, says that talks between SF and the government have failed or are at the point of failure.

**2 November** John Bruton meets Gerry Adams for talks in Dublin.
In Washington David Trimble calls on loyalist paramilitaries to 'take the courageous first step and the moral high ground by beginning the process of disarmament as quickly as possible'. The following day UDP councillor Gary McMichael writes in the *Belfast Telegraph*: 'I do not believe that a physical hand-over of guns is a solution – or at this stage even possible. But I am convinced that there will be no movement until republicans address the fears which exist within my community.'

**3 November** Michael Ancram and Martin McGuinness meet for discussions on the issues of all-party talks and arms decommissioning but fail to resolve the deadlock. After the government rejects the main elements of the latest Hume-Adams proposals, McGuinness says, 'What we must now do is appeal to the international community to convince the British government that the peace process must not be squandered.'
The NIO releases a document which it had circulated to all political parties and the US and Irish governments the previous week. The 'Building Blocks' paper aims to 'facilitate a shared understanding among all those involved of the building blocks for a twin-track approach to the way forward'. The paper suggests, 'All-party preparatory talks and an independent international body to consider the decommissioning issue will be convened in parallel by the two governments.' A target date for all-party negotiations might be announced, but achieving this target 'would depend on success in creating the necessary conditions to enable all parties to join in such negotiations constructively'. The international body would be asked to 'ascertain and advise on how unauthorised arms and other material which had been used to advance political ends could forever be removed from the political equation'. DUP deputy leader Peter Robinson later attacks the proposals, saying the jointly managed preparatory talks 'means that from now on there is effectively joint authority. That is totally unacceptable.'

**5 November** Gerry Adams says the British government has subverted the peace process to the point that it no longer exists. 'What we have now are two cessations of violence: one by the IRA, which is a complete military cessation which is now totally unanchored, and we have a conditional, qualified loyalist cessation.'

**7 November** The Act increasing the remission rate on the sentences of paramilitary prisoners from 33% to 50% is given royal assent.

**8 November** The SDLP releases a 'proposed statement to be made by both governments' which it had submitted to John Major in mid-October. The same proposals were also given tò Michael Ancram by Martin McGuinness. The suggestions include launching the preparatory phase of all-party talks no later than 30 November and asking former Senator George Mitchell to head an international body which would advise the governments on the arms question. This body would report on 'whether it has been established that a clear commitment exists on the part of the respective political parties to an agreed political settlement, achieved through democratic negotiations, and to the satisfactory resolution of the question of arms'. The proposals are rejected by both the UUP and DUP.

At a Sinn Fein rally in Belfast's Ulster Hall Martin McGuinness says, 'From our perspective, any formula which republicans could live with would require a date, as soon as possible, for all-party talks, the dropping of the precondition for Sinn Fein participation, and a project on the arms issue which resolved the matter to everyone's satisfaction.' David Trimble says the government's twin-track proposals are 'not acceptable in their current form ... In any event, there is no question of any negotiations without decommissioning.'

**9 November** In the Dail John Bruton confirms that he has put forward 'certain ideas' to the British government via a private letter to John Major in an attempt to move toward all-party talks in the short term.

A *Belfast Telegraph* editorial asks, 'Is it not time for the unionist parties to open up lines of communication with Sinn Fein? If the favoured twin-track approach of the British and Irish governments – heavily endorsed by the Americans – is eventually to come about in some form, there will be no way of avoiding all-party talks at some date in the future. Why not prepare for it now, by expanding the contacts that have already been made by unionists talking to loyalists, the SDLP and the governments in Dublin, London and Washington to include Sinn Fein?'

In a speech at Trinity College, Dublin, SDLP deputy leader Seamus Mallon says that decommissioning should be settled during negotiations. He also rejects unionist and Alliance calls for a new NI Assembly, saying, 'The offer of an internal election says effectively to nationalists, "If you will accept and seek election upon the unionist concept of the constitutional framework of Northern Ireland, then we can perhaps do business." Since the nub of the problem is that nationalists do not accept that framework as their own, and will not do so unless there is a new dispensation they can genuinely relate to, the election proposal is a means of making acceptance of an essentially unionist perspective the entry ticket for negotiations for nationalists.'

**10 November** In the Republic Gardai arrest two men after seizing a van bomb containing 1,300 lb of explosives a mile from the Co. Armagh border. Reports suggest that those arrested may belong to the Irish National Republican Army, which is connected with Republican Sinn Fein. Gerry Adams says the incident shows the need for all-party talks. UDP leader Gary McMichael describes it as 'the most serious development since the ceasefires'. The following week a further 14 lb of explosives, two mortar bomb launchers, a bag of detonators and ammunition are found on a farm near Castleblaney, Co. Monaghan.
David Trimble says the UUP will only talk to the British government in any twin-track talks process.

**11 November** In a speech to the Meath Association in London aimed at reassuring the nationalist community, John Bruton says, 'It is reasonable now to seek to, at last, begin the dialogue – on a clear three-stranded basis – between all the parties.' He adds that, 'The issues that are now stopping us from starting the talks are small and, in historical terms, little more than semantic. The Irish government have put forward fair, firm and reasonable proposals to move towards talks. We are ready to move forward now.' He also says that 'the absence of any adequate official expression of regret' for events in Derry in the late 1960s and early 1970s distorts present-day attitudes and that, 'The attitude towards the use of the Irish language, the flying of the union flag in a provocative or excessive manner, the design of official publications, are all examples of ways in which the Northern Ireland official system fails to give adequate recognition to the existence and legitimacy of Irish nationalism as an inherent part of Northern life.'

**12 November** Responding to John Bruton's speech, John Major states that Dublin had pulled out of a compromise deal on the issue of decommissioning weapons at the planned summit in September. The Prime Minister says, 'It wasn't the British government that backed away, it was the Irish government that didn't proceed with that meeting because it came under pressure from Sinn Fein and others ... The problem above all lies with Sinn Fein and Sinn Fein's complete reluctance to tackle the question, even with an international body, of how their arsenal of weapons and explosives are going to be taken out of commission.' UUP chairman Jim Nicholson also criticises Bruton's speech saying, 'If he wishes to retain the centre ground, he cannot change his view week by week or month by month. It is time for John Major to tell John Bruton that he will do what is best for Northern

Ireland and not listen to any diktats from Dublin which are orchestrated to help the pan-nationalist front.' Gerry Adams criticises Major saying, 'We have addressed every single issue which the British government has put before us.'

**13 November** An SDLP report recommends radical changes to the police including: changing the RUC name to the Northern Ireland Police Service; a new uniform; an end to the flying of flags over police stations; a change to the oath of allegiance and the disbanding of specialist units. The report also calls for the repeal of the Emergency Provisions Act and the Prevention of Terrorism Act.

**14 November** In the Dail John Bruton defends his London speech. Referring to Mayhew's 'Washington Three' condition he states, 'It was well known that the [Irish] government had not accepted the idea that a gesture was "necessarily something that should be insisted on before the commencement of talks".'
An Orange rally in Belfast's Ulster Hall organised by the recently formed 'Spirit of Drumcree' group passes motions calling for radical change within the Order, the resignation of Grand Master Martin Smyth and the severing of links with the Ulster Unionist Party.

**15 November** On the tenth anniversary of the signing of the Anglo-Irish Agreement David Trimble, Ian Paisley and Robert McCartney issue a joint statement on behalf of their parties declaring their 'unending opposition to that diktat which violated the Ulster people's constitutional rights' as equal citizens of the UK. The statement adds, 'We will not be coerced to negotiate within its parameters, or on the basis of its latest manifestation – the joint Framework Document – which we see as a one-way street to a united Ireland.'
In Washington Gerry Adams calls for peace talks on Northern Ireland using a similar format to those being held in the US in an attempt to end the war in Bosnia.

**16 November** A nineteen-year-old Strabane man is beaten and abducted from his home by a group of five masked men. It is suggested that the men may be part of an IRA gang. The man is found 36 hours later by police in Castlederg, Co. Tyrone.
Irish official sources say that John Bruton is satisfied that the British government is 'engaging on the issues raised' in his letter to John Major nearly two weeks earlier. It is reported that a letter from Major to Bruton has helped repair the rift which developed between the two premiers after Bruton's speech in London on 11 November.

**17 November** A total of 83 prisoners are released from NI jails as the result of the increase in remission of sentences from 33% to 50%. The new rules do not, however, apply to prisoners serving life sentences while those convicted before 1989, or serving five years or less, already receive 50% remission.

Reports suggest that a revised British plan aimed at achieving agreement with the Irish government on a twin-track approach to the peace process will be sent to Dublin within 48 hours. The plans are reported to include a target date for the entry of Sinn Fein into all-party talks approximately twelve weeks after the proposed international decommissioning body begins operation. SF could also raise its concerns about British army and RUC arms with the proposed body. The decommissioning body would report on whether it believed all parties had established that they were exclusively committed to peaceful methods – this would occur before inter-party talks began. The two governments would not be obliged, however, to accept the body's view. A British spokesman claims the proposals are 'rooted on the positions' which were already agreed with the Irish at the end of August and based on the government's 'Building Blocks' document released by Michael Ancram on 3 November. The *Times* notes (on 18 November) that, 'Mr Major believes that one of the key changes since September is that the preparatory talks will now have more meaning because of the tabling by the Ulster Unionists of proposals for an Ulster Assembly. Sinn Fein would be able to engage in such talks as an equal partner; it would have "parity of esteem".'

Four men from Castlederg, Co. Tyrone, are charged with four arson attacks including a fire at a Free Presbyterian Church. Two of the men are also charged with IRA membership.

In Washington Gerry Adams says that Sinn Fein 'will have to assert the supremacy of our strategy, which is a peace strategy'. He adds, however, that, 'If the British don't move speedily to set up all-party talks as soon as possible then we're all in deep trouble.' He also says that while SF is committed to the peace process, 'the wider republican community' is detaching itself from the process. On his return from America, on 19 November, Adams says that, 'The peace process no longer exists. The peace process has been subverted and undermined and eroded to the point where it has been reduced to a cessation.' He calls for all-party talks as soon as possible but says that any demand for the IRA to begin decommissioning arms as a precondition would be unworkable.

**18 November** After a heated debate between party members the SDLP annual conference votes to leave open the possibility of a future electoral pact with Sinn Fein. A British government source responds to the decision by remarking, 'The nationalist community has suffered unspeakably from the IRA campaign in Northern Ireland. Many find it abhorrent that anyone should think of an alliance between those two parties.'

**20 November** After separate talks with Gerry Adams and John Hume the Irish government replies to the latest set of British proposals. While the Irish are relatively happy with the British setting a target date for talks, there appears to be no progress on the issue (called 'Washington Three' in reference to Sir Patrick Mayhew's speech on 7 March 1995) of a partial decommissioning of IRA weapons before Sinn Fein becomes involved in all-party talks.

**21 November** The *Times* quotes a senior Irish source as saying of the latest British proposals, 'This deal is not quite good enough as far as we are concerned. But there are positive and helpful things in the proposals and we want to work on them.' A British official, however, comments, 'It is the case that our proposals may not be easy for everyone, it would be surprising if they were. It has to be overcome by people showing a bit of courage and imagination. We are prepared to do that, let's see if others are.'

In an interview with the *Independent* David Trimble compares Sinn Fein leaders with the Bosnian Serbs by saying, 'Martin McGuinness and Gerry Adams are the Karadzic and Mladic of Northern Ireland. They are not regarded as fit persons to sit at the table in view of their record. I don't envisage a situation of personal contact with those gentlemen. It is possible, if circumstances were right, there might be a talks process. But I don't see that in the short term. It is for that reason we have emphasised the advantage of going down the route of creating an elected body at which there could be the beginnings of a debate.'

A small explosion caused by a 'crude device' occurs outside Omagh courthouse.

**22 November** In Derry Sir Patrick Mayhew says SF and loyalist parties 'are welcome to participate' in political life in NI in accordance with their electoral mandate and political analysis. 'What they cannot expect to do is keep a foot in both camps, to sign up as it were to "democracy à la carte".' SF accuses Mayhew of playing word games.

Following a telephone conversation with John Major, John Bruton says it will be a 'waste of time' to begin the twin-track approach if it cannot deal with the British insistence that the IRA makes a gesture on the decommissioning of arms. On RTE Bruton states, 'You can't lay down the sort of immutable position that I felt that Sir Patrick was laying down today and expect that there is going to be a compromise. There must be mutability, not immutability, in this area.' Despite continuing telephone contacts between the two prime ministers over the following days, the two sides fail to reach agreement.

DUP leader Ian Paisley says that his party will not be involved in all-party talks while the IRA retains its weapons. He adds, 'There is this insistence to set a date for all-party talks. What is the use of that when half the people will not be at such a meeting?'

**23 November** The British ambassador to Washington, Sir John Kerr, claims that when President Clinton gave 'a visa and a handshake' to Gerry Adams the US administration believed the IRA would begin to hand over weapons.

**24 November** In the Irish Republic a referendum on the right to divorce is narrowly carried with 50.2% voting in favour and 49.8% against.

**25 November** The *Times* says the IRA has warned its members to prepare for a 'return to war' if efforts to break the current impasse on political talks fails.
Addressing the DUP annual conference in Craigavon, Ian Paisley warns of a British government sell-out to gangs of 'blood-soaked murderers presiding over arsenals of terrorist weaponry … Will we permit Ulster to be chloroformed into accepting the peace as a real peace? It is not peace … It is a surrender process which we must resist.' DUP deputy leader Peter Robinson attacks the UUP for 'lingering and dithering in the jaws of our sternest crisis'. He says that, 'Glengall Street has brought Ulster to the brink of disaster by its craven endorsement of the Downing Street Declaration, by being first, through Martin Smyth, to suggest talking with the IRA and by proposing all-Ireland executive structures through its talks team.'

**26 November** In a *Sunday Times* interview Fianna Fail leader Bertie Ahern says he would have 'avoided the mistake of joining with the British government in saying that Sinn Fein would have to make a substantial gesture on decommissioning before the start of all-party talks'. Ahern also says he would not have refused to meet John Hume and Gerry Adams together, claiming that, 'By doing so, John Bruton was abdicating as leader of nationalist Ireland.'

**28 November** The *Irish Times* reports that, despite frantic diplomatic activity, London sources say that, 'Only a miracle would enable agreement on the favoured twin-track strategy ahead of President Clinton's arrival'.
After a week of intense diplomatic activity involving London, Dublin and Washington, at approximately 8 pm John Major and John Bruton agree by telephone on a joint communiqué on the way forward for the peace process. Bruton flies to London and the communiqué is released at 10 Downing Street just before 11 pm. The communiqué marks the formal launch of the twin-track approach. The governments note their 'firm

aim' of achieving all-party talks by the end of February 1996. Invitations are sent to all parties to participate in intensive preparatory talks. At the same time an 'international body' is to be established to provide an independent assessment of the decommissioning issue. The governments ask this body to 'report on the arrangements necessary for the removal from the political equation of arms silenced by virtue of the welcome decisions taken last summer and autumn by those organisations that previously supported the use of arms for political purposes.' The body is specifically asked to advise on 'a suitable and acceptable method for full and verifiable decommissioning' and to 'report whether there is a clear commitment on the part of those in possession of such arms to work constructively to achieve that.' The body is asked to submit its report by mid-January 1996. The communiqué also notes that, 'Neither government, nor any other party co-operating with the work of the body, is bound in advance to accept its recommendations, which will be advisory.' Former US Senator George Mitchell is asked to chair the body. Harri Holkeri, a former Finnish Prime Minister, and General John de Chastelain (Canadian Chief of Defence Staff and former ambassador to the US) are also asked to serve on the international body.

UUP MP Ken Maginnis takes a sceptical view of the communiqué, stating, 'This is a botched-up job, a fudge, something that's been rushed through purely for Mr Clinton's benefit and, sadly, I think it's going to crumble.' Gerry Adams says Sinn Fein was not briefed on the details of the communiqué before it was released.

## The Launch of the Twin-Track Strategy

At first sight the late-night summit in Downing Street looked like a panic reaction to President Clinton's imminent arrival. When the dust cleared and the communiqué was issued, however, it appeared that the two premiers had fudged the issue and yet pulled off a coup.

What did the two prime ministers gain from their late-night tryst? The short answer is the support of the most powerful man in the world, President Clinton. The White House had studiously refused to support the British position on the decommissioning of arms. Now, however, there was little chance that the President would rebuke the British government for dragging its feet, as parts of Dublin's more nationalist press had been predicting, perhaps prompted by leaks from the American Embassy.

The British claimed that more objective attitudes on Ireland now prevailed in America's National Security Council, and also pointed out that the 15,000 British troops offered in support of President Clinton's Bosnia policy gave London additional leverage. Whitehall, however, still had some fears about Clinton's forthcoming speeches in Belfast and Derry.

Now President Clinton was at one with Major and Bruton. His support for a package which would seem to many to have been arranged in his honour ensured that Bruton's enemies in the Irish Opposition, Fianna Fail, and in Sinn Fein would have to tone down their criticism.

Sinn Fein and the Democratic Unionists were likely to have serious problems accepting the new proposal, but those who stood out against it would face the combined pressure not of two governments but of three – the third being that of the world's last superpower. This was rather more difficult for Sinn Fein than it was for the Democratic Unionists. Unionists, after all, were accustomed to living without political friends outside Ulster, whereas Sinn Fein had recently grown rather addicted to their support.

The Anglo-Irish Agreement, signed ten years earlier, was intended to end megaphone diplomacy, yet since the planned summit between Major and Bruton had collapsed in September, negotiations had been drowned out by a series of squabbles in London, Dublin and New York. The British issued a formal riposte at the United Nations to a speech by Dick Spring and there had been an unseemly row over a speech delivered by Bruton in London.

In recent years the negotiations had turned into a high-spirited game in which each side blackened the other's reputation before signing a deal. This was a game of poker at which John Major excelled. First there was the Brussels declaration of October 1993 against 'secret deals' and apparently against the united strategy of the Northern Ireland nationalists, both Sinn Fein and the SDLP. According to Sean Duignan, the then Taoiseach Albert Reynolds believed that Major was far more sympathetic to the plans put forward by Gerry Adams and John Hume than he could admit in public. As Duignan wrote, 'Hume-Adams was being declared dead in order to keep it alive.'

Then came the Downing Street Declaration of December 1993 in which the balance of advantage again clearly rested with John Major. This was followed by the Frameworks Documents of February 1995, the one hand in the game which the British side palpably lost. In its anxiety to sustain the republican ceasefire at the time, the British signed without achieving their principal negotiating objective, an explicit commitment from Dublin that in the event of an acceptable settlement it would remove from the Republic's Constitution the territorial claim to Ulster. Even so, Major gave himself an escape clause by insisting upon 'agreement of the parties' and a referendum on the Frameworks proposal.

But the latest progress was not all good news. John Bruton had once noted that, 'The worst possible scenario would be if the government initially set strict terms, but was forced to relax them under threat of a resumption of violence.' Yet the Irish government was hoping that the new international body would evade the precondition that talks could not begin without at least some disarmament by the IRA. The British, of course, hoped that the body would suggest a procedure by which the IRA could hand over arms. In the end, the result of this intensive diplomatic manoeuvring appeared to be that the IRA could no longer play the American card, or even the Dublin card, and that this might eventually lead to splits in the republican movement. Whatever happened next, Major had bought himself a few more months of peace, and time to plan the next masterly fudge.

**29 November** In London Bill Clinton gives his support to John Major and John Bruton, saying, 'Ireland is closer to true peace than at any time in a generation and risks taken by the Prime Minister and the Irish Prime Minister are the reason why.' He also declares, 'My message to the IRA is that the twin-track process has provided a mechanism for all the parties honourably now to bring their concerns to the table and be heard. In the end, peace means peace and we are all going to have to support that.'

**30 November** Bill Clinton becomes the first serving US President to visit Northern Ireland. He receives an almost universally warm welcome as he visits West Belfast (stopping on both the Shankill and Falls Roads and publicly shaking hands with Gerry Adams on the latter), East Belfast and Derry before returning to Belfast city centre and switching on the Christmas tree lights. In a keynote speech at Mackie's engineering factory in West Belfast he states, 'Here in Northern Ireland, you are making a miracle ... In the land of the harp and the fiddle, the fife and the lambeg drum, two proud traditions are coming together in the harmonies of peace. The ceasefire and negotiations have sparked a powerful transformation ... I want to honour those whose courage and vision have brought us to this point; Prime Minister John Major, Prime Minister Bruton and before him, Prime Minister Reynolds, laid the background and the basis for this era of reconciliation. From the Downing Street Declaration to the joint Framework Document, they altered the course of history. Now just in the last few days, by launching the twin-track initiative, they have opened a promising new gateway to a just and lasting peace. Foreign Minister Spring, Sir Patrick Mayhew, David Trimble and John Hume all have laboured to realise the promise of peace. And Gerry Adams, along with loyalist leaders such as David Ervine and Gary McMichael, helped to silence the guns on the streets ... Last year's ceasefire of the Irish Republican Army, joined by the Combined Loyalist Military Command, marked a turning point in the history of Northern Ireland. Now is the time to sustain that momentum and lock in the gains of peace. Neither community wants to go back to the violence of the past ... Both parties must do their part to move this process forward now.

'Let me begin by saying that the search for common ground demands the courage of an open mind. This twin-track initiative gives the parties a chance to begin preliminary talks in ways in which all views will be represented and all voices will be heard. It also establishes an international body to address the issue of arms decommissioning. I hope the parties will seize this opportunity.'

After condemning continuing paramilitary punishment beatings, Clinton continues, 'There will always be those who define the worth of their lives not by who they are, but by who they aren't; not by what they're for, but by what they are against. They will never escape the dead-end street of violence. But you, the vast majority, Protestant and Catholic alike, must not allow the ship of peace to sink on the rocks of old habits and hard grudges. You must stand firm against terror. You must say to those who would still use violence for political objectives – you are the past; your day is over.'

The President later holds separate private talks with the leaders of the five main political parties.

The European Court of Justice rules that the operation of the Prevention of Terrorism Act contravenes European Union law by breaching the freedom of movement guaranteed by the Treaty of Rome.

Former NI Ombudsman Maurice Hayes is named to oversee an independent review of the police complaints system.

**1 December** Leaving Belfast's Europa Hotel, Bill Clinton tells well-wishers who have gathered outside, 'I feel a great deal of gratitude for such a remarkable day.' Sir Patrick Mayhew says of the President's visit, 'He has lifted people's eyes to the horizon away from perhaps even the pebbles in front of their feet. He has given us a new scale and dimension to the whole of our affairs in Northern Ireland.'

In Dublin Bill Clinton meets President Mary Robinson and John Bruton and addresses the Irish parliament. After he is granted the freedom of the city, Clinton tells an 80,000-strong crowd, 'I want more than anything for the young people of Ireland, wherever they live on this island, to be able to live out their dreams close to their roots in peace and honour and freedom and equality.'

John Major tells the Conservative women's conference in London that, 'People who mean peace don't need guns.' He says it is time for the paramilitaries to 'start ridding themselves of guns and explosives' so all-party talks can begin. 'Can anyone who witnessed President Clinton's remarkable visit seriously contemplate a return to bombing and shooting?' he adds. Major calls on the NI parties to 'show open mindedness and to have the courage to step out of the bunkers they built during Ulster's troubles'.

As part of the twin-track process the British and Irish governments separately send invitations to preliminary talks to eight NI parties and to North Down MP Robert McCartney.

A man is shot and wounded in the arm after two INLA members burst into a house in the Falls area of Belfast. The man who was the intended target of the punishment attack escaped through the back of the house.

**2 December** At the end of Bill Clinton's visit to Britain and Ireland the *Times* comments, 'It was always hoped that this visit would be a significant moment in the Ulster peace process and would breathe life into the troubled negotiations. But few can have anticipated the emotion which his presence stirred on the streets of Belfast and Londonderry ... The spirit of the trip was captured by Catherine Hamill, a nine-year-old Roman Catholic whose father died in the Troubles. "My Christmas wish," she said, "is that we have peace and love and that it will last in Ireland forever." What might have seemed sentimental in a different setting was authentic in this context. This small child spoke for a Province whose people long for an end to the bloodshed ... More than any diplomatic agreement, the crowds on Ulster's streets were proof of something new and fragile which must now be nurtured with care.'

The army announces that 600 men serving with 45 Royal Marine Commando in Fermanagh have left NI. There are now approximately 17,000 troops in the province.

Following a SF party executive meeting Gerry Adams says the latest agreement 'marks a new phase of the peace process. The manner in which it was put together, and elements within it, have unsettled many nationalists and republicans who had hoped for firmer foundations upon which substantive progress could be made. Despite these reservations, Sinn Fein will of course be trying to make this next phase work.'

**3 December** It is reported that David Trimble has contacted loyalist representatives to encourage them to be first to decommission some weapons. The UDP and PUP later say there is 'no question' of loyalists handing in guns while the IRA remains armed.

A *Sunday Life* report claims loyalist paramilitaries fired six shots into a house in an attempt to frighten a man involved in a stabbing incident the previous weekend. Security sources say those in the house were not involved in the earlier incident.

**4 December** SDLP and UUP delegations led by John Hume and David Trimble meet for talks in Belfast. The previous day the two party leaders appeared together on television. During this programme John Hume commented on the Unionist proposal for a NI convention or assembly by stating, 'We've been down that road twice before. If we are going to have negotiations and you are going to elect a 90-member assembly to carry negotiations, it's just going to be a shouting match.'

Asked in a radio interview why the IRA will not decommission weapons if they will not be used again, SF member Mitchel McLaughlin says, 'The reality is that nobody can say that these guns will not be used again. The only time you can say that is when we can celebrate a permanent peace. What we have is a ceasefire situation ... We still have in place the political conditions which created that conflict.'

The home of a West Belfast Catholic family situated opposite a Protestant housing estate is attacked for the 56th time in nine years. The family say the latest petrol bomb attack, as well as earlier attacks, have been orchestrated by a local UDA leader. The attacks are condemned by UDP leader Gary McMichael. In February 1996, after a further spate of sectarian attacks, the family say they intend to leave their home.

A man is shot in the leg in a punishment attack near the Shankill Road.

**5 December** Replying to the Irish government's invitation to talks, David Trimble writes, 'We are not prepared to negotiate the internal affairs of Northern Ireland with a foreign government.' He calls on the Irish government to revoke the Anglo-Irish Agreement and remove its territorial claim to Northern Ireland. In a letter to John Major the UUP leader refuses to endorse the twin-track approach but says he will keep lines of communication open.

In a written reply a government spokesman tells the House of Lords that, in the fourteen months after the IRA ceasefire, there were 223 punishment beatings (148 carried out by republicans and 75 by loyalists) compared to 45 in the fourteen months before the ceasefire (37 carried out by loyalists and eight by republicans). In the same pre-ceasefire period loyalists carried out 82 punishment shootings (plus a further thirteen before their October ceasefire) and republicans 63. The government also says that there have been 137 arson attacks since the IRA ceasefire was announced compared to 65 similar attacks in the fourteen months before the ceasefire. UDP member John White says his party will 'continue to impress upon people to go to the police if they have complaints, and not to paramilitaries'.

**6 December** In Glasgow PUP member Lindsay Robb is convicted with two others of attempting to obtain guns for the UVF. Fellow PUP member Billy Hutchinson says his party is convinced that Robb is innocent but adds that, 'The ceasefire is 110% secure as far as the loyalists are concerned.'

**7 December** An IRA statement says, 'It is a matter of profound regret that rather than fulfilling its responsibilities, the British government, presented with this historic opportunity, has sought only to frustate movement into inclusive negotiations and has erected an absolute barrier to progress with its untenable and unattainable demand for an IRA surrender ... there is no question of the IRA meeting the ludicrous demand for a surrender of IRA weapons either through the front or the back door.'

**8 December** John Major criticises the IRA statement declaring, 'The IRA's intransigence is a slap in the face for hundreds of thousands of people in Northern Ireland and the Republic, who last week demonstrated their massive desire for peace.' DUP MP Peter Robinson says, 'It's only the IRA that can put out a statement indicating that they won't hand over one weapon or one bullet, and then accuse everybody else of being intransigent.' SDLP MP Joe Hendron claims that hardliners within the republican movement are stirring things up.

West Belfast soccer team Donegal Celtic withdraws from an Irish Cup game against the RUC's football team. The club had received a 'strong recommendation' from SF representatives not to play the game.

An alleged drug-dealer, named on an IRA death list, is shot dead in the Lisburn Road area of Belfast. On 11 December West Belfast MP Joe Hendron says the murder of Paul Devine constitutes a breach of the ceasefire.

**9 December** In a letter to the *Irish Times* Albert Reynolds comments on Dick Spring's Dail statement of 1 June 1994 that it was not possible for Sinn Fein to participate in constitutional talks 'without clear unequivocal and demonstrated disarmament by the IRA' and notes, 'This view was expressed without any prior consultation with me, was therefore just that, a personal view, and not government policy.'

**11 December** Sir Patrick Mayhew announces that, provided the ceasefires continue, £100 million will be redirected from the security budget to other areas of NI expenditure over the next three years. £180 million had already been cut from the security budget in the wake of the ceasefires. Public expenditure in Northern Ireland for the financial year 1996-97 will be £8,009 million.

**14 December** It is announced that Belfast's Crumlin Road prison is to close in the spring of 1996. Most of the remaining 250 prisoners (none of them paramilitary prisoners) are to be transferred to Maghaberry prison.

**15 December** As the members of the international body set up to examine the arms question arrive in Belfast, its head, George Mitchell, says that success is 'far from assured'. The body receives its first private submission from Sir Patrick Mayhew and later hears the views of the PUP.

The *Belfast Telegraph* quotes a republican source as saying that the target date for all-party talks at the end of February is a deadline for a decision on the future of the ceasefire. The source adds, 'If the British government then continue to insist on the surrender of IRA weapons before Sinn Fein can be included in talks the ceasefire will collapse ... Republicans are still fully committed to the search for a political settlement, but are not prepared to be humiliated as part of that process. If it is a choice between surrender and a return to war, the war will restart.'

**16 December** The international body receives submissions from the SDLP, UUP, the Alliance Party, UDP and the Workers' Party. The body also meets RUC Chief Constable Sir Hugh Annesley.

The UUP submission calls for the total decommissioning and disbandment of the IRA. David Trimble says the international body must be given details of the quantities of weapons held by paramilitaries. He also criticises recent statements by SF members saying, 'Republicans are effectively saying that if they have to prove they are committed to peace they will go back to war again.'

DUP deputy leader Peter Robinson says his party will not accept any political formula which admits Sinn Fein to all-party talks before all IRA weapons are surrendered.

**17 December** In Dublin the international body meets the Progressive Democrats, the Green Party, former Taoiseach Albert Reynolds and Father Alec Reid, a Catholic priest believed to have played a significant role in bringing about the IRA ceasefire.

In Derry Martin McGuinness says that SF will ask the body to request copies of the Stalker and Stevens reports from the British government. Sinn Fein wants the body to examine the issues of security force collusion with loyalists and 'shoot to kill' allegations.

**18 December** Following the meeting between the international body (later referred to as the Mitchell Commission) and SF Gerry Adams describes the meeting as 'very constructive and positive'. He also notes that they 'were not in there discussing the disposal of IRA weapons'. The body also meets representatives of the Irish government, Fianna Fail and Catholic and Protestant church leaders.

The FEC's annual report finds that while Catholics are under-represented in the NI workforce, the gap is closing. Over the last five years the Catholic proportion of the workforce has risen by 2.4% to 37.3%; 40% of the economically active population is Catholic. Catholics are, however, still twice as likely to be unemployed as Protestants.

Sir Patrick Mayhew begins another round of talks with local parties.

Fra Collins, a former IRA prisoner, is shot dead in the New Lodge area of North Belfast. The killers shout 'Up the IRA' as they run off. Reports suggest the murder may be the latest in the series of drugs-related killings.

**19 December** Chris Johnston, who was on bail in connection with a seizure of drugs in 1994, is shot dead in the lower Ormeau Road area of Belfast. Responsibility for the murder is claimed by a group calling itself Direct Action Against Drugs. The following day a senior RUC officer says they believe the killing of five alleged drug-dealers have been carried out by, or on behalf of, the IRA.

In Glasgow PUP member Lindsay Robb is sentenced to ten years' imprisonment for conspiring to obtain guns for the UVF.

Two men are found guilty of the murder of Margaret Wright in April 1994 in Belfast. In February 1996 the two are sentenced to life imprisonment.

**20 December** The Alliance Party meets British and Irish government ministers in the first meeting held under the twin-track approach.

SF says that it has made proposals to the Secretary of State for talks involving the leaders of the five main local parties to be held in January 1996.

The Irish government decides not to give permanent release to a further ten republican prisoners because of the recent murders in Belfast. Irish security sources also claim that the Gardai had foiled an attempt by IRA units to carry out a series of raids on cash shipments. SF vice-president Pat Doherty later describes the decision not to release the prisoners as 'astounding'.

**21 December** During a visit to NI John Major says most people in the North 'will find it laughable' that SF claim that it and the IRA are wholly separate organisations. Major later meets John Bruton for talks in Dublin.

NIO security minister Sir John Wheeler says that the murder of alleged drug-dealers and the IRA's targeting of police officers, racketeering and intimidation was 'not a breach of the military ceasefire'.

**22 December** West Belfast MP Joe Hendron calls on the IRA to stop murdering alleged drug-dealers and end punishment beatings. 'Republicans cannot be considered as true democrats while these activities are going on,' he adds.

In a speech to DUP members in Kilkeel, Co. Down, Ian Paisley backs the proposal for a NI Assembly and says, 'Let the IRA surrender all its murder arsenal and totally dismantle its organisation and cease to be. Then let its members go into a period of quarantine for at least five years as suggested by the former leader of the Official Unionist Party, giving full proof that they have really repented.'

**24 December** A *Sunday Times* report claims that Libya has provided Britain with details of how it had assisted the IRA in the past. The report says that over 130 tonnes of arms were shipped from Tripoli, £9 million in cash given to the IRA and twenty IRA activists trained by Libya. Among the Libyan weapons still believed to be held by the IRA are 650 Kalashnikov rifles, 20 armour-piercing machine-guns, a surface-to-air missile, 40 rocket-propelled grenade launchers, 500 detonators and two tonnes of semtex explosives.

The government pays £38,700 to cover the legal costs of the families of the three IRA members shot dead in Gibraltar in 1988.

**27 December** SF chairman Mitchel McLaughlin tells a republican rally in Rosslea, Co. Fermanagh, that, 'Britain is spoiling for a fight. Peace was, and indeed still is, within our grasp, but that grasp is rapidly loosening.'

In the latest of a series of murders believed to have been carried out by republicans, a 30-year-old man is shot dead in his home in West Belfast.

**30 December** Former UUP leader James Molyneaux receives a knighthood in the New Year's Honours List.

Deaths Arising from the Troubles: 9. Shootings: 50. Bombs planted: 2. Incendiaries: 10. Weapons Found: 118. Explosives Found: 5 kilos. Persons Charged with Terrorist Offences: 440.

# 1996

**1 January** As the Conservative government's majority continues to decline, Sir Patrick Mayhew says the UUP cannot expect special treatment in return for its promise not to bring down the government.

A man is shot dead while sitting in a car in Lurgan, Co. Armagh. The murder is claimed by Direct Action Against Drugs, believed to be a cover name used by the IRA. Three punishment attacks are also carried out, two in Crossmaglen and one in East Belfast. On 3 January columnist Kevin Myers writes in the *Daily Telegraph*, 'What is over is the ceasefire as understood by everyone that bright morning on 1 September 1994. Nobody likes saying this, because it appears to be unhealthy to announce such an unpleasant truth. But it is so.'

Albert Reynolds says he decided to open indirect negotiations 'with the people who controlled the violence on both sides' in attempt to bring peace in NI. Reynolds met loyalists, including Gusty Spence, for secret talks in a Dublin hotel. 'I asked them to write down for me what they were prepared to lose their lives for, what principles they wanted protected in any new evolving situation, and they did that.'

**2 January** In a *Belfast Telegraph* interview David Trimble says he is doubtful that all-party talks will begin in 1996: 'The further we get into 1996, the more the shadow of elections in both jurisdictions, Westminster and the Republic, will loom. I rather suspect that from early summer … onwards the prospect of those elections will begin to close down options. For that reason I am doubtful if we will see the beginning of an all-party talks process in 1996.'

**3 January** Newspapers report that a White Paper on policing reform in NI will suggest new lines of accountability for the force. The responsibilities of individual officers will be outlined and they will be expected, by law, to give due deference to the two traditions in NI. 24

locally autonomous police areas will be created and the RUC Reserve will be used to a greater degree in community policing. The number of police officers might be cut by 4,000. Financial and administrative responsibility will be transferred from the police authority to the Chief Constable.

UUP deputy leader John Taylor says the government should not talk or negotiate with republicans 'while the IRA continues to kill Catholics and, before long, Protestants in Northern Ireland'.

Families Against Intimidation and Terror say that the Protestant Action Force (believed to be a cover name for the UVF) has issued death threats against fourteen people allegedly involved in dealing drugs.

**4 January** SF chairman Mitchel McLaughlin says Gerry Adams has written to the British and Irish governments calling for multilateral talks to be convened among those parties prepared to attend them.

**5 January** The *Irish News* reports that between February and October 1995 SF raised $1,117,081 in the US.

Chief Constable Sir Hugh Annesley says the IRA has been responsible for six allegedly drugs-related murders since the ceasefires, beginning with the killing of Mickey Mooney on 28 April 1995 and culminating in the shooting of Ian Lyons on 1 January.

## The Direct Action Against Drugs Murders

Following President Clinton's visit to the province many observers were confident that his appeal for an end to punishment beatings would be heeded, at least during the deliberations of Senator George Mitchell's Commission on the arms issue. Instead there was a sharp increase of murderous violence in republican areas. Momentarily at least, Northern republicanism appeared to have returned to its ghetto roots with a vengeance.

Why did the republican leadership, anxious to preserve its links with the White House, not condemn activity that was, at best, seriously embarrassing? Why had a movement capable of hi-tech strikes against the Cabinet and City of London so changed its *modus operandi*? There were two possible answers to the puzzle. It was claimed on the one hand that republicans were under community pressure to take such action against the drug culture. Feeling against drug-dealers ran so high, it was said, that the movement lost credibility if it was not seen to act against them. It was also said that fathers approached the IRA asking for sons to be 'warned'.

But this could not fully explain the killing by 'Direct Action Against Drugs', a *nom de guerre* so unimaginative that it could only be intended to parody the peace process, of alleged drug-dealers against whom the RUC had already laid charges. More profoundly, the new wave of violence reflected a more complex problem – a changing balance of forces within republicanism.

The IRA faction which never really understood the logic of the ceasefires was becoming increasingly active. To be fair, this faction did not seem to have been informed definitively by the leadership that the war was over. Its increased assertiveness was reflected in the upsurge in violence which in turn helped to create a dangerously pessimistic mind-set in working-class nationalist areas, a mind-set which increasingly resigned itself to the possibility of another military campaign. To a greater extent than many believed, violence had long been accepted as part of the texture of life in certain areas of the province.

Although there was no competing leadership cadre, the Adams-McGuinness leadership was now looking increasingly tarnished. Having openly complained in January 1994 about the nature of the British stance on the arms issue, it rather surprisingly began to claim that it knew nothing of the very same British position which it had once bitterly denounced. It seemed to have little conception of the constraints under which British policy operated – except, of course, for an exaggerated notion of the influence which the slender majority of the Major government gave Unionists at Westminster.

For the first time, too, public doubts were being expressed by republicans about Sinn Fein leadership's obsession with entry to all-party talks on a constitutional framework agenda. However unpalatable this agenda might be to unionists, it irresistibly included the British government's commitment (in para. 20 of the Frameworks Documents) to 'uphold the democratic wish of a greater number of the people of Northern Ireland on the issue of whether they prefer to support the Union or a sovereign united Ireland'.

But the republican leadership still had some options. There was some hope that the report of the Dublin Forum for Peace and Reconciliation would reveal, at last, that Sinn Fein had signed up unambiguously for the principle of consent. This could have been linked to a 'no first strike' pledge of the kind already adopted by loyalist paramilitaries. It could also have been linked to an ending of the latest spate of shootings. By such moves Sinn Fein might have hoped to make a good impression on the Mitchell Commission. It might even have hoped that others – the British government and the unionists – would regard these as confidence-building measures which might act as a substitute for an early move on arms.

But many would remain sceptical about such a prospectus – in particular it was hard to imagine that Sinn Fein, whatever the private realism of some of its more astute minds, could formally accept the democratic legitimacy of Northern Ireland. The essence of the 25-year-old campaign of violence was the effort to coerce the Ulster unionist majority into a united Ireland. The settlement on offer bore a marked family resemblance to the Sunningdale package which republicans rejected in 1974. Anyway, the Irish state itself had not formally promised to drop the territorial claim on the North, so why should the republican movement?

This left only one visible alternative, an elected body of some type, as proposed by the Unionist leader David Trimble. While there was evidence of a certain softening of attitude in some quarters, the bulk of nationalist Ireland, given its cue by John Hume, remained unenthusiastic. The more relaxed, pro-active style of Unionist leadership – reflected in an unprecedented level of contact which both David Trimble and John Taylor gave the Irish media – might be capable of doing more to persuade nationalists that there was no lurking notion of a return to Stormont or, indeed, any other failed internal experiments. Such fears, however unrealistic, still animated grass-roots nationalists and gave the elites, who were considerably more sophisticated, no incentive to rethink their early negative position.

**7 January** In a television interview John Major calls on Sinn Fein and the IRA to stop punishment beatings and murders. SF spokesman Mitchel McLaughlin says his party is powerless to stop the attacks.

**8 January** The Belfast-based Committee on the Administration of Justice calls on MPs to oppose the NI Emergency Provisions Bill. The CAJ says renewal of emergency provisions is 'unnecessary, unhelpful and counter-productive'.

**9 January** The government announces that a review of the Emergency Provisions Act (which is renewed for a further two years) and the Prevention of Terrorism Act will begin shortly. The government also states that silent video recordings will be made of terrorist suspects during questioning at the Castlereagh, Gough Barracks, Armagh, and Strand Road, Derry, holding centres. SF calls for the three holding centres to be closed.
In Bangor, Co. Down, a man is beaten by a group calling itself Loyalists Against Thuggery. The victim of the beating suffers two broken arms and a broken leg. Several hours later the Protestant Action Force orders fifteen people from the Newtownards area to leave NI or face retribution. PUP member Billy Hutchinson says his party will do what it can to have the threats lifted.

**10 January** Sinn Fein releases 'Building a Permanent Peace', its submission to the international arms body. The submission states that the IRA might agree to dispose of its weapons with independent verification, but that this would not be considered until after a political settlement had been negotiated. After initially giving a guarded welcome to the proposals, Ken Maginnis of the UUP later says the SF message is 'unacceptable, unworkable and unattainable'.

**11 January** In Belfast Fianna Fail leader Bertie Ahern says the peace process 'has been disastrously mishandled and misjudged' by the British government.
The Workers' Party and the PUP meet for talks for the first time.
John Major meets the members of the international arms body in London as they prepare to finalise their report.
In a speech in Newcastle, Co. Down, SDLP MP Eddie McGrady says the UUP demand for an Assembly 'is cloaked in the guise of an attempt at movement and facilitation, but in reality is but an expression of Ulster Unionist policy to prevent a real settlement taking place'.

**12 January** The three members of the international arms body meet John Bruton and Dick Spring in Dublin.
A police officer loses an appeal against a £100 fine for breaching the RUC's disciplinary code by participating in marches by the Orange Order and Apprentice Boys of Derry.
Mitchel McLaughlin of SF says his party will give 'very serious consideration' to taking part in a rumoured 45-member elected forum for talks. Gerry Adams later says the idea of an assembly is a 'non-runner'.

**13 January** SDLP leader John Hume rejects the idea of a new assembly as a way of starting political talks, saying it would make it virtually impossible to reach agreement. UUP deputy leader John Taylor says Hume is now 'the obstacle to the peace process rather than being the one encouraging it along the road'.
A survey commissioned by the NI Tourist Board finds that 430,000 holiday-makers visited the North in 1995, a 68% increase on the previous year.

**14 January** The members of the Mitchell Commission meet loyalist and Alliance representatives in Belfast.
Newspaper reports claim that the IRA has decided to halt killings conducted under the Direct Action Against Drugs cover-name after pressure from nationalist and republican politicians.
A *Sunday Tribune* poll finds that 64% of Catholics see an elected

assembly as a means of involving SF and loyalist political parties in direct talks before the decommissioning of paramilitary weapons. Only 30% of Protestants support this proposition. The idea of a local assembly with power-sharing and cross-border institutions is supported by 40% of Catholics and 22% of Protestants. A power-sharing assembly, but without cross-border institutions, is supported by 33% of Protestants.

**15 January** Sir Patrick Mayhew, Dick Spring and John Hume meet at Stormont as part of the twin-track process. The Irish Foreign Minister says that all-party talks by the end of February is still the 'very firm aim' of both governments.

David Trimble and Ken Maginnis suggest that the international arms body ask the British and Irish governments for more time before producing its final report.

SF representatives meet the Mitchell Commission in Dublin. A SF spokesman says, 'This report, and more particularly John Major's response to it, will determine whether the process will survive.'

**16 January** A *Belfast Telegraph*/MRC Ireland opinion poll finds that 60% of those questioned favour all paramilitary weapons being decommissioned before talks between political parties are held. 23% believe some weapons should be decommissioned before talks while 13% say no weapons should be decommissioned. 95% of Protestants and 68% of Catholics say either that some weapons or all weapons should be decommissioned before talks. Further results of the poll find 70% support for the establishment of a new elected body as a step toward all-party negotiations (14% against) while 45% (74% of Catholics and 25% of Protestants) say the RUC must be reformed as part of the peace process.

The Mitchell Commission says it will report on 24 January.

**17 January** British and Irish government ministers meet a SF delegation for talks at Stormont.

Government figures give the NI unemployment rate for December 1995 as 11.4%.

**18 January** The RUC rejects a claim by Ian Paisley Jr of the DUP that it plans to make redundant 1,000 Protestant RUC officers with more than twenty years' service and to recruit Catholic officers instead.

Following a meeting with John Major and Sir Patrick Mayhew in Downing Street, Senator George Mitchell says of the decommissioning issue, 'The question is not whether this is going to be resolved in a single act or a single document or a single statement, rather whether the process of moving forward towards a just and lasting peace and reconciliation will be maintained. We believe and hope that it will be, and we hope that in some small way we can contribute to that.'

**19 January** Princess Anne performs the official opening of the new British embassy building in Dublin during a two-day visit to the Republic.
A man is beaten up by a loyalist gang at a flat in North Belfast. After inflicting injuries and bruises covering 98% of his body, the UFF later admits it had attacked the wrong man. A second flat is wrecked by loyalists when they discover that the man they were looking for was not there.
In an address to his constituency party in Newtownards, Co. Down, UUP MP John Taylor says his party must be 'ready at any time to discuss sensible co-operation, but not ideological schemes driven by the "dynamic" of a united Ireland ... Any co-operation with the Irish Republic is clearly dependent on constitutional change [to Articles 2 and 3] in the Republic.' He also says, 'For the leader of a major party to promise the return of Stormont is not to address the issues seriously. It is not something that can be delivered to unionists and only serves to relive the worst fears of nationalists.'

**20 January** Gerry Adams says the Mitchell Report 'has to remove preconditions. No matter what the Senator says, if ... John Major insists on the obstacle he has put up [decommissioning weapons], then it's all to no avail.'
Addressing the Upper Bann Ulster Unionist constituency association, David Trimble says a new elected body is necessary 'to establish the mandate and authority of the parties as they move towards any process of negotiation'. Noting that it would have no administrative or legislative powers, he says the primary role of such a body would be 'to debate and conduct factual inquiries on matters relevant to negotiations. This initial role could commence immediately after the elections and in advance of the resolution of the issue of weapons and the commitment to exclusively peaceful means.' Trimble insists, however, that substantive political negotiations can only take place after the decommissioning issue has been resolved.

**23 January** UUP deputy leader John Taylor says, 'Mitchell, if we are to believe the Irish leaks, has fudged the issue of decommissioning, has played into the hands of IRA-Sinn Fein, and therefore the only alternative way forward would be an elected body.'

**24 January** Ken Maginnis of the UUP and Pat McGeown of SF take part in a radio discussion in Belfast.
In an article leaking the details of the Mitchell Report, the *Irish*

*Independent* says that the British government faces 'a necessary climb-down' over the 'Washington Three' condition. The report, released several hours later, accepts that there is a commitment by those in possession of illegal arms to achieve full and verifiable decommissioning. The report concludes that paramilitary organisations will not decommission any arms before all-party talks and also states that, 'The parties should consider an approach under which some decommissioning would take place during the process of all-party negotiations, rather than before or after as the parties now urge.' It suggests that those involved in all-party negotiations affirm their commitment to a number of fundamental principles of democracy and non-violence. Parties should be committed to: democratic and exclusively peaceful means of resolving political issues; the total disarmament of all paramilitary organisations; that such disarmament must be verifiable to the satisfaction of an independent commission; renounce for themselves, and to oppose any efforts by others, to use force, or threaten to use force, to influence the course or the outcome of all-party negotiations; agree to abide by the terms of any agreement reached in all-party negotiations and to resort to democratic and exclusively peaceful methods in trying to alter any aspect of that outcome with which they may disagree; urge that punishment killings and beatings stop and take effective steps to prevent such actions. Among a number of possible confidence-building measures, the report notes that an elected body might be set up, 'if it were broadly acceptable with an appropriate mandate and within the three-strand structure, an elective process could contribute to the building of confidence'.

In the Dail Dick Spring welcomes the report, noting that it 'replaces the polemics which had sprung up around the so-called "Washington Three" debate with an alternative, more logical, and ultimately more promising approach. To solve both aspects of the problem in the way they suggest, is ultimately to solve the problem as a whole ... The next step is for the two governments working on the basis of the report and addressing also, of course, the various other issues in the political track to intensify still further the round of preparatory talks so as to achieve the launch of inclusive negotiations.'

In a Westminster debate on the Mitchell Report, John Major accepts the report but says the government can see no reason why paramilitaries should not begin decommissioning weapons and that the government's demand for the decommissioning of arms before talks remains valid. He states that the government is ready to introduce legislation to allow an elective process to go ahead as soon as practicable. Major says there are two ways in which all-party negotiations can be taken forward: 'The first is for the paramilitaries to make a start to decommissioning before all-party negotiations. They can – if they will. If not, the second is to secure a democratic mandate for all-party negotiations through elections specially for that purpose.'

Labour leader Tony Blair supports Major's position and comments, 'At the heart of this issue is how we move to all-party talks. For that to happen, there must be confidence – in particular, confidence among all parties – that violence has gone for good and been replaced by democratic debate. May I therefore reiterate our support for the view that that confidence cannot arise unless there is tangible evidence of the commitment to democratic means. We remain of the view that the simplest way of providing that tangible evidence is indeed the decommissioning of weapons. It is right in itself. People of all communities want it. It will strike any reasonable person as sensible. Senator Mitchell says that it will not occur, in his view, before talks. May I stress that, if that is so, it is incumbent upon those making it so to engage with other means of building confidence.'

John Hume attacks the election proposal and says, 'It would be utterly irresponsible for any party to play politics with the lives of those people [in NI]. It would be particularly irresponsible for a government to try to buy votes to keep themselves in power.' Major replies, 'From the outset of this process, I have made it clear … that what I care about is trying to prevent the killing, the bloodshed, the hatred, the abuse and the sheer nastiness that has dominated too much of the lives of British citizens in Northern Ireland over far too many years. I am prepared to take risks for that but I am not prepared to buy votes for it.'

David Trimble welcomes Major's proposal and calls for elections in April or May. Gerry Adams says, 'The Mitchell Report was the conclusion of one track of the twin-track which was set up to move us all into all-party talks by the end of February. In his reaction to this John Major has effectively dumped the twin-track process. He is quite clearly acting in bad faith by swapping one precondition to all-party talks for another.' SF says the Irish government has been 'ambushed' by John Major.

In Strasbourg John Bruton warns that elections in NI could be divisive and that the end of February remains the target date for the beginning of all-party talks.

## The Mitchell Commission Report

As the peace process staggered forward, a melt-down had once again been avoided. Why, though, had the Mitchell Commission not resolutely backed John Major's well-known stand on the arms issue?

There was a feeling in some quarters in Belfast that the evidence given by the RUC may have played a role in weakening the British government's position. If the Mitchell Commission heard from the RUC that the British government's insistence that at least some arms should be decommissioned by the IRA before all-party talks was impractical, this evidence may have had an impact on its findings. The real problem for the government lay not in the apparent waiving of its preconditions – Sir Patrick Mayhew had already opened the door to this possibility – but in the substitute confidence-building measures now proposed.

There was much noble assertion of peaceful and democratic principle in the Mitchell Report, but it should be noted that the reference to the need for all parties to 'abide by the terms of any agreement reached in all-party negotiations' had taken the place of the much firmer statement of the principle of consent which was to be found in the Downing Street Declaration. It was not impossible that Sinn Fein would sign up at the Forum for Peace and Reconciliation in Dublin, in support of this rather more vague principle of agreement.

Gerry Adams had been spared the immediate embarrassment of having to accept that the present partition of the island had a democratic basis, but this was only a postponement of the day when he was forced to face the implication that the status of Northern Ireland could not change without the consent of the majority of its people.

There were those in Belfast who believed that exactly the same thing had happened with decommissioning. It, too, was only postponed until the start of all-party talks. There was no doubt that the difficulties faced by Adams had been eased, but only for a time. In particular, attention should be paid to the notion in the report that commitments to exclusively peaceful methods would have to be honoured. As it stood, Sinn Fein could claim it had already agreed to much of the Mitchell formula, the most pressing difficulty would be the condemnation of punishment shootings and beatings. The real problem lay not with the political wing of Sinn Fein, but with the IRA, and this was the clue to the significance of the word 'honoured'. The rhetoric had to be followed by action to remove the element of threat and blackmail.

In the House of Commons Major moved to regain the initiative by promoting more warmly than he had done before the idea of an elected body. Crucially, John Bruton helped him by using restrained language on this topic.

It seemed clear that the British government's view was that in the absence of a first move on arms by the paramilitaries, the only other possible route to all-party talks was through the electoral process.

The truth remained, however, that the government itself needed to do more in the field of confidence-building. It needed to discuss with unionists much more frankly and realistically than it had in the past its broad vision of the political future for the province. If it could do this, the time won for the peace process would not be in vain. 'There are challenges for everyone,' was the vogue phrase of the day as officials strove to put the best face on the Mitchell Report. The overwhelming majority in Northern Ireland – 83% according to the latest poll – had been asked to accept what they had hitherto rejected: talks before any decommissioning got under way.

By supporting the election proposal, Major had made sure that the challenge was extended to the leaders of Northern nationalists. The British government would be reluctant to take an irrevocable decision unless it saw the Northern nationalists' opposition to an election somewhat reduced.

The Ulster Unionists were at their most placatory, saying that they had no intention of seeking a return to Stormont, or indeed any purely internal settlement. Major appeared to say in the House that much would depend on John Hume's capacity for generosity and flexibility.

**25 January** British government sources claim that in a telephone call two days earlier John Major had informed John Bruton of his plan to push the idea of a new NI body. Irish government sources later say that Major assured Bruton they would 'take the Irish side through' any House of Commons statement before it was made. The sources say that the text of the British statement was sent to them 30 minutes before it was delivered in the Commons and that they were unaware of the election proposal. John Major later writes to John Bruton in an attempt to heal divisions between the two leaders.

Sir Patrick Mayhew rejects nationalist criticism that the proposed elected body will be ineffective, saying it is better to have a 'shouting match than a shooting match'. Later, in the Commons, Mayhew announces that the government intends to create a Northern Ireland grand committee to improve the accountability of the NIO and NI departments. Nationalists interpret the announcement as part of a government move towards a unionist agenda.

In Strasbourg John Bruton says he is 'unwilling to entertain any change' to the joint British and Irish commitment to the 'firm aim' of all-party talks by the end of February.

**26 January** British and Irish divisions over the proposal of an elected body for NI are highlighted by the two countries' newspapers. While the *Irish Times* states that, 'A serious breach of faith' surrounded the announcement, the London *Times* says, 'An elected body, far from being a cul-de-sac, detour, or even road back to Stormont, is the most creative proposal yet advanced for moving the peace process forward.'

It is revealed that John Bruton had turned down a request for a meeting from David Trimble two weeks earlier because the UUP leader would not hold the meeting within the context of the twin-track approach.

Alliance leader John Alderdice attacks Dick Spring saying it would be a waste of time for unionists to talk to the Irish Foreign Minister at present: 'I don't believe they would find him open-minded or prepared to listen to what they have to say.'

Gerry Adams says SF is implacable in its opposition to elections at this time and also accuses John Major of having 'binned' the Mitchell Report.

UDP spokesman David Adams warns that if the suggested NI elected body fails to produce agreement, as he suspects the government intends, it may provide the government with the opportunity to implement the Frameworks Documents proposals which are opposed by all unionist parties.

At the Forum for Peace and Reconciliation in Dublin Sinn Fein delegates give provisional approval to a draft of a report which states that, 'The democratic right of self-determination by the people of Ireland as a whole must be achieved and exercised with and subject to the agreement and consent of a majority of the people of Northern Ireland.'

Councillor Eric Smyth becomes the first DUP Lord Mayor of Belfast to pay an official visit to his counterpart in Dublin.

**27 January** SDLP deputy leader Seamus Mallon says John Major 'has broken faith with not just the Mitchell committee which he helped to set up, but also with the Irish government, and he is well on the way to breaking faith and being at odds with the entire nationalist community in the North of Ireland'.

In Scotland Sir Patrick Mayhew repeats that all-party talks will not take place without elections to the proposed forum unless paramilitaries take the alternative route of decommissioning weapons.

**28 January** The *Sunday Business Post* quotes Dublin-based US sources as saying that White House officials are 'shocked and angered' by the apparent British dismissal of the Mitchell Report. A senior administration official says, 'Privately we share the shock and disappointment of the Irish government and of the various players involved that the whole report should be treated in such a cavalier fashion.'

**29 January** After Dick Spring accuses the British government of using 'divide and conquer' tactics, UUP MP John Taylor says Spring is 'endeavouring to stir nationalists up into a frenzy'.

Reports suggest that NI judges have protested to the Lord Chancellor against the decision to remove their police escort protection by July. Local MPs are also due to have their personal protection reduced in March.

SDLP representatives meet UDP and PUP members for talks for the first time. While the PUP supports the proposed election, senior member and former UVF commander Gusty Spence states, 'Never mind the objections of nationalists, we are not going down the road to the corrupt regimes of the past. We agree [with the SDLP] on that point.' John Hume and Seamus Mallon also meet UDP representatives for discussions.

US Senators Edward Kennedy, Christopher Dodd, Daniel Patrick Moynihan and Claiborne Pell nominate John Hume for the 1996 Nobel peace prize.

**30 January** Gino Gallagher, reputed to be the leader of the INLA, is shot dead in a social security office on the Falls Road. Security forces claim the murder may be the result of an internal feud, but this is rejected by the IRSP, the INLA's political wing.

Sir Patrick Mayhew and Gerry Adams meet at Stormont. Adams calls for the plans for an elected body to be dropped, but Mayhew rejects this suggestion. After the meeting Sir Patrick suggests that after the new NI forum is convened, negotiating teams would be established with the objective of reaching political agreement. Once agreement had been reached these groups would report back to the whole body for approval.

John Major meets John Hume and Seamus Mallon in London while British and Irish officials also meet in Dublin in preparation for a meeting between Sir Patrick Mayhew and Dick Spring.

In Washington NIO Minister Michael Ancram meets US officials for discussions and says all-party talks would be counter-productive if all groups were not represented: 'It still remains our firm aim to have all-party talks by the end of February, but what we can't do is to command.' Ancram says there will be no election in NI unless all parties agree.

**31 January** After a meeting with John Major at Downing Street Ian Paisley says the two main unionist parties would not participate in all-party talks if they were called immediately.

**1 February** Sir Patrick Mayhew and Dick Spring meet in London and attempt to repair some of the damage done to Anglo-Irish relations by recent developments. John Major later holds talks with David Trimble in the House of Commons. Trimble says that after elections his party will engage in 'dialogue' with Sinn Fein and adds, 'By taking the route of an elected body, one obviates the need for decommissioning before elections, but the need for decommissioning does not disappear.'

There are scuffles between police and mourners at the home of murdered INLA leader Gino Gallagher after a number of people wearing paramilitary uniforms appear as Gallagher's coffin is brought to the door. The following day the funeral proceeds with the coffin surrounded by a colour party wearing paramilitary uniforms but without masks.

In a BBC Spotlight programme on the RUC Martin McGuinness says that some members of the force might have a role to play in any new police service. Ken Maginnis of the UUP suggests that recruiting to the RUC be done on a 50% Protestant/50% Catholic basis, apparently contradicting the party's support for merit to be the main principle in recruitment practices.

In an *Irish Times* interview Democratic Party chairman Senator Christopher Dodd says he will support the idea of an election in NI provided it is not a delaying tactic but 'a legitimate device to provide some cover for unionist politicians to go to the table'. Gerry Adams later meets Bill Clinton in Washington. A White House statement says the President 'underscored the need for rapid progress to all-party talks' and 'encouraged all parties to remain committed to the search for peace and determined in its pursuit'.

**2 February** 57 shots are fired at the home of a policeman in Moy, Co. Tyrone. Police say they believe the IRA is responsible for the attack but an IRA statement denies involvement. DUP MP Revd William McCrea describes the incident as 'a serious breach of the ceasefire'.

Police Authority member Chris Ryder faces criticism from unionists after writing in a letter to the *Times* on 31 January, 'Roll on the day when the Union Jack and Irish tricolour fly side by side over Parliament Buildings at Stormont. Then we will have true peace.' Interviewed in the previous night's Spotlight programme, Ryder described the Police Authority as 'a performing poodle'.

In Dublin the Forum for Peace and Reconciliation publishes its report, 'Paths to a Political Settlement in Ireland: Realities, Principles and Requirements'. Sinn Fein does not subscribe to the report's clauses which say that the consent of a majority in Northern Ireland is required for any new agreement, describing this view as providing a 'unionist veto'. Alliance leader John Alderdice says the failure to find agreement effectively means that the forum is over. UUP deputy leader John Taylor claims, 'The Dublin Forum has served one purpose – it has exposed the reality that Sinn Fein is an obstacle to political agreement – even among nationalists.' Taylor later says there will be no all-party talks at the end of the month because the IRA has decided to retain its illegal arms.

In Dublin Martin McGuinness says that the British government has rewarded those parties which have refused to engage in dialogue while those who have tried to engage in discussions have had their views rejected.

Mitchel McLaughlin of SF and David Trimble share a platform for a debate on NI at the World Economic Forum in Davos, Switzerland.

**4 February** In a *Sunday Times* interview John Taylor says his party will talk to Sinn Fein after an election, provided SF pledges in its manifesto to use exclusively peaceful methods. Taylor says, 'We will enter into talks in the new elected body and the first priority will be to agree a method of phased decommissioning of firearms and explosives. Once we have a formula for decommissioning we can go into negotiations on other matters.' The newspaper also claims that David Trimble has stated privately that the attempt to draw SF into the democratic process is 'fatally mistaken' and that the IRA must be defeated.

In a television interview Senator George Mitchell warns there could be a split in the IRA if all-party talks do not begin soon. Martin McGuinness says there is no danger of a split.

**5 February** In an *Irish Times* interview John Taylor describes Dick Spring as 'the most detested politician in Northern Ireland ... a mouthpiece for Sinn Fein' and that, in the previous few weeks he could see 'no difference between Dick Spring and Gerry Adams'. David Trimble's refusal to meet Spring in his role as Irish Foreign Minister is criticised by the SDLP and London and Dublin officials. A British government source comments, 'A large number of people in Northern Ireland view the Irish government as their guarantor in negotiations and no solution is going to work without their co-operation.' On 7 February Trimble says of the election proposal, 'I don't see that we have to sell an argument for something that is so self-evidently right.'

**6 February** As bilateral political talks continue, a PUP delegation meets John Bruton and Dick Spring in Dublin. The PUP delegation stresses that the Irish government cannot expect to play a role in the internal affairs of NI. The UDP says it believes there is no value in going to Dublin to deliver the same message.

**7 February** Following a two-hour meeting with Sir Patrick Mayhew in Dublin Dick Spring suggests the peace process be carried forward by calling a conference similar to that held in Dayton, Ohio, on the Bosnian crisis. All political parties would be invited to the same building for two days of 'intensive multi-lateral discussions'. The purpose of the conference would be to reach general agreement on a basis and timetable for all-party negotiations. John Bruton suggests that the 'proximity talks' be held at Stormont by the end of the month.

Sir Patrick Mayhew states that the British government continues to support the idea of an elected body, 'not as a hurdle, but as a door to achieving the beginning of all-party negotiations'. NIO Minister Michael Ancram describes the proposal as 'at best premature'. The proposal is generally accepted by nationalist parties in NI but rejected by unionists. On a BBC television news programme David Trimble says the idea is 'a gimmick' brought forward to save face for Dick Spring who, Trimble says, 'has been making a fool of himself over the course of the last few days'.

**8 February** Commenting on the Irish government's suggestion for proximity talks at Stormont, Michael Ancram says, 'We have to deal with the politics of reality rather than the politics of wishful thinking. Anybody can call all-party talks at any time but, if the parties aren't prepared to come to those talks, you don't have all-party talks.' Mitchel McLaughlin of SF criticises the comments, saying, 'There is a growing body of opinion throughout the country and internationally that John Major has abandoned all pretence of sincerity about his desire to achieve a lasting settlement in Ireland.'

UDP leader Gary McMichael warns that loyalist paramilitaries could retaliate if the IRA kills two Protestants giving evidence in an IRA murder trial. McMichael later takes part in a debate with Pat McGeown of SF on a Ulster TV programme.

In Washington Dick Spring meets President Clinton and Vice-President Gore and stresses the urgency of proximity talks as the next step in the peace process. Spring says the President has agreed to consider the Irish proposals and that John Taylor's recent comments are 'over the top', noting that, 'Any thinking, rational unionist would realise that I'm actually reaching out to unionists.'

A White House statement records that, 'The President encouraged all parties to focus on the political track of the twin-track process in order to move rapidly to all-party talks.'

Sir Patrick Mayhew says that the end of February target date set for all-party talks in the twin-track process was in the context of 'co-operation from all the relevant parties in both tracks. We want to reach broad agreement on the way ahead by the end of February, and then to press ahead with any necessary legislation'.

**9 February** A *Guardian* article on NI argues that the British and Irish governments 'now have their alibis in place for when the "firm aim" target date – the end of February, jointly agreed last year – for beginning all-party talks passes without a resolution of the impasse. The British have advanced their "elective process" and the Irish have countered with "Dayton". Neither London nor Dublin will lightly wear the accusation that they didn't do enough.'

UUP MP Ken Maginnis and SF chairman Mitchel McLaughlin take part in a debate on BBC NI; the programme is not broadcast because of later developments. Senior UUP members are said to be outraged by Maginnis's decision to take part in a debate with a member of SF. David Trimble says he was not aware that the meeting was taking place. A republican source describes the debate as 'ground-breaking'.

In an *Irish Post* article former Labour NI spokesman Kevin McNamara says John Major will not risk his Commons majority to insist that unionists take part in all-party negotiations. McNamara also notes that

Major should have expected the 'united fury of nationalist Ireland' in response to his proposal for elections.

Interviewed on BBC Radio Ulster, Gerry Adams speaks of his 'Protestant brothers and sisters' and says that political progress can be made through all-party talks.

A *Belfast Telegraph* report notes that SF members Mary Nelis and John Hurl will be part of a delegation of NI councillors to Downing Street the following week.

At 5.40 pm Scotland Yard receives warnings from news agencies and Sky television that the IRA ceasefire is about to end. Several news agencies receive warnings that a bomb has been planted at South Quay railway station and attempts are made to evacuate the Canary Wharf area.

Shortly before 7 pm a statement from the IRA ending its ceasefire is authenticated. The statement reads: 'It is with great reluctance that the leadership of Oglaigh na hEireann announces that the complete cessation of military operations will end at 6 pm on February 9th, this evening. As we stated on August 31st, 1994, the basis for the cessation was to enhance the democratic peace process and to underline our definitive commitment to its success. We also made it clear that we believed that an opportunity to create a just and lasting settlement had been created.

'The cessation presented an historic challenge for everyone, and Oglaigh na hEireann commends the leaderships of nationalist Ireland at home and abroad. They rose to the challenge. The British Prime Minister did not. Instead of embracing the peace process, the British government acted in bad faith, with Mr Major and the Unionist leaders squandering this unprecedented opportunity to resolve the conflict.

'Time and again, over the last eighteen months, selfish party political and sectional interests in the London parliament have been placed before the rights of the people of Ireland. We take this opportunity to reiterate our total commitment to our republican objectives. The resolution of the conflict in our country demands justice. It demands an inclusive negotiated settlement. That is not possible unless and until the British government faces up to its reponsibilities.

'The blame for the failure thus far of the Irish peace process lies squarely with John Major and his government.'

At 7.01 pm a bomb, hidden in the underground car park of a six-floor office building near Canary Wharf, explodes killing two men, injuring more than 100 others and causing more than £85 million worth of damage. The blast, which leaves a crater 14 feet wide and more than 20 feet deep, is heard throughout East and North-East London.

In a statement John Major calls the explosion 'an appalling outrage. My first thoughts are with the casualties, their families and the emergency services. We will pursue relentlessly those responsible for this disgraceful attack.' Major calls on Sinn Fein to condemn those who planted the bomb and says that the atrocity 'confirms again the urgent need to remove illegal arms from the equation'. Tony Blair condemns the attack as a sickening outrage while Liberal Democrat leader Paddy Ashdown says it demonstrates that the IRA has moved against the popular will of the Irish people, North and South.

Sir Patrick Mayhew states that, 'Rather than face elections, they appear to have gone back to the bomb.' Later he adds, 'Those who have said the government hasn't moved fast enough are really saying, "You haven't responded to our threats fast enough so here's another one to smarten you up." '

John Bruton says the bombing is entirely unjustified and condemns it without reservation.

A statement by President Clinton says, 'I condemn in the strongest possible terms this cowardly action and hope those responsible are brought swiftly to justice ... As was clear during my visit to Northern Ireland last year, people want peace. No one and no organisation has the right to deny them that wish. The terrorists who perpetrated today's attack cannot be allowed to derail the effort to bring peace to the people of Northern Ireland – a peace they overwhelmingly support.'

A senior US adminstration official says that Gerry Adams telephoned the White House shortly before the London explosion. The official stated, 'He [Adams] said he was hearing some very disturbing news and he would call us back.'

David Trimble says, 'If there has been a resumption of violence then it has clearly been done in order to try and prevent elections in Northern Ireland. It is incredible that people who, for the last eighteen months, have been telling us they want to move into the democratic process should be resorting to violence.'

Ian Paisley says, 'I am sorry that so many people were gulled into believing the lies of the IRA and Sinn Fein that there will be no return to violence.'

Alliance leader John Alderdice says the situation is profoundly depressing and notes that if SF condones the London bombing it will again set the party outside the pale of democracy.

Joe Hendron, SDLP MP for West Belfast, suggests that there may be a split in the IRA, noting, 'I know that Gerry Adams was saying on local radio that the ceasefire was total and permanent. I suspect that this is perhaps a breakaway group from the IRA.' Dr Hendron says the British government has been 'playing with fire' over the Mitchell Report and the decommissioning issue.

No SF spokesman was immediately available to comment on the bombing and the ending of the ceasefire. Some time later Gerry Adams blames the British government and unionist leaders for the breakdown in the ceasefire and says SF's 'peace strategy' remains his party's main task.

In the Shankill area of Belfast shots are fired when loyalists, reacting to the IRA attack, attempt to hijack a car. The probable loyalist attack on a nationalist area is thwarted when the owner of the car refuses to hand over the vehicle. Veteran loyalist and PUP member Gusty Spence calls on loyalists not to react to the ending of the IRA ceasefire until the situation becomes clearer.

Police officers again wear flak-jackets while on patrol and the RUC says that patrols by armoured police vehicles will also be increased. Security around Belfast International Airport is also tightened.

## The End of the IRA Ceasefire

When the ceasefire was announced, Gerry Adams declared his conviction that a purely political way forward existed for the republican movement. The new relationship which had been forged with Irish America, John Hume's SDLP and the Irish government was the key. Nationalists spoke of the highly successful 'new departure' forged by Parnell in 1879 as the model for this altered strategy. Privately, also, some leading republicans said they had received a signal that the British would withdraw within ten years and some said that a deal had been struck to this end between the then Taoiseach, Albert Reynolds, and John Major.

Given these assumptions, the previous eighteen months had seemed like one disappointment after another; in essence, the British government refused to pressurise the unionists into all-party talks while an atmosphere of threat and undiminished republican armament remained.

When the Mitchell Commission finally forced the British government to drop its precondition on arms, John Major then embraced David Trimble's proposal for an elected assembly to negotiate a settlement. Nationalist Ireland was stunned; a unionist leader had shown the ability to set the agenda in a way which was not conceivable in the era of James Molyneaux, his predecessor.

Mitchel McLaughlin, chairman of Sinn Fein and an apparent 'dove', seemed to acknowledge that an electoral process was worthy of consideration. For others, it appears to have been the *casus belli*; the reality was that there was a return to violence not because senior republicans realistically thought it could bring about a united Ireland but because they thought it could bring about a 'peace process' on more favourable terms without problematical events like elections.

The belief was that the British would drop their points of principle and exert pressure on the unionists to go to the negotiating table. But even if the British government were to do so, as was unlikely, unionists would claim that all their previous reservations had been vindicated.

The actual choice of day for the return of violence could hardly have been more surprising. At midday Gerry Adams had been at his most peace-making on a local radio programme, speaking of his 'Protestant brothers and sisters'. Mitchel McLaughlin had taken part in a ground-breaking television debate with Ken Maginnis, the Ulster Unionist MP who had carried the coffins of so many of his constituents killed by the IRA.

It was yet another indication of the new era of dialogue which slowly appeared to be opening up. Tory MPs in Dublin spoke in a surprisingly kindly way of the Irish government's Dayton-style talks proposal. Most amazingly of all, it was announced that two Sinn Fein councillors were scheduled to visit 10 Downing Street as part of a delegation seeking economic aid.

In the wake of the Canary Wharf attack John Major called on Sinn Fein to condemn the bombing. Gerry Adams's statements contained no hint of condemnation. This may have indicated that the leadership of the republican movement was thinking of a new approach.

For some time Sinn Fein had been trying to create clear water between itself and the IRA. Even a favoured reverential phrase fell into disrepute: 'What is the republican movement?' Martin McGuinness had earlier asked a surprised Spanish journalist. His point was to stress that there was no unified movement of Sinn Fein and the IRA. This was a view John Major had pointedly rejected on 21 December 1995 during a visit to Ballymena.

The purpose of such a manoeuvre was clear enough – Adams would hope to retain his image as a peace-maker and, as he made clear in an RTE interview on 9 February, continue to meet prime ministers and presidents. This could prove to be an illusion, but the republican movement was, arguably, no stranger to the politics of illusion. In the first instance it was the reaction of the Irish government which would be most telling; it would be unfortunate if London and Dublin were to drift apart at this time, though the nationalist view of British and unionist intransigence could prove a dangerous ideological battleground.

The irony was that senior Ulster Unionists had been preparing themselves for talks in the summer – a speech by John Taylor in his Strangford constituency had offered a rough blueprint. At the same time, the British government offered much, not least a very soft negotiation of the Frameworks Documents, to keep the truce alive. For the time being the only good news appeared to be the restrained reaction of the loyalist paramilitaries.

**10 February** The *Irish Times* comments on the previous evening's events: 'Words are hardly adequate to condemn the bombing at Canary Wharf which has once more caused the world's television screens to fill with images of innocent people injured and mutilated in the name of Irish nationalism ... At one blow, the normality of peace has been undone and replaced once again by the fear of random violence ... A great deal has been achieved over the past eighteen months and the genuine peacemakers – in Ireland, in Britain and across the Atlantic – have not slackened in their resolve to bring this process through to a final and agreed settlement. If there remains a chance to put it back on course, those peacemakers must not now play into the hands of the extremists.'

The *Irish News* remarks, 'Irish unity is not worth the life of a single person. If there is to be a resolution of our problems we must reach it through democratic debate, not with bombs and bullets. This has been a tragedy for the peoples of Britain and Ireland ... We cannot allow our countries to descend once more to violence.'

The Belfast *News Letter* states, 'The ending of the IRA ceasefire last night will have a numbing effect on the great mass of people in Northern Ireland who had been savouring the fruits of relative peace and near normality in the province for the past eighteen months. But it is a development which will hardly surprise those who had enough wit to realise that the IRA ceasefire of 31 August 1994 was nothing more than a ploy by the Provo high command to wring major political concessions from the government for the narrow republican agenda.'

In a BBC radio interview Gerry Adams says he had no prior knowledge that the IRA was about to end the ceasefire and that he regrets what has happened.

An IRA statement admits planting the bomb at Canary Wharf, adding that, 'The regrettable injuries which occurred could have been avoided had the British security forces acted promptly on clear and specific warnings.'

The Irish government rescinds a decision to release nine republican prisoners due to be freed that day.

David Trimble calls on SDLP leader John Hume and the Irish government to break off all contacts with Sinn Fein.

John Hume says he is doing everything in his power to try to ensure a total and absolute cessation of violence and adds, 'My strong message to the leadership of the IRA is that since you say you believe in the right of the Irish people to self-determination, the Irish people also have the right to self-determine their methods, and – particularly during the visit of President Clinton, and particularly since the ceasefire – they have made their self-determination on methodology very, very, clear.'

The *Belfast Telegraph* asks, 'Is this really the end of the peace? That is the question that dominates everyone's thinking today, in the aftermath of last night's bomb outrage in London. The nightmare of the last 25 years has been revisited on scores of innocent victims in Canary Wharf, recalling the worst horrors of a quarter century of violence, but this is not the time for meekly accepting that all is lost. Along with the massive destruction caused by the bomb, the IRA has destroyed at a stroke whatever trust in the republican movement has been built up over the past eighteen months. If Sinn Fein knew nothing about the bomb plan, as it says, what are its relations with the IRA? Why should the views of its leaders be taken seriously, if they have no influence over the bombers?' John Bruton says the IRA must resume its ceasefire immediately otherwise Sinn Fein will be isolated in the political process. He warns the IRA that the Irish government is determined 'with all the force at its disposal to protect the peace in Ireland and Britain'. Bruton says that this time the IRA will not only have to end violence but make it clear that it is doing so on a permanent basis: 'It must stop permanently because if we are to restore the momentum of the peace process there cannot be this constant looking over the shoulder.' An Irish government statement adds that, 'Only those who take no part in violence, in the threat of violence, or in the support of violence, can take part in democratic negotiation ... The basis for previous government meetings with Sinn Fein was that a total cessation of IRA violence was already in place. That policy enjoyed support because it showed that violence was not an acceptable method of promoting a political programme. We are concerned to ensure that any meeting with Sinn Fein should be consistent with that long-standing policy.'

John Major comments, 'The IRA and Sinn Fein must say now that their campaign of violence has stopped and they will never resume it.'

President Clinton says the people of Ireland want peace and 'no one and no organisation has the right to deny them that wish. I am determined to do all that I can to make sure that the enemies of peace do not succeed.'

Gerry Adams says he learned of the breakdown in the ceasefire from the media: 'The IRA have never consulted Sinn Fein about operational matters and have never at any time involved us and I would never at any time wish to be involved or see our party involved in those matters.'

Security in NI is stepped up in the wake of the London bomb. The RUC mounts permanent checkpoints outside a number of police stations while army Land Rovers take part in joint patrols with the RUC in West Belfast. Police patrols are also increased on both sides of the border in an attempt to prevent IRA bombs being moved from the South to the North.

**11 February** A *Mail on Sunday* report claims that the decision to resume the IRA's campaign had been taken at a meeting of the IRA Army Council in Dublin the previous Thursday (8 February). An earlier vote to end the ceasefire, taken just before Bill Clinton's visit to Belfast, had been defeated on the casting vote of the then IRA Chief of Staff. The replacement of one member by another individual was believed to have changed the balance within the Army Council in favour of a return to the terrorist campaign.

In an interview with the *Observer* a leading SF member says John Major is 'prepared to put peace in Northern Ireland at risk just because he needs to shield himself on issues like the Scott report [into British arms sales to Iraq] and that means keeping the Unionists on board.'

Reacting to John Bruton and the Irish government's statement of the previous day, Gerry Adams comments, 'If he is saying to me that he will not meet me or any of the representatives of those who have voted for us unless the IRA ends its campaign, what room does that give to anyone, when the lesson is that marginalisation under Stormont and marginalisation in the twenty years since Stormont fell achieved nothing?'

Conservative MP Peter Temple-Morris says Gerry Adams should not be asked to condemn the London bomb: 'If you demand that from him you basically negate the whole peace process, and in neutering Adams and co. you invite something far more extreme to take their places.'

It emerges that MI5 had warned the government a month earlier to expect a renewal of IRA violence, but the security service had not expected the IRA campaign to resume until March. Security sources also claim that the decision to recommence the campaign was taken to avoid a split in the IRA.

**12 February** David Trimble meets President Clinton and Anthony Lake for talks in Washington. The President rejects Trimble's call for a ban on US visas for members of SF and an end to SF fund-raising. White House spokesman Mike McCurry says, 'Mr Adams is an important leader in this process because he speaks for Sinn Fein. It is hard to imagine a process making progress towards peace without the active involvement of Sinn Fein.'

In an interview with the *Irish Times* Gerry Adams says, 'It was the absence of negotiations and the consequent failure to address and resolve the causes of conflict which made the re-occurrence of conflict inevitable.' The newspaper also reports that republican sources in Dublin say the IRA has told its members that the London bomb was a 'one-off' incident, meant to affect the political process rather than to restart the conflict in the North.

In Belfast several thousand people attend a peace rally organised by Women Together. Another peace rally is held in Derry on 14 February.

In the Commons John Major says, 'No one, no one took more risks for peace than the government over the past two years, but we never lost sight of the fact that the IRA commitment had not been made for good. No responsible government could have done otherwise. That was why we and many others saw a start to the decommissioning of illegal arms as a way of creating confidence in Sinn Fein's acceptance of democratic peaceful methods, and showing that the violence had really ended. But all the time that Sinn Fein were calling for all-party talks, we knew that the IRA continued to train and plan for terrorist attacks … It remained ready to resume full-scale terrorism at any time. We could never be confident that its behaviour was that of an organisation which had decided to renounce violence for ever. The IRA peace was not true peace.

'I regret to say that the events of last Friday showed that our caution about the IRA was only too justified. The timing of the return to violence may have been surprising: the fact that violence could resume was not. We must now continue the search for permanent peace and a comprehensive political settlement in Northern Ireland. Let there be no doubt that the government's commitment to that is as strong as ever and will remain as strong as ever. We will work for peace with all the democratic political parties and with the Irish government. But a huge question mark now hangs over the position of one of the parties – Sinn Fein … In the absence of a genuine end to this renewed violence, meetings between British ministers and Sinn Fein are not acceptable and cannot take place. That is also the position of the Irish government. They have made it clear to Sinn Fein that their attitude and willingness to meet at political level will be determined by whether the IRA ceasefire is restored. We and the Irish government are at one on this: the ball is in the court of Sinn Fein and the IRA, if indeed that distinction means anything. It is for them to show, through their words and actions, whether they have a part to play in the peace process. I am not in the business of slamming doors, but the British and Irish peoples need to know where Sinn Fein stands.' Tony Blair says that whatever his differences with John Major, 'On this matter we shall stand four square together in the cause of peace.'

John Hume calls for referenda to be held in Northern Ireland and the Republic to ask whether people absolutely and unequivocally disapproved of violence for any purpose and whether they wanted all parties brought to the table to begin the process of dialogue to create lasting stability.

North Down MP Robert McCartney says, 'While there is a necessity to restore in some form the ceasefire, such a restoration and entering into further negotiations with Sinn Fein-IRA begs the question about whether further down the line, when it meets with another impasse, or some situation that does not meet with its approval, it will simply blast its out of the way in the manner of Canary Wharf?'

In a national television address John Major says he will continue working for a lasting peace in NI. He states that it is the government's aim to bring together all democratic parties for talks and that talks have not taken place already because Sinn Fein and the IRA did not give a commitment to put away their arms.

Ian Paisley Jr claims that the tax disc on the lorry used in the Docklands bomb was stolen from an English-registered lorry in Co. Armagh three weeks earlier and notes that this took place prior to the completion of the Mitchell Report on decommissioning.

Gerry Adams says responsibility for the London bomb 'lies squarely with the IRA', but John Major must accept his share of responsibility for the breakdown in the peace process. Adams states that in private discussions British representatives had said that there would be substantive talks three months after an IRA cessation and that the British government reneged on that position. He calls on John Major to 'show real leadership' and join with the Irish government to lead everyone into all-party talks and the substantive negotiations which were required to restore the peace process. Dick Spring welcomes John Major's statements, saying, 'Imposed elections would not work, but agreed elections on the right terms might.'

**13 February** The *Financial Times* gives details of proposals put forward to the democratic parties and the Irish government over the previous three weeks. After the poll those elected would only meet in a single forum in exceptional circumstances, there would be no legislative, executive or administrative functions and all-party talks would begin immediately.

After a meeting with John Major at Downing Street Ian Paisley agrees that proximity talks after an election are a realistic proposition.

A planned meeting between NI councillors (including two members of SF) and John Major is postponed indefinitely by Downing Street.

In Washington David Trimble says if SF took its seats in the proposed 'peace convention' there would be decommissioning running alongside the operation of a convention in which there would be substantive negotiations. Unionists would, however, need to be reassured that any new IRA ceasefire was permanent and that they had accepted the Mitchell principles.

In the Dail John Bruton says, 'The British government made a mistake in its response to the Mitchell Report. The unionist parties made a mistake in not sitting down with Sinn Fein and asking them the hard questions face to face, but a comparison cannot be drawn between political mistakes and the response to those mistakes that took human life. Killing is never justified as part of the political process. Killing is never justified as part of a negotiation. Killing is not an acceptable passport to negotiations. A government cannot allow murder, or the threat of murder, to set the political agenda ... As leader of the Opposition, before I became Taoiseach, I made an act of faith when I said in September 1994 I believed in Sinn Fein and I was willing to believe that the IRA had ended the killing for good ... I accepted that Sinn Fein was committed exclusively to advancing its cause by peaceful, democratic politics. I believed they had made an irreversible commitment to peace. That act of faith has now been thrown back in my face by the IRA.' Despite this, Bruton says that the Irish government has 'not shut any door on Sinn Fein' and that he is willing to authorise direct contact between SF leaders and Irish government officials. Dick Spring repeats his proposal for proximity talks to be held before any NI election.

Fianna Fail leader Bertie Ahern criticises the NI Secretary of State saying, 'A plausible case could be made for saying that Sir Patrick Mayhew's job was to manage the Northern Ireland peace process in a way that ensured the survival of the Tory government at Westminster rather than the survival of the peace itself.'

After a private meeting with Gerry Adams former Taoiseach Albert Reynolds says that he believes that if a definite date was set for all-party talks then the IRA would immediately call another ceasefire.

**14 February** Republicans call on John Bruton to talk to Gerry Adams in order to get the peace process back on track. A republican source says the IRA 'cessation' was 'the result of risks being taken by John Hume, Gerry Adams, the Irish government led by Albert Reynolds and the Irish-American lobby. It was a combination of their efforts that produced an alternative that was persuasive to the IRA and that kind of combined effort is needed again.'

**15 February** As security is increased across NI, 500 soldiers from the 1st Battalion, the Royal Irish Regiment, are flown into the province. A number of security roadblocks are also re-erected.

In an interview with *An Phoblacht* an IRA spokesperson says the end of the IRA ceasefire was caused by John Major's 'cynical misuse and betrayal of the historic opportunity offered by the Irish peace initiative ... The IRA leadership delivered a complete cessation of military operations on a clear, unambiguous and shared understanding that inclusive negotiations would rapidly commence to bring about political agreement and a peace settlement. The British government committed itself to this publicly. So too did the Dublin government.

'Let us be crystal clear about this. John Major reneged on these commitments, publicly given. He had acted in bad faith throughout the period of the IRA cessation, introducing one new precondition after another. He has betrayed the Irish peace process and has deliberately squandered this opportunity to resolve the causes of the age-old conflict between Britain and the Irish people. He did so to keep himself in power ...

'From all of this we could only finally conclude that the surrender or political defeat of Irish republicans was the actual agenda for the tactical engagement by the British government in the Irish peace initiative.'

The IRA spokesperson also criticises John Bruton, stating that he 'knew well the basis upon which we agreed to a complete cessation of military operations in August 1994. It was a quid pro quo understanding that all-party talks would commence rapidly. It was a clear and unambiguous understanding which the previous Taoiseach was clear about and which John Bruton was informed of when he assumed office.' Bruton and his predecessor, Albert Reynolds, later reject this assertion.

In the Dail Albert Reynolds claims that Major's rejection of the Mitchell Report and support for the Unionist proposal of a NI election 'was the straw which broke the camel's back'. Peter Robinson of the DUP criticises the remarks saying, 'Once again we hear Mr Reynolds whistling the IRA tune. The people who are responsible are those who masterminded the bomb, primed and placed and deliberately blew up not only two innocent human beings but the prospect of peace.'

John Bruton says that he and John Major have agreed on two major objectives: to secure the restoration of the IRA ceasefire and to work toward the start of all-party talks. Bruton says he has suggested five more issues aimed at achieving these ends: the creation of a way for SF to rejoin the process once the IRA campaign was over; the development of the proposal for proximity talks; how an election might lead directly to all-party talks; consideration of John Hume's proposal for referenda and how the role of the US administration might be deepened to help the peace process.

British and Irish officials meet in an attempt to reach agreement on a formula to bring about all-party talks.

Alliance leader John Alderdice says he will only support calls for an election in NI if it leads to all-party talks within two weeks. Alderdice says he can envisage a situation in which talks take place without a renewed IRA ceasefire provided no further attacks are launched.

An 11 lb IRA semtex bomb, planted in London's Charing Cross Road, is defused. The incident leads to a further tightening of security in the capital.

RUC sources claim the IRA ceasefire has now ended completely. A security source says that new IRA members have been recruited and are being trained in the Republic. Loyalist paramilitaries are also said to be gearing up for a return to terrorism in response to any IRA attacks.

In a speech in Belfast Gerry Adams reveals that he has written to John Major urging an immediate start to all-party talks. He also says that, 'Any willingness to accept the unionist election proposal would not augur well for the period ahead.'

**16 February** Some 4,000 people attend a trade union-organised peace rally at Belfast City Hall. There are minor scuffles between those attending the rally and SF supporters carrying placards calling for all-party talks. A peace group called No More Violence collects more than half a million signatures calling for the ceasefire to be reinstated. Dick Spring calls on people to wear a white ribbon to show their support for peace. The Republic also holds a one minute silence in support of a restoration of the IRA ceasefire.

A poll conducted for the *Irish Independent* finds that 85% of people in the Republic and 56% in NI want all-party talks immediately. In the South 11% oppose immediate talks while 38% in the North were also opposed.

In London Scotland Yard offers a reward of £1 million, donated by an anonymous organisation, for the capture of the Canary Wharf bombers. Armed police raid more than 30 houses and arrest four men in the hunt for IRA suspects.

Irish officials meet Gerry Adams to consider ways in which the IRA ceasefire can be restored. SF vice-president Pat Doherty declares, 'If the process broke down through a lack of negotiations, or indeed a refusal by the British government to initiate such negotiations, then there is a big responsibility upon the governments to abide by their commitments, and that then puts a very clear responsibility upon the IRA.'

David Trimble meets PUP leader Hugh Smyth and other members of his party for talks at Belfast City Hall. A Sinn Fein spokesperson later says, 'It seems incredible that David Trimble can talk to a loyalist party that has no democratic mandate while refusing to talk to Sinn Fein, which has more votes on Belfast City Council than his party.'

Former Unionist leader Sir James Molyneaux claims that any new IRA ceasefire will 'hit the buffers' once peaceful methods and consent are mentioned.

**17 February** Asked about the possibility of loyalist paramilitaries ending their ceasefire, PUP spokesman David Ervine says, 'I don't think they are preparing for war but they are getting themselves gathered, mentally, for the possibility of it.'

David Trimble writes to Dick Spring offering to discuss the consequences of the IRA resumption of violence and matters which affect the Irish government in relation to the proposed 'peace convention'. The Unionist leader says, however, that the Dublin government cannot play the role of co-sponsor in the elected talks body.

John Hume and Gerry Adams meet for talks. A joint statement says they have recommitted themselves to do their utmost to restore the peace process.

**18 February** The *Sunday Life* claims that the previous day the IRA Army Council had given free rein to its five bombing squads in England to resume their campaign. The Army Council was also reported to have voted against resuming attacks in NI for the present.

Commenting on the impact of the renewed IRA campaign on loyalists, David Ervine tells the *Sunday Times*, 'My biggest fear is that they [the CLMC] could drop the word "universal" from the terms of their ceasefire. That scares me because they could then take their battle to the South and start a cycle which would bring us God knows where. It is a dangerous thing for loyalists to witness, if the Provos look like they are getting something from the political leverage of violence. We could never carry a situation where the Provos were being talked to and were still letting off bombs.'

In West Belfast Gerry Adams tells a republican rally, 'At this very dangerous and risky period in our struggle, we offer the hand of friendship to John Major. We say to John Major – pull back from the abyss, we want to talk and we want peace. But we must have justice and we must have freedom and we must be treated as equals in this situation … We are going to face the British government with a united republican struggle and with demands for peace talks now, freedom and justice.'

At 10.40 pm the premature detonation of a 5 lb IRA bomb on a double-decker bus in the Aldwych in central London leaves one person dead and six injured. The man killed in the explosion is IRA member Edward O'Brien from Co. Wexford. An IRA hit list, bomb-making materials and 40 lb of semtex are later found at O'Brien's flat.

Ken Maginnis of the UUP says Gerry Adams's 'refusal to condemn these outrages has to be seen for what it is – part of a terrorist campaign intended to enable less than 5% of the electorate in Northern Ireland to dominate by violence the other 95%'.

**19 February** President Clinton says, 'These cowardly acts of terrorism are the work of individuals determined to thwart the will of the people of Northern Ireland.'

In an *Irish Times* interview Alliance leader John Alderdice says that for the IRA, 'the peace process was about achieving a united Ireland in short stages with the assistance of other nationalists. It was not about accepting the reality of the Joint Declaration, the Framework Documents, or any other accommodation with partition. On this analysis the bomb at Canary Wharf was always coming. The Forum Report and the Mitchell Report explain its timing, and the row which followed John Major's speech in the Commons gave it the best possible political context, but, if the IRA was not going to see the Irish peace process deliver its aims, then a return to violence was always an option and the threat of the return to violence was always more powerful than outdated republican argument.'

The *Times* reports that jobs created under the Community Work Programme, and funded by money saved from the NI security budget as a result of security cutbacks during the IRA ceasefire, may now be lost.

The *News Letter* reports that a special 'anti-terror' telephone poll set up by the province's five main newspapers has received more than 150,000 calls.

In a debate on the renewal of the Emergency Provisions Act Sir Patrick Mayhew states, 'The British government in this democracy will not be shifted from their chosen and democratic course by bombs or by the threat of bombs, or by any variety of violence ... The perpetrators of violence should realise that in this democracy they will make no political progress whatsoever by means of violence.' Mayhew also attacks Gerry Adams's 'sickening hypocrisy'.

Andrew Hunter, chairman of the Conservative backbench committee on NI, says, 'The IRA will get no concessions from this course of action. Clearly, we must consign the ceasefire to history.' Conservative backbencher Terry Dicks says the government 'should immediately embark on a policy of shoot-to-kill'.

Liberal Democrat leader Paddy Ashdown says the London bus bomb has 'put the final nail in the coffin of the ceasefire'.

The RUC officially confirms earlier speculation that plans to reduce the personal protection of senior politicians and judges have been dropped.

Representatives of more than 100 community, voluntary and church groups issue a joint statement calling for a renewed ceasefire and moves towards all-party talks.

Responding to the latest IRA bombing, Gerry Adams says, 'The peace process is over. What we have to do is rebuild it.'

## The End of the Peace Process

In the months which followed the London bombs, strenuous attempts were made to resurrect the peace process and coax the IRA into announcing another ceasefire. Public support for peace rallies throughout the British Isles and statements from the US administration added to the pressure for a renewed ceasefire. In response Martin McGuinness noted on 24 February that if a guaranteed date for all-party talks was given there would be a major onus on Sinn Fein to give a political analysis to the IRA which would recognise the need for 'an imaginative initiative to be taken'.

In a joint communiqué issued four days later, the British and Irish governments launched a package which they hoped would restart the peace process. A firm date for all-party talks, 10 June, was announced. Political parties would be asked to attend proximity talks (later renamed 'intensive multilateral consultations') to consider the structure, format and agenda for the all-party talks and whether there should be a referendum in both Northern Ireland and the Republic to demonstrate support for a political settlement. Discussions would seek to reach agreement on the form of election used to lead to all-party negotiations with elections to the negotiating forum to be held in May. Sinn Fein could take part in the negotiations provided it persuaded the IRA to renew its ceasefire. The communiqué also stated that, as a confidence-building measure in all-party negotiations, 'All participants would need to make clear at the beginning of the discussions their total and absolute commitment to the principles of democracy and non-violence set out in the report of the International Body.' If IRA violence resumed during the talks, Sinn Fein would be excluded. John Major also warned that if there was no agreement at these talks, the government would impose its own proposals.

Criticism that the governments had conceded ground as a result of the IRA bombs was rejected both by Bruton and Major, the latter stating that there were areas where he had compromised and that others had done the same. With the Ulster Unionists and the SDLP still on board (SDLP deputy leader Seamus Mallon calling the package 'the moment of truth for all paramilitary, terrorist groupings in Northern Ireland') and with American support for the latest proposals, Martin McGuinness could only reply that it was 'totally wrong and undemocratic' that Sinn Fein was not treated on the same basis as all other parties.

Yet the broad consensus of democratic parties in favour of the 28 February proposals was not as stable as might have been hoped. Relations between the Ulster Unionists and the Conservative government were decidedly chilly, not least as a result of the controversy over whether or not the Unionists had offered to support the government in the Commons vote on the Scott report into sales of British arms to Iraq in return for the government pursuing a more unionist agenda. The question of the 'modalities' of the decommissioning of paramilitary weapons also remained unresolved, while the paramilitaries themselves continued to make clear that actual decommissioning was not on their agenda, at least until all other issues were settled.

By March the prospects for peace, if anything, looked even less bright: disaffected loyalist paramilitaries threatened to 'execute' Sinn Fein and IRA members and 'create a balance of terror', an internal INLA feud resulted in four deaths by the end of May, with another in June, and the proposed 'proximity talks' failed to live up to their name with meetings eventually taking place in no fewer than ten different venues. The IRA meanwhile continued its campaign in London with a small explosive device detonating in Fulham, while hope of an early restoration of the ceasefire also appeared to be dashed on 7 March when an IRA spokesman told *An Phoblacht*, 'There is not the necessary dynamic to move us all away from conflict and towards a lasting peace.'

One of the few positive developments of the month took place on 11 March when Ulster Unionist leaders David Trimble and John Taylor met the leaders of the Irish government for talks in Dublin. Any benefits which may have accrued from this meeting were undermined four days later when a government document entitled 'Ground Rules for Substantive All-Party Negotiations' was sent to the parties while Unionist leaders were in America. The proposals, suggesting that the Irish government be joint co-ordinator of the negotiations, were perceived by unionists as another concession to nationalists and further soured relations between the UUP and the Irish government.

On 21 March the government announced that in the NI election to be held on 30 May voters would be asked to vote for a party rather than an individual candidate. The election would be held using the new constituency boundaries with the eighteen constituencies each returning five representatives. Two extra seats would be allocated to each of the ten most successful parties across Northern Ireland as a whole. The lifetime of the elected forum was initially limited to twelve months. This hybrid electoral system was criticised by all the main parties, Seamus Mallon calling it a 'monster raving loony election proposal', while Gerry Adams described the proposals as an 'anathema to nationalists'. The following day an INLA statement announced an end to its tactical ceasefire.

On the positive side, no party had withdrawn from the election and, on 23 March at the Sinn Fein ard fheis, Gerry Adams said his party should contest the 30 May election if the SDLP did so, although Sinn Fein's preference was to boycott the election. On 25 March the SDLP rejected Sinn Fein's calls for a joint boycott of the election, though Seamus Mallon said his party had not yet decided whether it would take part. The Irish government meanwhile attempted to assuage nationalist fears that the proposed forum would become another Stormont, and on 27 March John Bruton said in the Dail that he would do everything possible to 'insulate' the role of the forum in the negotiating process. On the issue of decommissioning he said, 'The priority being given to the Mitchell Report at the beginning of the discussions must not be construed to mean that this issue can be used to block discussions of other issues.' David Trimble also appeared to soften his previous position on the issue of decommissioning being resolved before other areas were discussed by stating on 29 March that there would be no 'log-jam' if the paramilitaries accepted the Mitchell Report.

In April, as discussions surrounding the mechanics of the election continued, the reality of street politics in Northern Ireland re-emerged when serious rioting occurred in Belfast after police prevented an Apprentice Boys of Derry march passing along the nationalist lower Ormeau Road. Nine days later, on 17 April, the IRA continued its London bombing campaign by exploding a device in the Earls Court area and on 24 April two IRA bombs containing more than 30 lb of semtex planted under Hammersmith Bridge partially detonated but caused only minor damage.

The end of the month saw an echo of the earlier controversy surrounding government contacts with paramilitary spokesmen when the *Sunday Times* revealed on 28 April that the government had opened a secret channel of communication with the IRA using former NIO Minister Michael Mates as a go-between. Mates later confimed that he had met a senior member of Sinn Fein, but said that the meeting was not undertaken at the government's initiative. The following day it was revealed that Mates had also met loyalist representatives for private talks.

The final day of the month also gave indications that the various political actors were moving further apart. On the loyalist side PUP spokesman David Ervine suggested that the Protestant paramilitaries' ceasefire was far from stable, although the following day UDP spokesman David Adams denied the loyalist ceasefire was under threat. Meanwhile John Bruton, in a speech perceived as an attempt to re-establish a nationalist consensus on the peace process, said that prior decommissioning of arms would not be allowed to stand in the way of progress towards full negotiations. He also declared there was 'no question of the government I lead conforming to, or acquiescing in, any unionist agenda of domination'.

By May the position of grass-roots loyalists appeared to be hardening in reaction to nationalist overtures towards Sinn Fein. On 5 May the Mid-Ulster UVF claimed to have planted three bombs at Dublin Airport and, although nothing was found, several flights were delayed while the airport was searched. This unilateral action by the mid-Ulster UVF led to a dispute between the UDA and UVF within the CLMC so that by the end of the month the status of the loyalist paramilitary co-ordinating body was unclear. The Ulster Unionists also appeared to harden their position on the arms question when David Trimble noted, on 24 May, that in the opening session of talks (which he said might last for days or weeks) his party wanted to see 'equipment of some sort' appearing.

Grass-roots nationalists also appeared to be drawing the line on any further compromise, and on 12 May leading republican Brian Keenan stated at a commemoration ceremony in West Belfast that republicans would have their victory: 'Do not be confused about the politics of the situation and about decommissioning. The only thing the republican movement will accept is the decommissioning of the British state in this country.'

On 16 May the British government appeared to nod in Sinn Fein's direction once again when, in an *Irish Times* interview, John Major said that he wanted Sinn Fein to be part of the negotiations but that it could not make a contribution without an IRA ceasefire. On the crucial question of arms he noted that decommissioning would 'need to be addressed at the beginning of the talks and agreement reached on how Mitchell recommendations on decommissioning can be taken forward, without blocking the negotiations'. This statement, which certainly went further than unionists and many Tory backbenchers were prepared to go in downplaying the importance of the decommissioning issue, was perceived as another attempt by the government to involve Sinn Fein in talks by encouraging a renewal of the ceasefire.

By 30 May, the date of the election, several key issues still remained unresolved. Attempts by nationalists and the Irish government to have the arms issue treated as a 'fourth strand' of discussions and separated from the other three strands were rejected by the British government and unionists while, despite Gerry Adams's statement on 20 May that Sinn Fein would agree to the Mitchell principles, there was no sign of the renewed IRA ceasefire which all parties (Sinn Fein excepted) believed was a prerequisite for all-party negotiations. The name of the individual, or individuals, who would chair the various strands of the talks had also to be resolved.

The outcome of the 30 May election provided few crumbs of comfort for the optimists, with a strong showing for the more extreme parties and a weak performance by those at the centre. Contrary to pre-election predictions, the Ulster Unionist Party remained the largest single party with 24.2% of the vote and 30 seats in the forum, the DUP with 18.8% received 24 seats, the SDLP 21.4% and 21 seats. Sinn Fein appeared to be the main winner in the election with its best ever showing (15.5%, 17 seats and 116,377 votes), a result which could be interpreted in different ways, either as a vote to reinstate the ceasefire or alternatively as showing support for the hard line taken by republican militarists. More predictably, and at least partly as a result of the nature of the electoral system used, one of the main losers was the middle-ground Alliance Party, which took 6.5% of the vote and seven seats. Robert McCartney's recently formed UK Unionists attracted 3.7% of the vote and won three seats in the forum. Four other parties, the PUP (3.5%), the UDP (2.2%), the Northern Ireland Women's Coalition (1.0%) and a Labour coalition (0.9%), failed to win any of the constituency seats but, by finishing among the ten most successful parties, each won two seats in the forum.

In the wake of the election Sir Patrick Mayhew again caused consternation among unionists by stating that he did not expect weapons to be handed in at the beginning of talks, leading Ulster Unionist MP Martin Smyth to comment that, 'Nobody believes the government because it keeps changing its tune on vital issues.' Last-minute difficulties also surfaced in the question of what part George Mitchell should play in the talks and it was not until the publication of a joint British-Irish paper on 6 June that the former Senator was handed the leading role of chairing the plenary sessions as well as the sub-committee dealing with decommissioning. Senator Mitchell's colleagues on the international body were also asked to participate – General John de Chastelain to chair strand two (North-South) talks, with Harri Holkeri acting as an alternate in any area which required an independent chairman. The plan was generally welcomed by nationalists but greeted with suspicion or hostility by most unionists who objected to Senator Mitchell's role in the talks.

Relations between the Irish government and Sinn Fein were also damaged by the murder of Garda Jerry McCabe during a mail van robbery in Country Limerick on 7 June. John Bruton was further angered by statements from Sinn Fein members that they would not condemn the incident because, they said, they would not indulge in 'the politics of condemnation'. It was not until 15 June that the IRA admitted that its members had been responsible for killing Detective McCabe.

In some areas relations between the UK and Ireland continued to improve, as demonstrated by President Mary Robinson's successful four-day official visit to Britain (the first by an Irish head of state) in early June. But despite these developments and optimistic pronouncements from Irish sources, there was still no sign of a renewed IRA ceasefire. Nevertheless, it still came as something of a shock when the IRA exploded a one-and-a-half tonne van bomb in the centre of Manchester on 15 June, injuring 200 people and causing damage estimated at £100 million. In the wake of the bomb British and Irish public and political opinion hardened noticeably against republicans and John Bruton declared that the IRA would have to declare an 'unconditional and irrevocable' ceasefire before Sinn Fein could be admitted to talks. Irish government opinion hardened further on 20 June when a major, and active, IRA bomb-making factory was discovered by Gardai at Clonaslee, Co. Laois.

The events of July 1996 proved particularly disheartening for those who believed that peace and political stability were within reach. On 6 July the RUC announced that it was re-routing the following day's Orange parade to Drumcree church in Portadown away from the Catholic Garvaghy Road. The broad unionist community saw the decision to re-route the march as a threat to its identity and believed the decision had been taken in order to appease republicans and therefore refused to accept it. Nationalists, however, viewed the decision, and the RUC's ability to stop the Orange march going through a Catholic area, as a test of the equal status of the Catholic community in Northern Ireland.

By 11 July, after three days of loyalist rioting across the province and a continuing stand-off between police and Orangemen at Drumcree, it had become apparent that the RUC and army (now back to a force of 18,500 men) were incapable of controlling an increasingly united and hostile unionist population. The subsequent reversal of RUC tactics, allowing the Orange march to proceed along the Garvaghy Road, brought an almost inevitable reaction from nationalists, with days of rioting in republican areas and the bombing of a hotel near Enniskillen by a republican splinter group on 13 July. By the end of the month there had been two deaths (Catholic taxi-driver Michael McGoldrick was murdered near Lurgan on 8 July, almost certainly by loyalists, and republican Dermot McShane crushed by an armoured car during riots in Derry on 13 July), a number of shooting incidents and a spate of sectarian attacks on churches and private property. On 13 July, when the SDLP announced that it was quitting the Northern Ireland Forum, the level of mutual contempt which existed between nationalists and unionists seemed greater than it had been for two decades.

With a UFF bomb scare in Dublin bringing the city to a standstill on 18 July and an INLA bomb threat in Lisburn the following day, the continuing loyalist ceasefire seemed to be in a precarious position, leading John Major to attempt to stabilise the situation by meeting a joint PUP-UDP delegation at Downing Street on 22 July. At the same time relations between the British and Irish governments hit rock bottom and communications between the two had largely returned to the type of 'megaphone diplomacy' which the Anglo-Irish Agreement had been intended to prevent; the same Agreement was also meant to improve the acceptability of the RUC to the Catholic community.

In August the damage which the previous month had done to community relations became, if anything, even more apparent. Many moderate Catholics now called for the disbanding of the RUC and agreed with the sentiments of Gerry Adams's statement on 5 August when he noted, 'The issue is bigger than marches. It has got to do with equal treatment. It has got to do with who governs this state.' Equally, as a flood of letters to the *Belfast Telegraph* and a number of incidents (such as a proposed boycott of Protestant shops by Catholics in border areas) illustrated, unionists believed they were being 'culturally cleansed' by a fully functioning 'pan-nationalist front'. While August saw fewer riots and overt sectarian clashes than the previous month, the situation remained one of stalemate rather than resolution. The pervasiveness of sectarian feeling was aptly commented on by the PUP's David Ervine on 19 August when he stated that the sectarian atmosphere existed at all levels, 'in the workplace, in the streets, it's certainly in the areas where Protestant and Catholic meet. It's almost to the point where we have created a form of tribal retreatment.'

With no IRA ceasefire and Sinn Fein's Irish peace process in tatters, the republican movement appeared to be back where it had started three years earlier. With Sinn Fein excluded from negotiations and with unionists critical of the role allocated to George Mitchell, the prospect of a comprehensive political settlement appeared slight, but then this had also been the case in 1993 when the peace process first began to gather pace.

Despite its apparent failure, the 1993-96 peace process had undoubtedly achieved more than many of the North's veteran cynics had believed possible. While the peace process had not 'solved' the Northern Ireland problem, at least it had (drugs murders and punishment attacks notwithstanding) provided more than a year of comparative peace and, for a time at least, offered the tantalising prospect of a final end to the Troubles. While the genuine desire for peace and political stability which existed among the overwhelming majority of the people of Northern Ireland, the Republic and Britain and the belief remained strong that there should be 'no turning back', the difficulty was, as ever, whether this desire could be converted into genuine compromise and a political agreement acceptable to all sides. A worrying development in this context was the growing belief of many Ulster politicians – from the Alliance Party's Lord Alderdice to Gerry Adams – that paragraph 47 of the Frameworks Documents implied a British willingness to impose joint authority on the province, even though this interpretation had been denied by Michael Aneram as far back as 15 March 1995 in an interview in the *Belfast Telegraph*. Nevertheless, the notion of an imposed solution continued to encourage some and to infuriate others.

# Glossary

| | |
|---|---|
| Ard fheis | conference of Irish political parties |
| CBI | Confederation of British Industry |
| CLMC | Combined Loyalist Military Command; loyalist para-military co-ordinating body formed in 1991 and comprising the UDA, UFF, UVF and Red Hand Commando |
| Dail | lower house of the Irish parliament |
| DUP | Democratic Unionist Party; led by Revd Ian Paisley |
| FEC | Fair Employment Commission |
| GAA | Gaelic Athletic Association |
| Garda (pl .-i) | Police in the Republic of Ireland |
| HMG | Her Majesty's Government |
| INLA | Irish National Liberation Army; republican paramilitary group formed in 1974 as a breakaway from the Official IRA |
| IPLO | Irish People's Liberation Organisation; republican organisation which has used Catholic Reaction Force as a cover-name, formed as a breakaway from the INLA in 1986 |
| IRA | Irish Republican Army, also referred to as Provisional IRA; formed in late 1969/early 1970 after a split with the Official IRA |
| IRSP | Irish Republican Socialist Party; political wing of the INLA |
| ITN | Independent Television News |
| ITV | Independent Television (British) |
| MP | Member of Parliament (Westminster) |
| NIO | Northern Ireland Office, British government department |
| NSC | National Security Council (US) |

| | |
|---|---|
| PUP | Progressive Unionist Party; loyalist party close to the UVF, led by Hugh Smyth |
| RTE | Radio Telefis Eireann; radio and television network in the Republic of Ireland |
| RUC | Royal Ulster Constabulary; the Northern Ireland police force |
| SAS | Special Air Service; elite regiment of the British army involved in a number of controversial operations in Northern Ireland |
| SDLP | Social Democratic and Labour Party; the largest nationalist party in Northern Ireland, led by John Hume |
| SF | Sinn Fein ('Ourselves Alone'); republican party close to the IRA, led by Gerry Adams |
| UDA | Ulster Defence Association; the largest Protestant paramilitary organisation, founded in 1971 and declared illegal in 1992 |
| UDP | Ulster Democratic Party; loyalist party close to the UDA, led by Gary McMichael |
| UDR | Ulster Defence Regiment; locally based British army regiment formed in 1970 to replace the discredited Ulster Special Constabulary (the B Specials), amalgamated with the Royal Irish Rangers in 1992 to form the Royal Irish Regiment |
| UFF | Ulster Freedom Fighters; overtly military wing of the UDA which emerged in 1973 and was involved from an early stage in murders and other terrorist activities; the UFF was a proscribed organisation during the period when the UDA remained legal |
| UPUP | Ulster Popular Unionist Party; small unionist party led by Sir James Kilfedder |
| UUP | Ulster Unionist Party; the largest unionist party, also referred to as the Official Unionist Party, led by James Molyneaux until 1995 and since then by David Trimble |
| UVF | Ulster Volunteer Force; loyalist paramilitary organisation |
| VAT | Value Added Tax |

# Bibliography

Aughey, Arthur and Duncan Morrow (eds), *Northern Ireland Politics* (Longman, London, 1996)

Bew, Paul, Peter Gibbon and Henry Patterson, *Northern Ireland 1921-1994: Political Forces and Social Classes* (Serif, London, 1995)

Bew, Paul and Gordon Gillespie, *Northern Ireland: A Chronology of the Troubles 1968-1993* (Gill and Macmillan, Dublin, 1993)

Duignan, Sean, *One Spin on the Merry-Go-Round* (Blackwater Press, Dublin, 1995)

Flackes, W.D. and Sydney Elliott, *Northern Ireland: A Political Directory 1968-1993* (Blackstaff, Belfast, 1994)

Hickman, Mary (ed.), *Northern Ireland: What Next? Conference Report* (University of North London Press, London, 1995)

Jarman, Neil and Dominic Bryan, *Parade and Protest: A Discussion of Parading Disputes in Northern Ireland* (Centre for the Study of Conflict, Coleraine, 1996)

Mallie, Eamonn and David McKittrick, *The Fight for Peace: The Secret Story Behind the Irish Peace Process* (Heinemann, London, 1996)

McIntyre, Anthony, 'Modern Irish Republicanism: The Product of British State Strategies', *Irish Political Studies*, Vol. 10, 1995.

Purdy, Ann, *Molyneaux: The Long View* (Greystone Books, Antrim, 1989)

Rowan, Brian, *Behind the Headlines: The Story of the IRA and Loyalist Ceasefires* (Blackstaff, Belfast, 1995)

Sinn Fein, *Setting the Record Straight* (Sinn Fein, Belfast, 1993)

*A Citizens' Inquiry: The Opsahl Report on Northern Ireland*, Andy Pollak (ed.), (Lilliput, Dublin, 1992)

*Paths to a Political Settlement in Ireland: Policy Papers Submitted to the Forum for Peace and Reconciliation* (Blackstaff, Belfast, 1995)

## Official Publications

The Chief Constable's Annual Report 1993-1995 (Police Authority for Northern Ireland, Belfast, 1994-1996)
Frameworks for the Future (HMSO, Belfast, 1995)
Parliamentary Debates, Official Report (Hansard) House of Commons, Sixth Series, Volumes 226-272
Dail Eireann, Parliamentary Debates, Official Report, Volumes 432-462
Forum for Peace and Reconciliation: Report of Proceedings of Public Sessions (Stationery Office, Dublin, 1995-1996)

## Newspapers and Magazines

*Belfast Telegraph*
*Daily Mail*
*Daily Telegraph*
*Fortnight*
*Financial Times*
*The House Magazine*
*The Guardian*
*The Independent*
*The Independent on Sunday*
*Irish Independent*
*Irish News*
*Irish Press*
*The Irish Times*
*Mail on Sunday*

*An Phoblacht*
*News Letter*
*NI Brief*
*The Observer*
*Parliamentary Brief*
*Sunday Business Post*
*Sunday Express*
*Sunday Independent*
*Sunday Life*
*Sunday Press*
*Sunday Telegraph*
*Sunday Times*
*Sunday Tribune*
*The Times*

# Index